Reference Only

THE CAMBRIDGE COMPANION TO SEAMUS HEANEY

Seamus Heaney is a unique phenomenon in contemporary literature, as a poet whose works (such as his *Beowulf* translation, and volumes of poems such as *Electric Light* and *District and Circle*) have been high in the best-seller lists for decades. Especially since winning the Nobel Prize for Literature, he has come to be considered one of the most important English-language poets in the world. This *Companion* gives an up-to-date overview of his career thus far, and of his reception in Ireland, England and around the world. Its distinguished contributors offer detailed readings of all his major publications, in poetry, prose and translation. The essays further explore the central themes of his poetry, his relations with other writers and his prose writing. Designed for students, this volume will also have much to interest and inform the general reader and admirer of Heaney's unique poetic voice.

A complete list of books in the series is at the back of this book.

THE CAMBRIDGE COMPANION TO
SEAMUS HEANEY

EDITED BY
BERNARD O'DONOGHUE

CAMBRIDGE UNIVERSITY PRESS
Cambridge, New York, Melbourne, Madrid, Cape Town, Singapore, São Paulo, Delhi

Cambridge University Press
The Edinburgh Building, Cambridge CB2 8RU, UK

Published in the United States of America by Cambridge University Press, New York

www.cambridge.org
Information on this title: www.cambridge.org/9780521547550

First published 2009

Printed in the United Kingdom at the University Press, Cambridge

A catalogue record for this publication is available from the British Library

Library of Congress Cataloguing in Publication data
The Cambridge companion to Seamus Heaney / edited by Bernard O'Donoghue.
p. cm.
Includes bibliographical references and index.
ISBN 978-0-521-83882-5
1. Heaney, Seamus, 1939– – Criticism and interpretation.
I. O'Donoghue, Bernard. II. Title.
PR6058.E2Z5745 2008
821′.914–dc22
2008040775

ISBN 978-0-521-83882-5 hardback
ISBN 978-0-521-54755-0 paperback

CONTENTS

CONTRIBUTORS

GUINN BATTEN is an associate professor of English at Washington University in St Louis. She is the author of *The Orphaned Imagination: Melancholy and Commodity Culture in English Romanticism* and several published essays on contemporary Irish poetry. A former editor for the Wake Forest University Press's Irish poetry series, and the co-author of 'Irish Poetry in English, 1945–2000' for *The Cambridge History of Irish Literature*, she is writing a book on ethics and the crisis of autobiography in English Romanticism as they are revised in contemporary Irish poetry.

RAND BRANDES was born in Batesville, Indiana and educated at Hanover College (BA) and Emory University (MA and PhD). He is the recipient of two Fulbright Fellowships to work with Seamus Heaney in Dublin. Along with Michael J. Durkan (1925–96), he has published *Seamus Heaney: A Reference Guide* (1996) and *Seamus Heaney: A Bibliography 1959–2003* (2008). He is the Martin Luther Stevens Professor of English at Lenoir-Rhyne College in Hickory, North Carolina.

FRAN BREARTON is Reader in English at Queen's University Belfast, and assistant director of the Seamus Heaney Centre for Poetry. She is author of *The Great War in Irish Poetry* (2000) and *Reading Michael Longley* (2006), and is currently working on a study of Robert Graves and twentieth-century poetry.

NEIL CORCORAN is King Alfred Professor of English Literature at the University of Liverpool. He previously taught at the universities of Sheffield, Swansea and St Andrews. A revised, enlarged edition of his book on Seamus Heaney was published as *The Poetry of Seamus Heaney: A Critical Study* (1998), and recent publications include *Elizabeth Bowen: The Enforced Return* (2004) and *The Cambridge Companion to Twentieth-Century English Poetry* (2007).

PATRICK CROTTY was born in Fermoy, Co. Cork, in 1952 and educated at University College Cork and the University of Stirling. He is the editor of *Modern Irish Poetry: An Anthology* (1995) and of the forthcoming *New Penguin Book of Irish Verse*. He is Professor of Irish and Scottish Literature at the University of Aberdeen.

JOHN WILSON FOSTER was born in Belfast and educated at the Queen's University and the University of Oregon. Among his books are *Fictions of the Irish Literary Revival* (1987), *Colonial Consequences* (1991), *The Achievement of Seamus Heaney* (1995) and *Irish Novels 1890–1940* (2008). He is Professor Emeritus, University of British Columbia, and in 2004–5 was a Leverhulme Visiting Professor to the United Kingdom.

DILLON JOHNSTON has published two editions of *Irish Poetry after Joyce* (1985 and 1977), and *The Poetic Economies of England and Ireland* (2001), as well as many essays, mostly about Irish and British poetry. He was founder and director of Wake Forest University Press. He currently lectures in the graduate program at Washington University in St Louis.

ANDREW MURPHY is Professor of English at the University of St Andrews. He contributed the *Seamus Heaney* volume (1996) to the British Council's 'Writers and their Work' series. His other books include *But the Irish Sea Betwixt Us: Ireland, Colonialism, and Renaissance Literature* (1999) and *Shakespeare for the People: Working Class Readers 1800–1900* (2000).

BERNARD O'DONOGHUE is a Fellow in Medieval English at Wadham College, Oxford. His study *Seamus Heaney and the Language of Poetry* was published in 1994. He has published five volumes of poems, and his *Selected Poems* was published in 2008.

HEATHER O'DONOGHUE was born in Stockton-upon-Tees, Co. Durham, and grew up in Middlesbrough. She was educated at Westfield College, University of London, and Somerville College, Oxford. She is currently Vigfusson-Rausing Reader in Old Icelandic at the University of Oxford, and Vice-Principal of Linacre College. She is the author of *The Genesis of a Saga Narrative* (1991), *Skaldic Verse and the Poetics of Saga Narrative*: *An Introduction to Old Norse-Icelandic Literature* (2004) and most recently, *From Asgard to Valhalla* (2007), a study of the reception history of Old Norse myth. Her present project is a book about the influence of Old Norse myth on poetry in English.

DENNIS O'DRISCOLL has worked as a civil servant since the age of sixteen. His eight books of poetry include *New and Selected Poems* (2004), a Poetry Book Society Special Commendation, and *Reality Check* (2007–8). A selection of his essays and reviews, *Troubled Thoughts, Majestic Dreams*, was published in 2001. He is the editor of *The Bloodaxe Book of Poetry Quotations* (2006) and its American counterpart, *Quote Poet Unquote* (2008).

JUSTIN QUINN was born in Dublin in 1968, and educated at Trinity College. He is the author of four collections of poetry, most recently *Waves & Trees* (2006), and he has written two studies of twentieth-century American poetry. His books include the *Cambridge Introduction to Modern Poetry, 1800–2000* (2008); translations of the contemporary Czech poet, Petr Borkovec, *From the Interior* (2008); and, as editor, *Irish Poetry after Feminism* (2008). He is Associate Professor of English and American Literature at the Charles University, Prague.

DAVID WHEATLEY was born in Dublin and lectures at the University of Hull. He has published three collections of poetry, and edited the poetry journal *Metre* with Justin Quinn. His *Contemporary British Poetry: An Introduction* is forthcoming from Cambridge University Press.

ACKNOWLEDGEMENTS

My primary thanks are to Seamus Heaney, for providing the incomparable subject-matter and for his hallmark generosity and goodwill towards the project. I am deeply grateful to all the contributors who have borne delay with patience. I have drawn on Dennis O'Driscoll's noted infallibility more than once. Ray Ryan, Maartje Scheltens and Christopher Hills of Cambridge University Press were also very generous with their expertise. Lindeth Vasey was an extraordinarily efficient and reassuring reader and copy-editor. Wadham College and the Oxford English Faculty kindly allowed me a period of leave to work on the project, and I was given a generous grant by the English Faculty for research support. I am greatly in the debt of Drs Tara Stubbs and Heather O'Donoghue for addressing my word-processing incompetence. Without them the book would have never reached its quietus.

NOTE ON THE TEXT, AND ABBREVIATIONS

Most of Heaney's works have been published both in Britain and Ireland, and in America. When there is any divergence, I have given the British Isles English titles and dates of publication as the editions most readily available. In the 'Further Reading' I have given the English or Irish place of publication first because, when there is any difference in publication dates, those are always earlier.

Abbreviations

Titles of books frequently referred to, especially individual volumes of poetry and the four collected volumes of prose essays.

B	*Beowulf*
CP	*Crediting Poetry*
DC	*District and Circle*
DD	*Door into the Dark*
DN	*Death of a Naturalist*
EL	*Electric Light*
FK	*Finders Keepers*
FW	*Field Work*
GT	*The Government of the Tongue*
HL	*The Haw Lantern*
N	*North*
OG	*Opened Ground*
OL	*An Open Letter*

P	*Preoccupations*
RP	*The Redress of Poetry*
SA	*Sweeney Astray*
SI	*Station Island*
SL	*The Spirit Level*
ST	*Seeing Things*
WO	*Wintering Out*

CHRONOLOGY

(*Italics* denote political events)

13 April 1939	Born on a farm, 'Mossbawn', in Tamniarn, Co. Derry, Northern Ireland, to Patrick and Margaret Heaney. Eldest of nine children – two girls and seven boys.
1945–51	Attends the local Anahorish school, a mixed primary school with Catholic and Protestant pupils. Played Gaelic Football for St Malachy's, Castledawson up to minor level, at age 18.
1951–57	Attends, as a boarder, St Columb's College, Derry City.
1953	Family moves from Mossbawn farm to 'The Wood', at the other end of the parish, following the death of his brother Christopher (an incident commemorated in both his early poem 'Mid-Term Break' and the late poem 'The Blackbird of Glanmore' in *District and Circle*).
1957–61	At Queen's University Belfast, doing a degree in English. Graduates with First Class. First poems published in Queen's literary magazines.
1961–2	Studies for a postgraduate teachers' training diploma at St Joseph's college of education, Andersonstown, Belfast. While at St Joseph's, writes an extended essay on literary magazines in the North of Ireland, and is led to the collections of the Linen Hall Library, Belfast, and the works of the Ulster poet John Hewitt, and the British poet Ted Hughes.
1962	Begins teaching at St Thomas's Intermediate School, Ballymurphy. The headmaster, the short-story writer Michael McLaverty, introduces Heaney to the poetry of

	Patrick Kavanagh. Registers for a part-time postgraduate degree at Queen's. Begins writing in earnest. In November 1962, 'Tractors' is published in the *Belfast Telegraph*; other Irish journals, including the Queen's University magazine, *Interest*, soon publish other poems.
Spring 1963	'Mid-Term Break' is published by *Kilkenny Magazine*.
Autumn 1963	Leaves school teaching and returns to St Joseph's as a lecturer in English. Meets poet and lecturer Philip Hobsbaum at Queen's, and becomes part of the 'Belfast Group'. The group would meet in Hobsbaum's flat until his move to Glasgow in 1966; 1966–1970 they would meet at Heaney's flat. Its members included at various points Michael Longley, Derek Mahon, Stewart Parker and James Simmons, and later Paul Muldoon and Frank Ormsby.
1965	Mary Holland publicises the Belfast Group in the *Observer* in London, as part of the Belfast Festival.
August 1965	Marries Marie Devlin, whom he had first met in October 1962.
November 1965	The Belfast Festival publishes Heaney's first slim collection, *Eleven Poems*.
1966	Awarded a lectureship at Queen's following Hobsbaum's departure. Begins to write topical articles for the *New Statesman* and the *Listener* and to make broadcasts for BBC radio and television. Becomes known for his cultural and political communications. The Manchester publisher Phoenix Pamphlet Poets publishes *A Lough Neagh Sequence*.
May 1966	Faber publishes first full-length poetry collection, *Death of a Naturalist*. Receives the Gregory Award for Young Writers and the Geoffrey Faber Prize, setting the pattern of prizewinning which was maintained by all his poetry volumes.
July 1966	Son, Michael, is born. Writes about Belfast in the 'Out of London' column in the *New Statesman*, focusing on political rather than cultural issues.

February 1968	Second son, Christopher, is born.
5 October 1968	*Civil rights march in Derry City – first major violent clash of the 'Troubles'.*
24 October 1968	Writes a piece in the *Listener*, 'Old Derry's Walls', in sympathy with the marchers, and a satirical song, 'Craig's Dragoons', for Radio Eireann.
June 1969	Second volume, *Door into the Dark*, is published. Wins the Somerset Maugham Award.
12 August 1969	*Sectarian clashes in Derry; would become known as the 'Battle of the Bogside'.*
14 August 1969	*The British Army enters Derry.*
January 1970	*The Provisional Irish Republican Army is officially formed in Dublin.*
1970–1	Spends the academic year at the University of California, Berkeley. Returns to Northern Ireland in September 1971.
1971	*The Provisional IRA's bombing campaign is stepped up.*
1972	Publication of *Soundings*.
30 January 1972	*'Bloody Sunday', in which thirteen civilians are killed by the British Army in Derry.* Would write a lament for the dead, 'The Road to Derry', and would commemorate the event in 'Casualty', published in *Field Work*.
August 1972	Having resigned from Queen's, the Heaneys rent from Anne Saddlemyer a cottage in Glanmore, Co. Wicklow, where Heaney begins work as a freelance writer (rejoicing in the local association with J. M. Synge).
November 1972	Publication of *Wintering Out*.
1973–7	Hosts, intermittently, a radio show, *Imprint*, on Radio Eireann.
April 1973	Daughter, Catherine Ann, is born.
October 1973	Visits Denmark, where he sees the bodies of the Bog people at the museum at Silkeborg.

1975	The Belfast/Honest Ulsterman Press publishes prose-poetic sequence *Stations*, completed in May and June 1974, as a pamphlet. The publication reflects a vital moment in his career when he acknowledges the impact of sectarianism on his poetry. Ted Hughes's sister, Olwyn, publishes a limited edition of the whole series of bog poems – as *Bog Poems* – from her Rainbow Press.
June 1975	Publication of *North*.
October 1975	Joins the English department at Carysfort, a teachers' training college in Dublin.
November 1976	The Heaneys move to Sandymount, Dublin.
1976–81	Employed as Head of the English Department at Carysfort.
1979	Spends a semester teaching a poetry workshop at Harvard University as one of several temporary successors to the American poet Robert Lowell, who had died in 1977. Publication of *Field Work*, thought to have been influenced by the poetry of Lowell (Heaney had given an address at his memorial service in London). Lowell had praised *North*, while an elegy to him is included in *Field Work*.
1980	Joins the Board of the Field Day Company, founded by his close friend, the playwright Brian Friel and the actor Stephen Rea to produce Friel's *Translations* outside the commercial theatre. A director of Field Day along with the poets Tom Paulin and Seamus Deane. Publication of *Selected Poems, 1965–1975*, and *Preoccupations: Selected Prose 1968–1978* (in October).
1980–1	*Ten Republican prisoners die on hunger strike, including Heaney's neighbour Francis Hughes, from Bellaghy.*
January 1982	Begins five-year contract at Harvard, teaching one semester a year.
1983	As a director of Field Day, Heaney publishes, in Ireland, *Sweeney Astray* (started in 1973), a version of the long

	medieval Irish poem, *Buile Suibhne* ('the madness of Sweeney'). Publishes a pamphlet poem, *An Open Letter*, dissociating himself from the adjective 'British' (Blake Morrison and Andrew Motion had included him in their 1982 edition of the *Penguin Book of Contemporary British Poetry*).
1984	Elected to the Boylston Chair of Rhetoric and Oratory, Harvard University, which he holds until 1996. Heaney divides his time between Dublin and America, running poetry workshops at Harvard for four months of the year.
October 1984	Publication of *Station Island* and of *Sweeney Astray* in England. Death of his mother, commemorated in 'Clearances'.
1984	Publication of *Hailstones*.
1986	Death of his father, commemorated in 'The Stone Verdict'.
1987	Publication of *The Haw Lantern*, which wins the Whitbread Award.
1988	Publication of *The Government of the Tongue: The 1986 T. S. Eliot Memorial Lectures and Other Critical Writings*.
1989	Publication of *The Place of Writing*.
1989–94	Takes up five-year appointment as Professor of Poetry at Oxford; lectures published as *The Redress of Poetry: Oxford Lectures* in 1995.
1990	Publication of *New Selected Poems 1966–1987*, and of *The Cure at Troy: A Version of Sophocles's 'Philoctetes'*; performed by Field Day Company in Derry.
1991	Publication of *Seeing Things*.
1994	Co-edits *The Rattle Bag*, a poetry anthology for older children, with Ted Hughes.
31 August 1994	*IRA ceasefire.*
1995	Awarded the Nobel Prize for Literature. Publishes *Crediting Poetry*.

1996	Publication of *The Spirit Level*. Commonwealth Literature Award. Named Whitbread Book of the Year.
1998	*Good Friday Agreement reached on 10 April between the British and Irish governments and most Northern Irish political groups, restoring devolved government to Northern Ireland; seen as making an official end to the 'Troubles'. Omagh Bombing: the exploding of a Real IRA bomb in Omagh, Co. Tyrone on 15 August, in which 29 people were killed.*
1999	Publication of the translation of *Beowulf*, which also is named as Whitbread Book of the Year.
2001	Publication of *Electric Light*.
2002	Publication of *Finders Keepers: Selected Prose 1971–2001*.
2003	Opening of the Seamus Heaney Centre for Poetry at Queen's University Belfast.
2004	Publication of *The Burial at Thebes*, a translation of Sophocles' *Antigone*, to mark the centenary of the Abbey Theatre in Dublin.
2006	Publication of *District and Circle* which wins the T. S. Eliot Prize.

1

BERNARD O'DONOGHUE

Introduction

When Seamus Heaney was awarded the Nobel Prize for Literature in 1995, the citation famously paid tribute to his combination of 'lyrical beauty and ethical depth which exalt everyday miracles and the living past'. This captures with remarkable economy not only Heaney's pre-eminent strengths, but also the two imperatives between which his own commentary and the criticism of him have fluctuated. In the Preface to *Finders Keepers: Selected Prose 1971–2001* Heaney described the choice between the ethical and the aesthetic again, quoting from his Foreword to the prose collection *Preoccupations* in 1980: 'How should a poet properly live and write? What is his relationship to be to his own voice, his own place, his literary heritage and his contemporary world?' By quoting the earlier Foreword verbatim, Heaney was making it clear that his abiding concerns have remained unchanged.

The Nobel citation also summarises the issues that this book aims to account for. Heaney's most recent collection of poems *District and Circle* (2006) – and Heaney's titles are carefully considered, as Rand Brandes's essay here shows – marks a point, forty years on from his first full-length volume *Death of a Naturalist*, at which he circles back to the local district in which that highly localised volume was placed. In those forty years Heaney has published at least twelve major individual volumes of poems, three series of *Selected Poems*, several dramatic translations and a large body of critical prose. Not surprisingly, taking stock is not a simple matter: by now, in 2008, there is a very considerable bibliography on him to account for, as well as his own works, and several critical approaches of varying schools of thought and degrees of approval.

A comparison with Yeats is revealing (indeed it has been found hard to avoid): Heaney is now the age Yeats was in 1934, twelve years after he had won the Nobel Prize (it is thirteen years since Heaney's) and a year after the publication of *The Winding Stair*. At the corresponding stage Yeats too was a major international figure, and he still had a significant body of poetic work ahead of him. Yet there was no study of Yeats in existence, though a number of important shorter discussions had appeared, such as in Edmund Wilson's *Axel's Castle*. By now the number of specialising books on Heaney is too large to itemise because it is likely to be out of date as soon as it is published. For example there are at least sixteen books whose title is simply *Seamus Heaney*, as well as many others with titles in which the poet's name occurs. If it is suspected that this is merely a change in the times, and that there are simply more books published, this quickly proves not to be the explanation. No other current poet is nearly as much written about as Heaney has been, since the appearance of the first book devoted to him, Blake Morrison's in 1982, the same year in which the introduction to Morrison and Andrew Motion's *Penguin Book of Contemporary British Poetry* saw the emergence of Heaney as one of the factors that made a new anthology timely.

In this introduction I will principally be tracing the poet's own poetic writings and his reception, in keeping with the emphasis of the book. In this connection another Yeats comparison might be made: Heaney has been a busy career-teacher of literature as well as writer, rather than 'a man of letters' in the way that Yeats was (the term is no longer current, nor is the lifestyle). While a large body of critical prose work survives from the 1880s at the very beginning of Yeats's writing life, nothing of comparable substance exists in Heaney's case, despite the fact that he is recognised as a major critic-practitioner nowadays (his distinctive gifts as a critic are established by David Wheatley in his chapter here; John Wilson Foster paid lavish tribute to those gifts too, calling Heaney's 'the best Irish literary criticism since Yeats'[1]). But, while Heaney was a regular reviewer, especially for the *Listener* from 1966 onwards, it was the late 1970s before any more extensive critical writings appeared, culminating in the publication of *Preoccupations* in 1980.[2] And 1977 has significance as the year when he first published critical work of some length and when he first gave one of the many interviews which emerged over the years.

So, although Heaney's status as critic-practitioner is of undoubted significance, the emphasis in this book is on him as poet, and to a lesser extent as poet-translator engaging with other poets. Heaney was twenty-six when *Death of a Naturalist* appeared in 1965: young, but not prodigiously so. The reception of that book quickly established him as a major new talent, writing with brilliant linguistic fidelity and evocativeness, mostly about his country upbringing in County Derry. The next book, *Door into the Dark* (1969), confirmed this reputation, in some poems even enhancing it. From the first his gifts were recognised as being of a very specifically poetic kind, founded on an alert eye and linguistic precision. In his *New Statesman* review of *Death of a Naturalist*, Christopher Ricks said, 'the power and precision of his best poems are a delight, and as a first collection *Death of a Naturalist* is outstanding'. C. B. Cox in the *Spectator* said the poems give us 'the soil-reek of Ireland'. This tactile accuracy continued to be noted as Heaney's particular strength in reviews of the next book: sometimes the praise sounds a shade stereotyping, but the purport is clear. In *The Times Literary Supplement*, Douglas Dunn said of *Door into the Dark* (1969) in a much-quoted effusion that the poems were 'loud with the slap of the spade and sour with the stink of turned earth'. Ricks continued in his previous vein in the *New Statesman* by saying – perhaps with a glint of warning – that Heaney would 'have to reconcile himself to the fact that *Door into the Dark* will consolidate him as the poet of muddy-booted blackberry-picking'.

His gifts could be summarised in a phrase from Gerard Manley Hopkins, passed on to Heaney by the teacher-writer Michael McLaverty, of which he is fond: 'description is revelation' (*N* 71). And, while several commentators made even grander claims for *Wintering Out* in 1972 (Neil Corcoran calls it 'the seminal single volume of the post-1970 period of English poetry'[3]), Heaney's characteristic strengths were mostly seen as the same: exactness of description and evocation. In *Wintering Out* the descriptive precision was put to further purposes: to evoking the places of his upbringing, often through a semantic dismantling of their etymologies, in the 'placename poems' such as 'Broagh' and 'Anahorish'. But there is another perspective which always has to be considered in describing the development of any Northern Irish writer in the current era. The most significant departure from the previous volumes in *Wintering Out* was a more developed sense of a political context. The poet was writing in a fraught period of history in Northern Ireland. Having grown up as the young 'naturalist' on a farm in County Derry, in a world where the country poet might trace at leisure the Wordsworthian 'making of a poet's mind', Heaney had moved to Belfast as a gifted student of English at Queen's University in 1957. But the last third of the twentieth century, when Heaney's work attained major status, was the most violent period in Northern Irish history. He was a member of a remarkable poetic generation who lived it, at least to begin with, 'bomb by bomb', in Derek Mahon's famous phrase.[4]

Seamus Deane observes that, although 'political echoes are audible in *Death of a Naturalist* and in *Door into the Dark*, there is no consciousness of politics as such, and certainly no political consciousness until *Wintering Out* and *North*'.[5] What soon came to be a matter of controversy was the use to which Heaney put – or should put – his undoubted gifts. The change from the descriptive bucolic in the relatively untroubled anti-pastoral of the early poems happens somewhere across the two volumes *Wintering Out* and *North*. The challenge now was to represent the wider public context as well as to evoke locality. Heaney found, to repeat a line of Yeats which Heaney has often drawn on himself, a 'befitting emblem of [the] adversity'[6] in the riven Northern Irish community when he read in 1969 *The Bog People* by P. V. Glob, a study of what seem to be ritual killings in Iron Age Jutland. Glob's book was illustrated by dramatic photographs of the victims of the killings, whose bodies had been preserved in the bog water. The first Heaney poem to reflect on these images was 'The Tollund Man' in *Wintering Out*, in which he imagines visiting Aarhus where the bodies are kept. There, in 'the old man-killing parishes' of Jutland, the poet will recall recent brutal killings in Northern Ireland and he will feel 'lost, / Unhappy and at home' (*WO* 48).

This poem is a trailer for what is seen as the first substantial change in Heaney's poetic corpus, with *North* in 1975, at once his most admired and most controversial single volume. The dilemma for the Northern Irish writer has often been noted, by Michael Longley and others: if they wrote about the violence, they were accused of exploiting suffering for their artistic purposes; if they ignored it, they were guilty of ivory-tower indifference.[7] Heaney said in his interview with John Haffenden, 'Up to *North*, that was one book' (*Viewpoints*, p. 64), in an attempt perhaps to escape the two-stranded stereotyping of the early work, from the bucolic to the symbolising of violence, by bracketing off together the four volumes that between them manifested the two stereotypes. Certainly the more or less unanimous chorus of critical praise becomes less certain after *North*. This sense of uncertainty extends to Heaney himself; several critics, including Seamus Deane and Terence Brown, see guilt as a major factor in the poet's self-characterisation from this point onwards. One of the reviews of *North*, by Ciaran Carson in the *Honest Ulsterman*, has been endlessly quoted as a representation of the case against 'the Bog Poems', as they were called from the first. According to Carson, Heaney had laid himself open to the charge (in fact Carson did not literally level it himself) of being 'the laureate of violence – a mythmaker, an anthropologist of ritual killing ... the world of megalithic doorways and charming noble barbarity'.

Other highly influential voices read *North* differently. Anthony Thwaite in *The Times Literary Supplement* saw it as a superior continuation of the linguistic and descriptive virtues in the earlier books, with 'all the sensuousness of Mr Heaney's earlier work, but refined and cut back to the bone'. Even more momentously, Robert Lowell, in the London *Observer*, called it 'a new kind of political poetry by the best Irish poet since W. B. Yeats'. The parallel with Yeats (Clive James and John Wilson Foster had prophesied it in 1972) in fact applies equally to Carson's accusation and to Lowell's tribute. The case against *North* was primarily what has been called 'the aestheticisation of violence', a charge most famously made in Irish poetry against the conclusion of Yeats's 'Easter 1916', that, in the bloody fighting in Dublin, 'a terrible beauty is born'. And if the sentiment of guilt, seen in Heaney by Deane,

Brown, Heaney himself and others, seems like the inevitable confessional product of a Catholic upbringing, we might recall that Yeats, coming from a very different background, shared it in precisely this context, rendered sleepless (at least poetically) in old age by wondering 'did that play of mine send out / Certain men the English shot'. In an admiring but dismayed review of *North* in the *Listener*, Conor Cruise O'Brien made the same charge against Heaney as he had made in a brilliant and influential essay against Yeats ten years earlier.[8] Heaney, according to O'Brien, has used his exceptional capacity for exact description of 'the thing itself' to evoke in an unbalanced way the suffering of the Catholics of Northern Ireland: 'there is no equivalent Protestant voice'. In each case the poet is being accused of using fraught public events to serve a personal cause.

By the late 1970s, when Heaney was a much more noticeable prose commentator and interviewee, the poet himself wished to change course, away from the political, or at least to be recognised as doing so. If 'up to *North*, that was one book', his new book *Field Work* was attempting a different kind of style and subject. Partly that book can be seen as a delayed accounting for a major change in Heaney's life, his moving with his family to Wicklow in the Irish Republic in 1972. His departure from the North of Ireland had been pursued by insults from extremist opponents on the Unionist side (recalling for some readers the Citizen's catcalls after the departing Bloom in the 'Cyclops' chapter of Joyce's *Ulysses*), and even with some misgiving by his friends (a state of affairs lamented in the powerful poem 'Exposure' at the end of *North*: 'my friends' / Beautiful prismatic counselling / And the anvil brains of some who hate me'). The publication of *North*, three years after the move to Wicklow, meant he could hardly be accused of abandoning the issues of Northern Ireland. But by 1979, he wished to make a new beginning, one which he described in an interview with James Randall in formal terms but with the reminder that 'a formal decision is never strictly formal': 'in the new book *Field Work*, I very deliberately set out to lengthen the line again because the narrow line was becoming habit ... I wanted to turn out, to go out, and I wanted to pitch the voice out ... a return to an opener voice and to a more – I don't want to say public – but a more social voice.'[9] The antithesis then is not so much between public and private as between two kinds of public position: the political and what he calls the social.

From this point onwards Heaney's writing is increasingly linked to this kind of self-commentary. It is clear now that the public-local opposition interlocks with the political-aesthetic in a complicated way, and the critical discussion of him has centred on that since. But, if *Field Work* is seen, as the poet pleads here, as the start of a post-*North* era in the work, it is in significant ways a continuation of the established previous concerns too. Amongst the most admired poems in *Field Work* – indeed in the whole corpus – are two great elegies for victims of the Northern violence, 'The Strand at Lough Beg' and 'Casualty'. These are the poems which address with the greatest directness the questions of guilt and involvement raised in the most unflinching of the Bog Poems, such as 'Punishment' where the poet – 'the artful voyeur', in the poem's terms – admits to understanding the 'tribal, intimate revenge' of the people who barbarically tarred and feathered Catholic girls who went out with British soldiers. 'Casualty' returns to that issue, or stays with it: was Louis O'Neill, the fisherman who was blown up by a bomb after he ignored the curfew imposed by the IRA after Bloody Sunday (seven years earlier than *Field Work*, it should be noted), guilty of some breach of local piety? 'Puzzle me / The right answer to that one' is what O'Neill's voice in the poem says (*FW* 23).

The poems in *Field Work* that attempt a new beginning – a new bucolics, it seems, circling back to the home district of *Death of a Naturalist* – are outweighed by the public poems: something that the complex claims in the Randall interview seem to concede in the terms 'public' and 'social'. We might remember too that as early as 1972, in his brief introduction to his anthology *Soundings '72*,[10] Heaney had made a strong bid for artistic freedom, three years before *North*:

> I am tired of speculations about the relation of the poet's work to the workings of the world he inhabits, and finally I disagree that 'poetry makes nothing happen.' It can eventually make new feelings, or feelings about feelings happen, and anybody can see that in this country for a long time to come a refinement of feelings will be more urgent than a reframing of policies or of constitutions.

There is something forced though about this inversion of the normal understanding of Auden's phrase about Yeats, 'poetry makes nothing happen', which is usually taken to mean that poetry cannot be politically effective. Heaney is saying 'poetry can make something non-political happen'; but that is not an obvious sense of 'nothing' in this context. Clearly the urgency of policies and constitutions in Northern Ireland in 1972 could not be so easily dismissed, as we have seen. And the wish that *Field Work* in 1979 should mark the starting point of a similar new freedom was equally doomed. As it happened, the late 1970s, followed by the hunger strikes of the early 1980s, was one of the worst periods of the Northern Troubles: hardly a point at which a guilt-inclined and socially aware commentator like Heaney could avoid public attitudes, however much he wanted to escape the 'responsible *tristia*' weighed in 'Exposure'. Unsurprisingly, Heaney's next books, the linked works *Station Island* (1984) and *Sweeney Astray* (1983), are again deeply concerned with issues of public answerability and guilt. The central section of *Station Island* – which is much the longest single volume of

Heaney's – shares the volume's title, describing a Dante-influenced purgatorial pilgrimage to Lough Derg in County Donegal, a demanding penitential programme that Heaney undertook three times when he was young. The question of guilt is obviously central here as the narrator/poet encounters figures from his own past life and the literary past.

By this time too criticism of Heaney is not simply a matter of reviews of individual volumes, laudatory or disapproving as the case might be. There is now a more wide-ranging criticism of Heaney whose work is seen in more general terms, as the exemplary instance of the Yeatsian conflict between artistic freedom and public responsibility. Often the criticism in this area has been remarkably simple-minded: strikingly more so, it might be said, than the poet's own subtler, well-weighed deliberations. Heaney has often praised Yeats for his ability to live in doubt, between stark alternatives, and Heaney has himself been praised for the possession of this modernist virtue (by Ian Hamilton for instance, or in *The Sunday Times* by John Carey – one of Heaney's most consistent and most perceptive advocates). But Declan Kiberd argues in a crucial essay that a virtuous political standpoint is not simply a matter of claiming to be in doubt:[11] something we will hear Heaney claiming later on in *The Spirit Level* and *Electric Light*. Principally dealing with the poetry of this period, Neil Corcoran published an acute essay on this recognition of Heaney as the test case for such issues for poetry in English.[12] It becomes increasingly clear over the next decade that this responsibility – one, as we have seen, that he would have liked to evade from the first – weighed heavily on Heaney. The dialectical, dramatic framework of the 'Station Island' sequence is a useful medium for the discussion of this. Heaney returns to 'The Strand at Lough Beg' in a fiction in which Colum McCartney, the murdered cousin addressed in that poem, accuses the poet of a failure to take his social and familial pieties seriously enough, choosing rather to stay in Jerpoint 'with poets' while his 'own flesh and blood / was carted to Bellaghy from the Fews' (*SI* 82). Worse, the attempt to escape the Troubles had made him 'confuse evasion and artistic tact', whitewashing ugliness and drawing 'the lovely blinds of the *Purgatorio*' to saccharine McCartney's 'death with morning dew' in the great elegy. So, just as artistic freedom wishes for its own jurisdiction, social and familial responsibility claim their rights too.

But the sequence begins and ends with powerful pleas for artistic freedom. The opening poem meets another Sweeney, the old sabbath-breaking tinker Simon Sweeney, who memorably advises the poet to 'Stay clear of all processions!' (*SI* 63). The last encounter is with the ghost of James Joyce who also thinks this peasant pilgrimage is 'infantile', adding that 'you lose more than you redeem / doing the decent thing' and urging the poet to 'fill the element / with signatures on your own frequency' (*SI* 93–4). Some critics (such as Michael Allen in the *Irish Review* and Denis Donoghue) have reacted to this in puzzlement, noting, reasonably enough, that this is what Heaney was doing anyway. A surprisingly large number of other critics have taken Joyce as having the last word here, indicating that Heaney will hereafter abjure 'the decent thing' and become the unanchored artist. This view ignores the well-balanced dialectic of the sequence: the Dantesque power and anger, for example, of the great narrative of William Strathearn who was treacherously gunned down in his shop ('Station Island', VII) – the most fully Dantesque piece Heaney has ever written. Joyce may have the last word, urging Heaney to forget about the 'decent thing'; but it is not the only word, or even, in my judgement, the most persuasive word. And of course, like the figure of Colum McCartney in 'The Strand at Lough Beg', this Joyce, we should remember, is Heaney's invention.[13]

The volume twinned with *Station Island* was the translation of the medieval Irish epic *Buile Suibhne*, the story of an Ulster poet who is exiled for sacrilege. The issues of poetic vocation, religious duty in the loosest sense, and public responsibility could hardly be more effectively staged; Heaney saw immediately that 'there was something here for me', as he said in an interview with Dennis O'Driscoll in the Irish periodical *Hibernia* in 1983. Sweeney in the Irish poem achieves a kind of freedom, with a profound topographical knowledge of the whole of Ireland, but at the price of an increasing rootlessness; the need for a sense of place now usurps the sense of self, recalling the placename poems of *Wintering Out*. Successful as Heaney's version, *Sweeney Astray*, was mostly thought to be (there were a few dissenting voices), many commentators have felt that the best product of this encounter with the medieval text was the curiously personal and intricate series of poems called 'Sweeney Redivivus' – Sweeney reborn – which was section three of *Station Island*. We can take it that the revived Sweeney figure in that sequence was what Heaney himself described Sweeney as: 'a figure of the artist, displaced, guilty, assuaging himself by his utterance', adding that 'it is possible to read the work as an aspect of the quarrel between free creative imagination and the constraints of religious, political and domestic obligation'.[14] In later volumes, Heaney replaces Sweeney with the Tollund Man as his alter ego, as we will see.

The Sweeney poems, then, have the same art theme as before, but from this point on there is a slightly different, more defiant emphasis. There is still the guilt, but the poet (through the figure of Sweeney) is getting impatient with the old accusations against him as 'a feeder off battlefields'. This impatience will be sounded most loudly in *The Spirit Level* in 1996. More generally, the 'Sweeney Redivivus' poems are a sustained reflection on writing itself, and its relationship to the experiences (such as those of Heaney's childhood) on which it is founded; many review headings seized on the significant rhyme 'Heaney's Sweeney'. These poems also deal for the first time with a different idea of escape (another Yeatsian term): not into art but into a kind of liberating scepticism. In Neil Corcoran's words, in this section Sweeney 'becomes the opportunity for Heaney to voice contrary and hostile emotions of his own, emotions exhilaratedly free from what he appeared to value in much of his earlier work as his deepest attachments, obligations and responsibilities'.[15]

However, the following volume, *The Haw Lantern*, even if it is – as Michael Allen says – a continuation of what Heaney was doing already, does mark a move into a different area for his next 'images and symbols adequate to our predicament' (Heaney's version in his essay 'Feeling Into Words' of the Yeatsian 'befitting emblem of adversity', *P* 56–7). A contributory factor was Heaney's move to Harvard in 1984 which had brought him into contact with a wider contemporary literary community than the Irish or English milieu to which he had previously been largely attentive. In particular he became more intently aware of a world where the literary and public imperatives did seem to come together, and where it was respectable – even obligatory – to take sides: the Cold War world of repression and samizdat. This same awareness was prominent in the contemporary critical work *The Government of the Tongue*. In Russia, Poland and Czechoslovakia, political poetry could be written and the writer could proudly claim to be an 'internal exile', a term which might seem extreme and over-glamorising in an Irish context without the validation of a wider political world. 'The Master' in 'Sweeney Redivivus' was the first major tribute to one of these exiled protest poets, Czesław Miłosz (described, just before the end of his life, by Heaney as the greatest living poet). Significantly, even as authoritative a Heaneyist as Neil Corcoran understandably 'presumed' that the subject of 'The Master' was Yeats; the literary ground was still assumed to be Ireland.[16]

There were other major events in Heaney's life to be taken into account: in the early 1980s he joined the board of Field Day, the theatre company founded by the playwright Brian Friel and the actor Stephen Rea. Field Day was a very successful venture, designed to take dramatic performances on tour throughout Ireland; involvement in it was seen as a move into a more public artistic arena, one whose aspirations were linked to notions of republicanism in various senses (the 'sweet equal republic', imagined by Tom Paulin in the long poem 'The Book of Juniper' at the end of *Liberty Tree*).[17] Involvement in the theatre, particularly in prompting two major Sophocles translations, *The Cure at Troy* and *The Burial at Thebes*,[18] has an important place in Heaney's life thereafter, even if it did not distract him from his primary poetic purpose in the way that Yeats complained that his engagement with 'theatre business, management of men' did.[19] Still with his major concern, the publication in 1988 of *The Government of the Tongue*, his most concentrated critical book, offered a sustained exploration of the rights and obligations of the writer, whether in the East or the West. The celebrated prefaced essay begins with an anecdote that dramatises the artistic/social choice with tact and precision: in 1972 Heaney and his friend David Hammond were on their way to a recording studio in Belfast to make a tape of songs and poems when a series of exploding bombs filled the air with noise and sirens. Hammond could not sing, 'the very notion of beginning to sing at that moment when others were beginning to suffer seemed like an offence against their suffering ... and we both drove off into the destroyed evening' (*GT* xi).

Generally speaking, the volume from the year before this political book of essays, *The Haw Lantern*, was (apart from 'Clearances', the wonderfully lucid sequence of elegies for Heaney's recently dead mother) less enthusiastically received than any other single Heaney volume up to that point. Before, critics had sometimes agonised about Heaney's place as poet: whether he ought to take a more or less committed stance towards Irish politics. The question was how his gift ought to be used; the gift itself was unquestioned. John Bayley had declared the poems in *Station Island* (a volume whose politics have sometimes been questioned) to be 'as beautiful as anything he has written, and wider in breadth'; Paul Muldoon, a reader who has sometimes been readier than most to scrutinise Heaney's achievement with a degree of friendly scepticism, called *Sweeney Astray* 'a masterful act of repossession'. But the reaction to *The Haw Lantern* seems to be questioning in a new way. Michael Allen, in the review I have mentioned already, assumes a tone of exasperation: 'What has happened to Heaney? It is as though James Joyce let him off the hook when he told him at the end of *Station Island* "to fill the elements with signatures of your own frequency".' J. D. McClatchy has an odd explanation, in an oddly militaristic metaphor, for his impression that this book is 'something of a disappointment': that the poet (like the Arthurian Lancelot) is doing badly on purpose: 'I would say that it had been written with damp powder, except for my lingering suspicion that the poet himself may deliberately have wanted at that point in his career, by means of this rather slight book of mostly occasional poems, to defuse again the megaton reputation many had made for him' – in marked contrast to Muldoon's acerbic scolding in a review of *Station Island*: Heaney 'should resist more firmly the idea that he must be the best Irish poet since Yeats'.

McClatchy's view can hardly be the explanation, since the occasional poems were the most admired in the book. But the new questioning does seem to be linked to an overall view of what might be called 'the Heaney project': what the poet saw his whole vocation to be. Reviewing *The Haw Lantern*, Ian Hamilton (who had been less impressed than most by *Death of a Naturalist*: 'a strange, featureless first collection') saw Heaney's cautious scepticism about vocation as a strength, the great modernist virtue of doubt: 'there is always a touch of "Why me?"' But in his next book *Seeing Things* in 1991, Heaney took one of the most decisive positions he has ever assumed. Already in *The Haw Lantern* there was some claim for artistic freedom, as there had been in 'Sweeney Redivivus' and at many points throughout Heaney's career, as we have seen. But in *Seeing Things* this bid for freedom does not go outside experience; it suddenly sees it as having been implicit in experience from the first.

The claim is most famously made in 'Fosterling', a poem in which Heaney returns to the model of Wordsworth, displacing Dante and the East Europeans whose allegories had dominated Heaney's poetry – and prose – in the 1980s. Various stages of his career have been seen as decisive points of change: Heaney's own observation that 'up to *North* that was one book'; Foster's suggestion that the poetry takes a different course after 1980. But the clearest declaration of change comes in 'Fosterling': 'me waiting until I was nearly fifty / To credit marvels' (*ST* 50). In fact Heaney has been a great appreciator of marvels throughout his career, presenting the marvellous in the ordinary, captured in the much-quoted phrase from the medieval Fenian legends 'the music of what happens'. In 'Fosterling' he characterises his previous understanding as having been 'the doldrums of what happens', declaring that it is now 'time to be dazzled' and for the 'heart to lighten'. Once again, we are tempted to say with Michael Allen that this is what Heaney has always done, ever since the visionary artisan-poems of the early volumes where the family marvelled, for example, at the 'Midas touch' of the thatcher who turned the roof to gold (*DD* 20). But Heaney's declarations of artistic purpose are always a matter of emphasis, a balance of preferences between various imperatives: 'two buckets were easier carried than one'. This principle of balance was the central concern of his Oxford lectures, delivered as Professor of Poetry between 1989 and 1994, and published as *The Redress of Poetry*.

Nevertheless, *Seeing Things* was seen as biased towards the celebration of the marvellous by invoking artistic licence, to an extent that caused it to be regarded with some suspicion by those who were anxious that Heaney should remain the exemplary voice of the conflict between public duty and artistic freedom. What was hard to resist was the quality of the poems in the book as it explored the visionary ('seeing') capacity of the poet. Many critics and readers (for example, Helen Vendler in her brief, suggestive 1998 study of Heaney) have seen the most perfect representation of this visionary perspective in Number viii in the sequence of forty-eight twelve-line poems called 'Squarings' which make up the last section of *Seeing Things* (before its inspired conclusion with the Charon episode of Dante's *Inferno* III).[20] This beautiful parable recounts the story of a vision by medieval monks in Clonmacnoise in which they see a ship sailing above them in the air. The anchor gets snagged in the altar rails; one of the crewmen climbs down but fails to release it, so the monks free it. The ship moves on and the crewman climbs back up 'out of the marvellous as he had known it' (*ST* 62).

The story represents with wonderful aptness the capacity of two cultures and worlds, however unalike, to collaborate. This remarkably positive turn in Heaney's poetic position must be seen in the context of an improvement in the political situation in Northern Ireland, culminating in the 1994 IRA ceasefire. The context is important because it shows that in *Seeing Things* Heaney was not turning his back on public issues (as is evident from Poem xxxvi in 'Squarings' about fear on a civil rights march); he was taking a positive view, one which is encapsulated in one of his most quoted lines, from *The Cure at Troy* whose title and theme of course are very significant. Perhaps the time is coming at last 'when hope and history rhyme': a line which was quoted at significant moments by Bill Clinton and Mary Robinson amongst others.

The heart does not simply 'lighten' though. The recurrent image in *Seeing Things* is of a false sense of security, or a false sense of insecurity. The car in the civil rights poem 'gave when we got in / Like Charon's boat under the faring poets' (*Squarings* xxxvi; *ST* 94), echoing the insight about boats in the book's title-poem:

> What guaranteed us –
> That quick response and buoyancy and swim –
> Kept me in agony. (*ST* 16)

Modernist doubt is not to be so lightly dispelled. Charon, in Dante's version from *Inferno* III, is the last boatman in this book of passings over (he will implicitly become significant again in *District and Circle*). And sure enough, the next book *The Spirit Level* (1996) allows itself to express considerable pessimism, even an uncharacteristic spleen. Since *Seeing Things* indeed, Heaney has become increasingly pessimistic, often in relation to politics and especially, since the start of the new millennium, in the international arena. What varies is the temper with which the pessimism is expressed, from rueful to angry. *Electric Light* in 2001 is dominated by the pastoral genre; but it is pastoral seen as a grim politics, as I argue in my chapter here (and, more significantly, as Heaney himself argues in his Irish Academy lecture).[21] So, when *District and Circle* is dominated by the chthonic and the transition to the afterlife (yet again, we find ourselves noting: Heaney has always been concerned with this), this is not so much in relation to his own ageing – though that of course gives the theme an increasing poignancy – as to what he sees as the gloom of the world of the early twenty-first century, dominated by an increasingly world-dominant but also rudderless imperial West. In the 1980s Heaney's international politics looked eastward; in 'Known World' in *Electric Light*, Heaney tells us that when he visited Belgrade what he found sinister was the 'west-in-east'. In the later poetry, the West, one might conclude, will take on some of the oppressive role of the totalitarian East of the 1980s writings.

The power of some of the poems in *The Spirit Level*, especially 'Mycenae Lookout' with the echoes of 'Punishment' in its fierce 'Cassandra' section, has tended to dominate discussion of the volume. But the book has notably positive qualities too. It manages to integrate the domestic and local within the public in a new way, especially in the volume's finest poem 'Keeping Going', in tribute to the poet's brother Hugh. Two tragic events, understated as they are, dominate the poem: the accidental death of Hugh's daughter (uncannily reminiscent of the death in 'Mid-Term Break'), and the killing of a Royal Ulster Constabulary reservist on his way to work, witnessed by Hugh. But the poem's title, and its conclusion, manages to win an optimistic message from the tragedy, with implications for the possibility of public peace. Like those in Mahon's poem who lived through adversity 'bomb by bomb', this exemplary figure has 'kept going', and the poem pays tribute to his 'stamina' and his achievement in being able to 'stay on where it happens' (*SL* 12). This celebration of quiet, stoical endurance occurs at other places in the book – for example in the beautiful poem about the blind neighbour, 'At the Wellhead', or the great poem of friendship 'A Call'. But in this book of balances – noted already as the dominant theme of *The Redress of Poetry* – these tributes to the ordinary are set against a series of poems of defiance and self-justification, like 'Mycenae Lookout' and 'Weighing In'. The balancing of artistic freedom with ethical responsibility has shifted its ground, perhaps because the poet no longer feels the necessity to make a case for the adequacy of art to our predicament. *Seeing Things* has suggested that artistic vision is an end in itself, no longer required to make its case.

But *Electric Light* reminds us, once again, that responsibility is not so lightly discarded, just as it wasn't despite the advice of Heaney's Joyce in *Station Island*. Some poems make the bid for freedom, notably 'Known World' with its recalled conference of light-headed poets, beginning '*Nema problema!*' and ending '*Nema problema! Ja!* All systems go.' But in between there is a problem, and the poem admits, in lines that summarise the dilemma of 'Keeping Going', that

> That old sense of a tragedy going on
> Uncomprehended, at the very edge
> Of the usual, it never left me once ... (*EL* 21)

'In Belgrade' the poet, as I have said, has found his 'west-in-east', just as many years before the northern world of Glob's Bog People had made Heaney feel 'lost, / Unhappy and at home'. *Electric Light* is again dominated by tragedy, not with the anger of *The Spirit Level* but in despair: the murder of Sean Brown, heard about in Greece, makes us think of an early prophetic line of Heaney's 'that kind of thing could start again' (*DN* 41). It is a book too of eclogues (a forum for political debate as well as the bucolic) and elegies: elegies for Heaney's poetic friends – Ted Hughes, Joseph Brodsky and Zbigniew Herbert – and relatives, in the beautiful, distanced title-poem about his grandmother and another poem about his father, 'anointed and all', recalling Hopkins's 'Felix Randal'. For the first time the 'real names' can be used without qualification because all of Heaney's interests come together, as he walks in the shadow of death.

There is of course a major poetic work of Heaney which bears the same relation to *Electric Light* as *Sweeney Astray* does to *Station Island*. Translated works have often interrelated with new poems (if translation is not 'new') in Heaney, and his version of *Beowulf* in 1999 was one of his most acclaimed successes.[22] There are major infiltrations from *Beowulf* in *Electric Light*, especially the optimistic and spiritual Song of Creation, drawn on in 'The Fragment' (*EL* 57), and more tellingly the desolate story of Hrethel whose son accidentally kills his elder brother.[23] The melancholy of *Beowulf* fits grimly well into much of the spirit of *Electric Light*, even if it is limiting to speak of Heaney in terms of content only: as from the first, his formal powers of description and evocation remain unrivalled – for example in the simile of the burning newspapers in 'The Little Canticles of Asturias' in *Electric Light*: 'breaking off and away / In flame-posies, small airborne fire-ships' (*EL* 24).

District and Circle reinforces the death-shadowed theme, with much of the book taking place in the Underground or afterlife. Charon, who lurked as a threat in the artistic paradise of *Seeing Things*, is now a dominant presence in this book of crossings over. But here too the descriptive power is undimmed, as in the title-poem's description of 'strap-hanging' in the Tube in lines which bring together an astonishing number of Heaney's themes and techniques:

> I reached to grab
> The stubby black roof-wort and take my stand
> From planted ball of heel to heel of hand
> As sweet traction and heavy down-slump stayed me. (*DC* 18)

There is the buoyancy of the boat in 'Seeing Things', or of Charon's boat – kept in agony by what guarantees us; the repetition of the heel; the sense of weight; and the powerful physical evocation of the 'roof-wort' – a neologism that could not apply to anything else, except perhaps to the 'old kale stalk' in 'The Harrow-Pin' in the same book. The poem invites comparison with Rilke's 'Orpheus', in the way that worldly experience translates without strain into the transcendental, 'transported / Through galleried earth with them, the only relict / Of all that I belonged to' (*DC* 19).

Just as earlier changes of emphasis in Heaney's poetry were prompted by political events, such as the intensification of the Troubles in the early 1970s or the ceasefire in 1994, one major international event affected the temper of *District and Circle*, the 9/11 attacks in New York. The poem which most reflects this, both in its pre-published form and in the book itself, was the version of Horace's Ode 1.34, 'Anything Can Happen', in which Jupiter 'galloped his thunder cart and his horses / Across a clear blue sky' (*DC* 13).[24] As in the other volumes since *Seeing Things*, art is not asked to make its case. But the balance between the private and public perspectives ends in this book with the earthly defeat of the private, in the recurrence of poems set in the underworld (with Seferis, Cavafy and the tinwhistle-playing Charon in the title-poem), recalling Yeats's late revenant poems such as 'Cuchulainn Comforted', the poem Heaney would choose to represent Yeats at his best.[25] There are more encouraging and durable things too: the Horatian metal (an unlaboured *aere perennius*) of the implements in the translation from Eoghan Rua Ó Súilleabháin and in the hopeful millennial anvil linked to it. But once again the book ends on a note of foreboding that tilts the balance towards the tragic: 'I said nothing at the time / But I never liked yon bird' (*DC* 75–6). The tragedy at the edge of the usual is still not leaving the poet.

But *District and Circle* is only the latest Heaney, and already not the last. To keep in step with Yeats, there are still the volumes after *The Winding Stair* to come: the period of which F. R. Leavis questioned whether it was 'Late Yeats and Greatest?'

In a poet who has been as much written on as Heaney, the representation of criticism in a book like this must inevitably be partial. It may be that the theme I have given most prominence to in this introduction – the Yeatsian concern with art and life – is unduly over-represented in the essays too. I have not been concerned to give a balanced introduction to all the periods of the poet's work, since the work up to 1990 has been very fully accounted for in the existing criticism, as is evident in the bibliography. Thus, an essay is devoted by John Wilson Foster to the work of Heaney's middle age, from *Seeing Things* to *Electric Light*. Heaney's standing as a poet-practitioner in the tradition from Coleridge to Eliot is widely recognised, so David Wheatley's essay on his criticism is of the first importance. Similarly, the influences from Wordsworth and Yeats are given centrality as, I would suggest, the guides of whom Heaney is most aware; the influence of Dante might have been addressed more particularly, but that too has been given a good deal of attention. The general emphasis here is probably on Heaney in Irish traditions, both literary and historical. Within the literary tradition, Andrew Murphy casts his net backwards while Dillon Johnston looks at Heaney amongst his poetic contemporaries, giving particular prominence to themes shared with his southern contemporaries such as Thomas Kinsella. In the public context Patrick Crotty looks at the wider critical reception of Heaney, first amongst his Irish poetic predecessors and contemporaries, and then in his own right; Dennis O'Driscoll adds to this the poet's own contributions to the debate about his reception. Similarly privileged information is provided by Rand Brandes's exploration of titles that Heaney toyed with and changed. Beyond an Irish tradition, discussions of Greek, Eastern European and Germanic influences are clearly indispensable. Fran Brearton's essay ventures into an area of gendered imagery where Heaney's practice (like that of several of his Northern Irish contemporaries) has been scrutinised. Guinn Batten's essay serves in some ways as a rejoinder to this, seeing an idea of feminine nourishment derived from Wordsworth as a prompt to the poetic imagination. Throughout though, whether the poet is negotiating with the ancient Classics, the Northern Past, or the international present, or with the English and Irish literary traditions, the distinctive strength and emphasis of this writer is indeed to show how 'lyrical beauty' is the vehicle for 'ethical depth'.

NOTES

1. John Wilson Foster, *The Achievement of Seamus Heaney* (Dublin: Lilliput Press 1995), p. 2.
2. For Heaney's miscellaneous earlier prose writings, up to 1991, see 'Uncollected Articles and Reviews, etc.', in *Seamus Heaney: A Collection of Critical Essays*, ed. Elmer Andrews (London: Macmillan 1992), pp. 257–9. Exceptions to my perhaps over-generalising view about the paucity of early extended criticism are the brilliant British Academy Chatterton lecture on Hopkins in 1974, 'The Fire i' the Flint: Reflections on the Poetry of Gerard Manley Hopkins' (reprinted in *P* 79–97), a discussion which gives a good foretaste of what Heaney's distinctive critical strengths will be; and the considered review of *The Penguin Book of English Pastoral Verse* in *The Times Literary Supplement* (see my chapter on 'Heaney's Classics and the Bucolic' here).
3. Neil Corcoran, *English Poetry Since 1940* (London and New York: Longman, 1993), p. 182.
4. Derek Mahon, 'Afterlives, for James Simmons', in *Collected Poems* (Oldcastle: Gallery Press 1999), p. 59.

5. Seamus Deane, 'Seamus Heaney: The Timorous and the Bold', in *Celtic Revivals* (London: Faber and Faber, 1985), p. 175.
6. *Yeats's Poems*, ed. A. N. Jeffares (London: Macmillan, 1989), p. 310. The famous line comes at the end of Section II of 'Meditations in Time of Civil War', Yeats's most effective political poem. For Glob's book, see p. 205 n. 5.
7. See Frank Ormsby, *A Rage for Order: Poetry of the Northern Ireland Troubles* (Belfast: Blackstaff Press, 1992), p. xvii (quoting Michael Longley from the *Radio Times*, 20–26 October 1979).
8. Conor Cruise O'Brien, 'Passion and Cunning: An Essay on the Politics of W. B. Yeats', in *In Excited Reverie*, ed. A. N. Jeffares and K. G. W. Cross (London: Macmillan 1965), pp. 207–78; reprinted in *Passion and Cunning and Other Essays* (London: Paladin Grafton Books, 1990).
9. 'An Interview with Seamus Heaney' (James Randall), *Ploughshares* 5: 3 (1979), p. 21.
10. *Soundings '72: An Annual Anthology of New Irish Poetry* (Belfast: Blackstaff Press 1972), n.p.
11. See Declan Kiberd, 'Multiculturalism and Artistic Freedom: The Strange Death of Liberal Europe' (1993), in *The Irish Writer and the World* (Cambridge: Cambridge University Press, 2005), pp. 250–68.
12. Neil Corcoran, 'Seamus Heaney and the Art of the Exemplary', *Yearbook of English Studies* 17 (1987), pp. 117–27; incorporated into a longer chapter 'Examples of Heaney', in *Poets of Modern Ireland: Text, Context, Intertext* (Cardiff: University of Wales Press, 1999), pp. 137–55.
13. It has not, I think, been sufficiently noted that Joyce's closing words to Heaney in this section are closely modelled on Virgil's last words to Dante at the end of *Purgatorio* Canto 27.
14. Michael Allen, 'Writing a Bare Wire: *Station Island*', in *Seamus Heaney*, ed. Michael Allen, Macmillan Casebook Series (London: Macmillan, 1997), p. 120.
15. Corcoran, *Poets of Modern Ireland*, p. 108.
16. Allen, *Seamus Heaney*, p. 123.
17. Tom Paulin, 'The Book of Juniper' (1981), collected in *Liberty Tree* (London: Faber and Faber 1983), p. 27.
18. Seamus Heaney, *The Cure at Troy: A Version of Sophocles' 'Philoctetes'* (Derry: Field Day Theatre Company, 1990); *The Burial at Thebes. Sophocles' 'Antigone'* (London: Faber and Faber, 2004).
19. W. B. Yeats, 'The Fascination of What's Difficult', *Yeats's Poems*, ed. Jeffares, p. 188.
20. Heaney tells us that at one point he hoped to complete twelve groups of twelve, making 144 poems in all. He has not commented whether stopping at 48 had Bach's 'Well-tempered Klavier' in mind (like Eliot's *Four Quartets* perhaps). If the suggestion is not too fanciful, the adjective 'well-tempered' might describe the spirit of the sequence well.
21. Seamus Heaney, 'Eclogues *in extremis*: On the Staying Power of Pastoral', *Proceedings of the Royal Irish Academy* 103C:1 (2003), pp. 1–12.
22. *Beowulf* shares with *The Spirit Level* the unusual accolade of winning the Whitbread Book of the Year award: one rarely given to poetry.
23. It is striking how Heaney adjusts in small ways the wording of his translation in *Beowulf* for the section which he reproduces substantially in 'On His Work in the

English Tongue' in *Electric Light*, as if he believes a different register of language is appropriate for the translation of epic from lyric.

24. Published as a separate pamphlet in various translations: *Anything Can Happen: A Poem and Essay by Seamus Heaney with Translations in Support of Art for Amnesty* (Dublin: TownHouse, 2004). The linking of a public event with art is noticeably foregrounded in this full title.
25. Seamus Heaney, 'Yeats as an Example?' (1978), reprinted in *P* 98–114.

2

RAND BRANDES

Seamus Heaney's Working Titles: From 'Advancements of Learning' to 'Midnight Anvil'

'"Polder", how do you pronounce "polder?"' was the topic of discussion between Seamus Heaney and his editor at Faber and Faber, Charles Monteith, who advised the poet to 'Never call a book by a title that people aren't sure how to pronounce.'[1] 'Polder' never made it to the bookstores; neither did 'Easter Water', another working title for the same volume. But the collection of poems did finally appear under the title *Field Work* (1979). As well as receiving sound marketing advice, Seamus Heaney has been highly attuned to the mystical potential of book and poem titles (as well as the look of the book).[2] For Heaney, 'working titles' are titles that 'work', as in successfully embodying the spirit of the poem or book in a way that resonates with the reader. But most obviously, 'working titles' are titles that serve as emblems capable of calling forth the essence of the book or poem from memory. In addition, 'working titles' are provisional titles, like 'Polder', that after serious consideration by the poet have been replaced because of internal and external pressures.

Heaney has said of the process:

> What usually happens is that I start to look for one [a title] once a 'critical mass' of poems gets written. I find that if I have a working title at that stage – say when half a volume is in existence – the title itself can help in shaping, or at least inclining and suggesting, the poems to come.[3]

If a title can help engender the 'poems to come', then it must also play a role in shaping the books to come. Writing great poems is one thing; giving them great titles is another; but assembling them with authority and vision into a dynamic whole takes more than mere talent. Ultimately, to compose one 'great' Yeatsian book out of all the books he has written is the final stroke of the Magus.[4] What informs Heaney's 'great book' is the notion of the poet as shaman and seer, as well as promoter and protester. Heaney has said that:

> publication is rather like pushing the boat out; then the boat/book turns into a melting ice floe and you have to conjure a second boat that turns into a melting floe under your feet. All the stepping-stones that you conjure disappear under the water behind you.[5]

Heaney's titles, in outline form, document the poet's quest as revealed in the riddles and rhymes of the soul as it invents for itself a way through a violent world in search of enlightenment. He has consistently resisted titles that were too self-referential, too literary, too colloquial and too close to the book titles of other poets. Heaney is hyper-conscious of the dialogue between books – books that move from self-discovery to self-consciousness to self-revelation.

Examined in chronological order Heaney's published titles reveal an uncanny foreknowledge of future titles; it is as if the 'flicker-lit' underworlds of *District and Circle* (2006) were already inscribed in the lantern-lit darkness of *Death of a Naturalist* (1966). Acknowledging the poet's publishing sixth sense is not designed to mystify the authorial and commercial realities of literary production, but to emphasise how the book titles have come to shape our fundamental perception of a possible Yeatsian wholeness informing Heaney's work and world. Heaney's individual volumes to date can be read as chapters in a book about an artist coming to terms with a world both familiar and strange, material and mystical, political and poetic, prehistoric and postmodern. No other poet writing in English has so deftly charted the political and personal changes in consciousness and material conditions in the second half of the twentieth century as has Heaney.

In *Death of a Naturalist*, Heaney's first full-length volume of poems, we witness the birth of the poet. The book's title, taken from the poem 'Death of a Naturalist', prepares the reader for the anti-pastoral, coming-of-age poems that follow. Heaney's first published poems, 'Reaping in the Heat' and 'October Thought' (Michaelmas 1959) and 'Nostalgia in the Afternoon' (November 1959) appeared in the Queen's University publications *Q* and *Gorgon*, respectively, when the poet was only twenty. At twenty-five, Heaney sent the manuscript of 'Advancements of Learning' to Irish publisher Liam Miller of the Dolmen Press late in 1964. 'Advancements of Learning', the working title of *Death of a Naturalist* in the making, refers to a poem with a similar title, 'An Advancement of Learning'. The poem describes the poet's encounter with a rat and his overcoming his fear of the 'rodent' and all it represents to the pubescent boy who 'stared him out' (*DN* 19). Ironically, what the child of the poems learns is that life can be scary and violent as in 'The Early Purges', 'Turkeys Observed' and 'Dawn Shot'. It can also be disappointing as in 'Blackberry Picking': 'It wasn't fair / That all the lovely canfuls smelt of rot' (*DN* 20); full of historical injustices as in 'For the Commander of the "Eliza"'; and personally painful as in 'Mid-Term Break'. As a result of the ironic potential of the working title of the Dolmen manuscript, 'Advancements of Learning' is almost too literary and self-conscious for the elemental ambiance of the book as it later became. The poet's awareness of this literary liability also appears in the working title of the poem 'Death of a Naturalist', which first appeared in *Poetry Ireland* (Spring 1965) as 'End of a Naturalist'. In addition to sounding more final than the poem suggests, 'End' is a much more abstract and literary term than 'Death'. In the subtle shift from 'End' to 'Death', we see one thing that the poet has learned – that his writing is rooted in the natural world.

In a virtuoso performance and with much bravado, 'Digging' establishes the poet's most significant and versatile metaphor for the creative endeavour and the search for truth – digging. The metaphor is multi-faceted and capable of simultaneously embracing seemingly contradictory notions. While it is healthy to loosen the soil to plant and harvest, to dig into one's psychic past, to explore one's history through archaeology, mythology and etymology, it can also be painful and destructive. On the surface 'Digging' examines the natural longing for familial and communal continuity – my ancestors worked the land, so I should work the land – while acknowledging that the very awareness of the past results in an increased consciousness that separates the poet from it and its comforts. The moral and aesthetic education of the poet is at the heart of Heaney's *Death of a Naturalist* as suggested in the working title 'Advancements of Learning'. From the opening poem of the book, 'Digging', to the closing poem, 'Personal Helicon', the poems are driven by the tensions between childhood innocence and insecurities and the adult realities and reconciliations. In the 'Advancements of Learning' manuscript, the final poem was 'Fisher', a poem lacking the authority of 'Personal Helicon', one working title of which was 'Apprenticeship' – again a title which offered an ending to the book that was too literary. 'Personal Helicon' does not resolve the sense of guilt and betrayal exposed in 'Digging', but it does reframe it. Between the first and last poems Heaney turns over in his mind the lessons that he has learned about life, love and language. With each poem we observe a growing awareness of the wonderful, weary and worrisome world clearly presented in the last lines of the book: 'I rhyme / To see myself, to set the darkness echoing' (*DN* 57). Ironically, the poet is illuminated by descending into the darkness. The lyric is the light that leads the way. This light appears in Heaney's second volume *Door into the Dark*.

As with many of the poems in *Death of a Naturalist*, *Door into the Dark* (1969) documents the mechanical modernisation of Northern Ireland and the disappearance of traditional trades and practices. In poems such as 'The Outlaw', 'The Forge' and 'Thatcher', the trade/practice represents not only a 'dying art', but also a lost set of social and aesthetic values with which the poet identifies. The mysteries of these arts, where the forge is an 'altar' (*DD* 19) and the thatcher has a 'Midas touch' (*DD* 20), are metaphors for a creative process more common and communal in the 'old world'. *Door into the Dark* was always *Door into the Dark* and did not have a provisional title.[6] The mythic potential of the title probably secured its place since many of the poems emerge out of the land itself. In these poems we see the poet's first encounters with the mythic darkness associated with the female fecundity of the land. 'Undine' and 'Rite of Spring' clearly anticipate the 'bog poems' in *North*. Heaney first published 'Rite of Spring' as 'Persephone'.[7] In addition to diminishing the mythic magnitude of the poem as suggested by the Greek Goddess, 'Rite of Spring' enhances the sexual undercurrent of the poem. This undercurrent flows through the volume's 'Lough Neagh Sequence', which was published on its own as a pamphlet in 1969.[8] The pamphlet's front cover has an image of a Celtic brooch with eel-like interwoven engravings while quotations from volume II of *The Fishes of Great Britain and Ireland* (1880–4) introduce the poem. Like many of Heaney's most successful poems, 'A Lough Neagh Sequence' relies upon the mythologising and de-mythologising of the poetic material. The fishermen are real people working in a real place (represented by the quotations), and they are part of a prehistoric drama of death, rebirth and global renewal (represented in the brooch).

While *Door into the Dark* seems in retrospect to be a transitional book where the poet was trying to overcome the success of *Death of a Naturalist*, *Wintering Out* (1972), with its two sections, is structurally and poetically more complex and accomplished. A much more bleak and political book, the title *Wintering Out* obliquely alludes to the famous opening line of *Richard III*, 'Now is the winter of our discontent ...'[9] The reference to a corrupt state plagued by an unsolved murder sets the tone (often pessimistic) for most of the poems in Part One. The phrase 'wintering out' appears in the fifth poem, 'Servant Boy': 'He is wintering out / the back-end of a bad year' (*WO* 17). The boy, and his latent hostility, look to the disenfranchised of Northern Ireland in the 1970s where the boys now spray-paint on the city walls of Derry 'Is there a life before death?'[10] However, the poems in Part Two seem to have initially shaped the poet's thinking about the book. The working title of *Wintering Out* was 'Winter Seeds', an image taken from one of the book's most famous poems 'The Tollund Man': 'His last gruel of winter seeds / Caked in his stomach' (*WO* 47). For all of the poem's ambivalence and ambiguity, 'winter seeds' is relatively optimistic. The poet contemplates the possibility that the violence in Northern Ireland, when seen in the context of prehistoric Europe, may carry within it the seeds of a new life and hope. Although 'The Tollund Man' appears in Part One where the poet explores the complexities of personal and communal identity through references to land, language, history and myth, the optimism of 'winter seeds' corresponds to the more personal poems of Part Two.

The poems of Part Two in *Wintering Out* seem to be written in the spirit of *Door into the Dark*; so, if the poems in Part Two had appeared as Part One, there would be a natural progression from one volume to the next. However, any hint of a normal life of self-integration and communal harmony in the poems of Part Two is qualified by the violence and social and political pressures of Part One. Thus some of the strangeness, suffering and hurt of poems like 'Limbo', 'Bye-Child' and 'A Winter's Tale' are rooted in the world of Part One. Even 'Wedding Day', the first poem of Part Two and one that could have appeared in the first two volumes, seems lonely and unpromising following 'Augury', the last disturbing poem of Part One. 'Augury', whose central image is a 'diseased' fish, was published as 'As We Roved Out', a much more ironical title alluding to the first line of a famous song by the same title.[11] Not only is the human world plagued, but also the land itself. Part Two ends with 'Westering', in which the poet is looking at a map of the moon and recalls a drive through Donegal on Good Friday. Six thousand miles from Ireland in California (where many of the poems were written during the poet's 1970–1 tenure at the University of California at Berkeley), there is no solace to be found on the moon, in a nostalgic longing for home, or the promised comforts of religion. The wasteland of *Wintering Out* is manifest in the closing image of 'untroubled dust', which flashes back to the poisoned lands of Part One (*WO* 80). The poet passed through the *Door into the Dark* and into the half-hell of *Wintering Out*, but he had not yet reached the nadir of his descent. This would come in *North*, published in 1975.

With the death of ritual come the rituals of death embodied in the recurring images of decomposition and dismemberment that pervade the poems of *North*. If the poet has imagined himself an archaeologist, uncovering the bog bodies of the Tollund Man's prehistoric kith and kin, he also sees himself as a political geologist, historian and witness to the crimes and injustices of the Northern Ireland conflict. The language of *North* is anatomical and geological. The poems describe a soulless world in which the competing ideologies produce a complete objectification of the human body. In *North* the living die and the dead come to life. The Troubles grind on with a geological inevitability; man and earth are ground down under Ice Age thinking, the run-off of which seems to produce a quagmire. As suggested in the title *North*, north is a non-place, a direction which if followed ends in death. However, it is also important to note that the poem from which the book title is taken had two working titles: 'North Atlantic', and 'Northerners'.[12] The former suffers from being too vague or general (not ambiguous), while the latter is too specific and anthropocentric. These titles were apparently never working titles for the book itself. *North* was always *North*.

In *Wintering Out* the dedicatory poem produces a pessimistic subtext that informs even the more optimistic poems of the volume. Likewise in *North*, the simple rituals and rewards of family love and communal life presented in the two poems of dedication work to qualify the violence and despair recorded in the poems that follow. Central to the book are the eight poems that were published separately as *Bog Poems* by the Rainbow Press run by Olwyn Hughes, the sister of Ted Hughes, who published *Crow* in 1970. *North* is Seamus Heaney's *Crow* – a mythological descent into an apocalyptic underworld in which the poet must confront the Goddess in all of her terrible beauty and exorcise his demons if he is to be reborn in his future poems. Of all of the *Bog Poems*, 'Punishment' is the most provocative and controversial. The poem has been used to accuse Heaney of various negative traits including sexism, atavism and violent nationalism. The poem's working title, 'Shame', describes the Catholic community's attempt to 'shame' its female members who fraternise with British soldiers by shaving their heads and pouring hot tar on them.[13] Of course, 'shame' is also what the poem implies the Catholic community should feel itself for its primitive, brutal behaviour. Unable to separate himself from either the girl or the community, the poet feels the shame of both. However, 'Punishment', unlike 'Shame', increases the distance between the poet and the poem while diminishing the accusatory tone of the working title. This tone was even stronger in the closing stanza of an early version of the poem published in *Broadsheet* (March 1973): 'into your meek gaze / I commit the stone-casters / and your punished sisters / weeping under the lamp-post'. Ultimately, by changing the poem's title and closing stanzas, the poet has affirmed in principle if not action his connection with the Catholic community, leaving the shame behind in another poem. In *North*, the poem's concluding confession, though self-incriminating, does not exonerate the community; this is one demon that will have to wait to be fully exorcised.

Field Work (1979) records the poet's sense of release and relief after his battles with the dark side in *North*. Though laced with elegies and re-examinations of empire, *Field Work* is a work of respite and the search for solace. The book's working titles, 'Polder' and 'Easter Water', foreground the significant shift in the poet's attitude. While *Field Work* follows up more closely on the anthropological themes of *North* and looks back to the agricultural and agrarian motifs of *Death of a Naturalist*, 'Polder' introduces us to the poet's wife and love life and a new procreative link to the land. Unlike the life and death struggles with the Earth Goddess/Bog Queen, 'Polder', which means land that is reclaimed from water, refers to the poet's renewed embrace of the land as suggested in the poem: 'I have reclaimed my polder' (*FW* 51). The poem was published with two alternative first lines different from that of the trade edition, which reads 'After the sudden outbursts and the squalls' (*FW* 51). The earliest version appeared in the *Honest Ulsterman* in July/October 1978, 'After the dyke-burst and receding floods', followed by the *Paris Review* (Spring 1979), 'After the outbursts and terrible squalls'. The working book title and the poem title 'Polder' provide a clearer context than does *Field Work* for the book's central sequence, *Glanmore Sonnets*. Published separately in a limited edition as the *Hedge School, Sonnets from Glanmore*, it presents Glanmore as a site of rural education, which is what the Hedge School was during Penal days – the *Glanmore Sonnets* 'centre' the poet and the book.[14] The *Glanmore Sonnets* are the *Bog Poems* re-imagined and reclaimed.

'Easter Water', the other working title for *Field Work*, is taken from the poem 'In Memoriam Francis Ledwidge'. This title is admittedly hopeful in its suggestion of rebirth, reconciliation and meaningful, not meaningless, suffering. However, it is, ironically, more contentious than the other two titles. The Christian reference to Easter stirs up sectarian anxieties while also being too optimistic: 'Where you belonged, among the dolorous and lovely ... / Easter water sprinkled in outhouses'.[15] Like 'Winter Seeds', 'Easter Water' was probably discarded for its hopefulness; thus marketing and memory became the main issue as in 'Polder'. Ledwidge is described in the poem as 'our dead enigma' and represents the part of the book where family and friends (literary and not) feel torn apart by the perplexities of the ongoing strife in Northern Ireland.[16] This strife comes to a head in the book's final poem 'Ugolino', Heaney's translation from Dante's *Inferno*. Allusions to Dante appear earlier in the book in the epigram to 'The Strand at Lough Beg' and in 'An Afterwords'. In contrast to the earlier pastoral and playful allusions to Dante in these two poems, in 'Ugolino' Dante becomes a paradigm of the exiled European political poet confronted with religious violence and seeking justice. The image of Ugolino's cannibalism reflects the state of affairs in Northern Ireland, and weirdly reminds one of the book's opening poem's 'alive and violated' oysters that were carried to Rome where the 'glut of privilege' ruled ('Oysters', *FW* 11). For those who read the Faber and Faber edition of *Field Work*, 'Ugolino' sets the stage for the deeply Dantean book *Station Island*. However, between 'Ugolino' and *Station Island*, American readers encounter for the first time in Heaney's books a section of 'notes' in the Farrar, Straus and Giroux edition. Apparently, the choice of *Field Work* over 'Polder' and 'Easter Water' was not the only concession made in the name of marketing and the poet's growing international audience.

Much of the poet's self-questioning or doubt, which informs *Station Island*'s (1984) central sequence, is in response to the self-confidence that had brought him this far. He had also spent a significant amount of time with all of his previous poems as he compiled his selected works as in *Selected Poems 1965–1975* (1980). Middle-aged and feeling the weight of his own success, Heaney knew he must recreate himself if he was to continue writing. His first move during this period to break free of the world he had created came with the 1983 publication of the Field Day pamphlet, *An Open Letter*, in which he baulked at being included in the *Penguin Book of Contemporary British Poetry*. The hunger strikes had just ended, and one of his Derry neighbours, Francis Hughes, was the second to die. The political situation in the North magnified the poet's sense of guilt in response to his success. Sometimes his frustration made it into his poetry as in 'Ulster Quatrains: Sectarian Water; Sectarian Latin; Sectarian Alphabet'.[17]

In each of *Station Island*'s three sections, the poet envisions the road ahead by looking back. Heaney explores three possible ways of moving his work forward. The first option in Part One is to continue to do what he already does well. The second in 'Station Island' is to examine his failings and limitations – sometimes in light of an alternative future, as in the young Priest of Section IV. The third option in 'Sweeney Redivivus' is to leave it all behind – the obligations, the responsibilities, the decorum – and dedicate himself to writing for the joy of it. Though Heaney argues that Sweeney's aloofness is an analogy for the poet freed from social constraints, it is really the ancient Irish scribe Moling, who writes down Sweeney's story and lives it vicariously, that serves as Heaney's alter ego.[18] In each section Heaney looks to those writers who have written under similar historical pressures, such as Chekhov, Joyce and Miłosz, for possible ways to proceed. He also recalls those moments and people that shaped his moral and artistic development, such as his childhood teacher Master Murphy.

Ironically, the first inklings of 'Station Island' appeared in Heaney's notebooks in 1966. The working title of what would become 'Station Island' almost twenty years later was 'Lenten Stuff'.[19] When the poem finally began to emerge in the early 1980s, Heaney had tried several combinations of 'Station Island' poems in numerous periodicals. The arrangements varied, as did the versions that actually made it into the book. One sequence of three 'Station Island' poems published in the *Hudson Review* offers a clue to how Heaney put the long poem together. The poems appear under the title 'Station Island' and include a note that says that 'these are the opening sections of a longer poem'.[20] The final 'Station Island I' appears as the first poem in the sequence but is vastly different from the collected version. For instance the *Hudson* version begins: 'It was a close grey morning', and line five becomes the first line of the collected version, 'A hurry of bell-notes', which is less narrative and more dramatic. While the second poem of the *Hudson* series appears as poem II in 'Station Island' and is close to the collected version, the third poem remains uncollected but describes the same scene in *The Haw Lantern*'s 'From the Frontier of Writing', locating the poem on the road at a roadblock. The would-be pilgrim says: 'The light flotsam of his intonation / skimmed past me like a bit part in Shakespeare, / Cockney as Keats or O What a Lovely War. / How different were the words / *home, Christ, ale* and *master*, on his lips and on mine!' The soldiers let 'the bible-thumpers' through, and the poet reflects on the experience. Contributing to the power of 'Station Island' is the poet's ability to maintain a tone and diction that complements the seriousness of journey; the shift in tone in the *Hudson Review*'s third poem is obvious, as is the overt politicising of the scene. 'Station Island' ends with Joyce telling the poet, as others have in the poem before him, to assert his independence and to strike out on his own. Using Joyce at this point in the poem is much more effective than the brief allusion in the rejected section. In Part III of *Station Island*, 'Sweeney Redivivus', Heaney does break on through to the other side. The Purgatory foreshadowed in *Field Work* is left behind for Sweeney's pre-Christian, anti-authoritarian world.

Once the poet accepts Joyce's advice and hits the road with Sweeney, he goes international. The border crossings and language barriers of Northern Ireland are exported in Heaney's work as part of the new globalisation. The poet's training in the North prepared him for the new frontiers of writing that inform *The Haw Lantern* (1987). In fact, *The Haw Lantern* covers much of the same ground as *North* but under the auspices of late-capitalism and multinational geopolitics – forces that produced people like Nelson Mandela, Osama bin Laden, Bob Marley ... and Heaney himself. The imminent breakup of the Soviet Union and the rise of neo-nationalism are transposed onto the tribalism of Northern Island, whose Troubles foreshadowed those of the rest of the world. Post-structuralism and postmodernism, which also influence *The Haw Lantern*, were the cultural responses to the world out of which Heaney writes.

The 'haw lantern' is Sweeney's lantern, 'a small light for a small people' (*HL* 7). The poet's quest for truth and justice, and even insight and vision, continues in this volume. The public search for 'one just man' is counterbalanced by the personal search for compassion. *The Haw Lantern* had two working titles: 'Alphabets' and 'The Stone Verdict'. The autobiographical poem 'Alphabets' opens the book, and like 'The Stone Verdict', appeared in a pamphlet along with seven other *Haw Lantern* poems in a collection entitled *Hailstones*.[21] 'Alphabets' traces the poet's trajectory from the prelinguistic world of the poet's birthplace, Mossbawn, to the professor's podium at Harvard. The moral development of the poet corresponds to his political and poetic development, which is framed by a historical transformation from a pre-modern to postmodern world. Even though education is a central theme of the book, along with post-structuralist linguistics, and hints at the allegorical poems influenced by Eastern European poets, 'Alphabets' as a book title appears too self-conscious and literary following *Station Island*. In contrast, while the moral tone of 'The Stone Verdict' seems to follow logically from the purgatorial and penitential world of *Station Island* and foregrounds the unforgiving nature of stone, it is too explicitly judgemental and prescriptive. An external factor also affecting 'The Stone Verdict' working title was the 1985 publication of Irish poet Richard Murphy's *The Price of Stone*. Heaney wanted a title that was ambiguous and autonomous: *The Haw Lantern* met both of these requirements. In addition, as with *Death of a Naturalist* and later volumes, Heaney's initial tendency is to go for literary and bookish titles that he later reconsiders.

Looking back at Heaney's writing life, there seem to be at least three overlapping stages: an initial period where one feels that poems are 'begotten' and 'engendered'; next, poems that come out of a sense of inadequacies, longing and loss; and then poems that argue for letting go and 'not caring' – as in Patrick Kavanagh's understanding of 'not caring'. *Seeing Things* (1991) leaves the disappointed light of the haw lantern behind for the extravagant light that is all too familiar and all too rare, as portrayed in 'Markings': 'Youngsters shouting their heads off in a field / As the light died and they kept on playing ... Some limit had been passed, / There was a fleetness, furtherance, untiredness / In time that was extra, unforeseen, and free' (*ST* 8). It seems that Joyce's advice in *Station Island* to 'let others wear the sackcloth and ashes. / Let go, let fly, forget. / ... Now strike your note' (*SI* 93), while previewed in 'Sweeney Redivivus', has been partially realised in *Seeing Things*. One reason of course that it took so long to let go is the death of the poet's mother in 1984, which added gravity to *The Haw Lantern*. Another reason is that, as in the period between *Field Work* and *Station Island*, the period between *The Haw Lantern* and *Seeing Things* was extremely productive, re-immersing the poet in his past work as well as classical Greek and Roman literature. In addition to publishing in periodicals and anthologies many of the poems that appear in *Seeing Things*, Heaney also wrote introductions to works on Wordsworth, Pádraic Fallon and the W. B. Yeats section of the *Field Day Anthology*. From 1987 to 1991 Heaney's major publications included: *The Government of the Tongue: The 1986 T. S. Eliot Memorial Lectures and Other Critical Writings*; *The Place of Writing*; *New Selected Poems 1966–1987*; *The Redress of Poetry: Oxford Lectures*; and *The Cure at Troy: A Version of Sophocles' 'Philoctetes'*. Writing under the pressures of prose and public performances, Heaney's longing for release and revelation is virtually realised in the visions of *Seeing Things*.

The structure of *Seeing Things* is one of Heaney's most complicated. The book is framed by two of his translations: 'The Golden Bough' (from Virgil's *Aeneid*) and 'The Crossing' (from Dante's *Inferno*). These two bookends, about journeys to the underworld and inspired by the death of the poet's father in 1986, buttress the book's two parts, the second of which is the forty-eight poem poetic sequence, 'Squarings'. *Seeing Things* had two working titles, 'Squarings' and 'Lightenings', the titles of two of the four sections of 'Squarings'. Neither made it into print as book titles, but they were viable options. However, as Heaney comments: 'but when I wrote the "Seeing Things" poem – I think in the summer of 1990, after I came home from Harvard, early summer – I suddenly knew that I had the name of the volume'.[22] Both of the working titles, while pointing to major themes and images in the book, could not evoke the ocular ambiguities of the book in its totality. In addition to 'Settings' and 'Crossings', the other two 'Squarings' sections, Heaney had published groups of the poems under the titles 'Holdings' and 'Resolutions'.[23] The title-less twelve-line poems gave the poet great flexibility when organising the poems in the book. Without titles to separate and isolate the poems, the poems can then play off of each other like musical notes creating improvised chords and melodies. If Heaney had given every poem in 'Squarings' a title, as he did in some periodical publications – xxi is 'A Rent' and xxxvii is 'Quoting' – the play of angles, light and music would be lost.[24] Roman numerals reinforce the form of the poem and the poems' formality as the poet playfully declares in xxxviii: '"Down with form triumphant, long live," (said I), "Form mendicant and convalescent. We attend / The come-back of pure water and the prayer-wheel"' (*ST* 98).

Seeing Things is driven by a spiritual openness and creative extravagance that can accommodate the 'marvellous' of the everyday and extraordinary and stand up to the political realities of the age and the death of loved ones, like his father. Having been tempered by his mother's death in which he found meaning in absence, Heaney takes the next step and wilfully begins to open spaces around him. Imagining freedom is not imaginary freedom; it is the only way forward for those who want to experience the fullness of being and realise their dreams. As Heaney writes in 'The Settle Bed', 'whatever is given / Can always be re-imagined, however four-square, / Plank-thick, hull-stupid and out of its time / It happens to be' (*ST* 29). Many of the poems of Part One were published in variant forms in *The Tree Clock* in 1990. In addition to refocusing the reader's attention on the constellation of love poems that bolster and balance the light-headedness of the book, *The Tree Clock* also highlights the 'things' that the poet sees into and through. Of these, 'The Pitchfork' looks most clearly back at the poet's roots and foreshadows his future. As with the 'star-ship' of 'The Milk Factory' in *The Haw Lantern*, the poet presents another Star Trek-like image: 'he would see the shaft of a pitchfork sailing past / Evenly, imperturbably through space, / Its prongs starlit and absolutely soundless'.[25] Alluding to the death, we assume, of his father in the poem, the poet takes an everyday implement and draws out of it its physical and spiritual essence. What the pitchfork has to offer the poet is another manifestation of the freedom he desires, 'Where perfection – or nearness to it – is imagined / Not in the aiming but the opening hand.' The poet must let go of his father, who, like the house he built, was 'A paradigm of rigour and correction' (*ST* 91). Like the hand letting go of the pitchfork shaft, the poet must stay open to what lies ahead in the *Spirit Level*.

The visionary energy of *Seeing Things* and the implicit desire for enlightenment continue the vision quest outlined in Heaney's book titles and provide a perfect portal into *The Spirit Level* (1996). Despite the absence of a significantly explicit political element in *Seeing Things*, Heaney did not shift his gaze for long, and the political was to be more robustly incorporated in *The Spirit Level* from a broader international perspective. *The Spirit Level* carried the working title 'The Flaggy Shore' into the summer of 1995 when the majority of the poems had already been assembled into a manuscript – well before Heaney was awarded the Nobel Prize in October 1995. This title is taken from the opening lines of the book's final poem, 'Postscript': 'And some time make the time to drive out west / Into County Clare, along the Flaggy Shore' (*SL* 82). Though not identified on most maps as such, the 'flaggy shore' is on the Atlantic coast south of Galway City. Heaney liked the title because it was 'windier and stronger' than *The Spirit Level*.[26] But perhaps the West of Ireland kitsch that it approached encouraged the poet to remain open to a title that unconsciously resonated with the majority of the poems and continued the spiritual momentum of *Seeing Things*. *The Spirit Level*'s transcendence continued the progression from *North*'s darkness, to *Field Work*'s healing, to *Station Island*'s penitence and relaunch, to the *Haw Lantern*'s dawnlight truths, to *Seeing Things*'s revelations. From this perspective *The Flaggy Shore* could sound like old-school Heaney.

The first *Spirit Level* poem Heaney published in a periodical in 1992 (the year after the publication of *Seeing Things*), was 'Weighing In'.[27] This poem considers the importance of balance in all aspects of one's life – a central theme in *The Spirit Level*. The allusion to entering a debate rationally by 'weighing in' on an issue is balanced by the more brutal allusion to 'weighing in' before a fight. The poet presents both sides of the argument, whether one should turn the other cheek like Jesus or deliver a 'quick hit'. The level of frustration is evident in the poem: 'Passive suffering makes the world go round'; and 'Still, for Jesus' sake, / Do me a favour, would you, just this once? / Prophesy, give scandal, cast the stone' (*SL* 22).The poem resolutely concludes: 'I held back when I should have drawn blood ... At this stage only foul play clears the slate.' The personal references are unclear, but the political implications of the poem are not. The political situation in Northern Ireland was growing tense, and for those who had lived through the previous twenty-five years, the situation seemed interminable. In December of 1993, Heaney was a signatory of a letter calling for the adoption of the Hume–Adams initiative, and in September 1994 he wrote an essay, 'Light Finally Enters the Black Hole', describing his feelings about the recently announced IRA ceasefire.[28] If the poet had stopped caring in *Seeing Things*, 'Weighing In' is one possible political and personal position.

Immediately following 'Weighing In' in *The Spirit Level* is 'St Kevin and the Blackbird', a poem that takes the opposite position on balance and self-sacrifice. Originally published as 'Diptych' in 1992[29] and perhaps playing on the idea of an outdated hagiography, 'St Kevin and the Blackbird' utilises the 'Squarings' structure to complement the sense of balancing perspectives. The poem asks if the Saint is in constant suffering or in constant forgetfulness, as he holds the eggs of a blackbird in his hand until they hatch. As an image of patient suffering, he preaches the Christian ideal challenged in 'Weighing In'. As with previous Heaney volumes, *The Spirit Level* has a long poetic sequence at its core which helps turn the cluster of poems into a constellation. 'Mycenae Lookout' expands the theme of waiting, metaphorically and historically. The poem's narrator, like the poet, has been relegated to watch and wait for war to end: 'I balanced between destiny and dread' (*SL* 30). Even though it ends with the ablutions of 'His Reverie of Water', 'Mycenae Lookout', which had the more scientific and suggestive working title 'Mycenae Wavelengths', follows the Freudian argument that as long as we are sexual creatures, we will have war.[30] Heaney's travels to Greece and Italy during this time and his increased immersion in classical texts by Sophocles, Homer, Virgil and Horace placed the Northern Ireland conflict within a more historical, less mythological, European context. From this historical perspective the Northern Ireland conflict both acquired and lost significance in *The Spirit Level*. As the probabilities of peace grew dim in the late 1990s, Heaney responded with *Electric Light* – an ironic title tinged with tragedy.

An underlying sense of tragedy informs much of Heaney's work; even in the most quotidian of poems one feels the presence of Anglo-Saxon doom and Greek catastrophe in the disappointments and disillusionments. Tragedy gives Heaney's poems much of their immanence; the fear and pity evoked by tragedy that Joyce talks about in *A Portrait of the Artist as a Young Man* add gravitas to the lightest of subjects. Heaney alludes to the historical continuity of the theme in 'Known World' from *Electric Light*: 'That old sense of a tragedy going on / Uncomprehended, at the very edge / Of the usual, it never left me once ...' (*EL* 21). Tragedy is behind all three of *Electric Light*'s working titles – 'The Real Names', 'Known World' and 'Duncan's Horses', the last taken from a line in the poem 'Known World' and alluding to a scene in *Macbeth* full of chaos and anarchy:

> Duncan's horses, plastered in wet, surge up,
> As wild as the chestnut tree one terrible night
> In Mossbawn ...
>   My mother rocking and oching
> And blessing herself –
>   The breach in nature open. (*EL* 48)

While perhaps rejecting 'Duncan's Horses' as too politically melodramatic, or too Anglo-centric, for the entire volume, Heaney also mentions that this title was too close to Derek Walcott's *Tiepolo's Hound* – a volume that shares the themes of colonialism and the role of art and the artist. As with the rejected working title 'The Stone Verdict', Heaney wants a title that will be able to operate in its own creative space. Like 'Duncan's Horses', the 'Known World' also alludes to Elizabethan imperialism and thus presents similar thematic, if not imagistic, problems. On the other hand, even though 'The Real Names' also evokes Shakespearean touchstones, the working title's inwardness and self-consciousness – Heaney's 'personal stars within the Shakespearean galaxy' – cannot accommodate the larger themes in the book.[31] Nonetheless, 'The Real Names' does reflect the myriad of private and public allusions dotting the book – dots that even readers familiar with the poet's work will have difficulty connecting. The cast of characters is immense as are the changes of scene. The electric light of the published title is sometimes a torch, a spotlight, a stage light or a floodlight, as it applies to each poem. Like *The Haw Lantern*, which it reflects, *Electric Light* searches for people of purpose and moral character as it simultaneously exposes humanity's self-destructive nature. If there has been a 'breach in nature', it is in the ethical life of the individual cut off from community and ritual. 'Duncan's Horses', 'Known World' and 'The Real Names' are useful in decoding the matrix that is *Electric Light*.

Composed around the year 2000, *Electric Light* is a millennial book, not in its sense of expectation and exultation, but in its secular and anticlimactic blend of Yeats's cold vision and Hardy's detached resignation: 'Post-this, post-that, post-the-other, yet in the end / Not past a thing. Not understanding or telling / Or forgiveness' (*EL* 61). If the title refers to Heaney's memories of rural electrification, it also refers to the demystifying effect it represents in his life. *Electric Light* is the light of the operating table and the morgue; it is the light of reality that says we are mortal as suggested in poems, such as 'Would

They Had Stay'd', 'Audenesque' and 'Seeing the Sick'. The bodies in the book assert their thingness, their elemental objectification. Following the sense of freedom and transcendence in *The Spirit Level*, *Electric Light*, while occasionally luminous, brings us back to earth where the 'plaster child [Jesus], in nappies, / Bare baby-breasted little *rigor vitae*, / Crook-armed, seed-nailed, nothing but gloss and chill – / He wasn't right at all' (*EL* 14–15). This is Heaney's 'Second Coming'. Christianity, even when viewed from its Virgilian dreamland in 'Bann Valley Eclogue', has failed the poet and the world.

The poet who recorded the post-colonial repercussions of Northern Ireland has traced them through eleven individual volumes (excluding translations and 'selections') and over five hundred poems from Belfast to Baghdad. These shock waves of the soul have produced a poetry that accommodates the 'murderous as well as the marvellous', and where, as he says of Osip Mandelstam, 'lyric poetry' is a form of political 'resistance'.[32] Regardless of where in history or the world his imagination takes him, it is always rooted in the memories of his childhood home, a centre of decency and discretion. This sense of rejuvenating, not ingrown, rootedness is at the core of Heaney's most recent volume *District and Circle*.

The pre-millennial anxieties of *Electric Light* become manifest in the post-millennial atrocities of *District and Circle*. Heaney had committed to the title *District and Circle*, referring in part to the green- and yellow-coded underground lines that serve London's Earls Court and St James's Park, before the terrorist attacks of 7 July 2005. He had taken these lines during a 'summer of vacation work in London', the memories of which contribute to the underground motif running through the volume.[33] The 'Tollund Man', a long-time resident of Heaney's underworld, reappears in first person in the volume's central sequence 'The Tollund Man in Springtime'. One of the book's fleeting working titles, 'Braird', was in response to 'the lyrical lift I [Heaney] felt as I wrote the Tollund Man poems and a lot of the stuff that follows them in the book'. 'Braird', 'meaning as it does new growth, as of corn or leaves', appears in the book's opening poem 'The Turnip Snedder' and in the elegiac poem to his sister, 'The Lift'. *District and Circle*'s primary working titles, however, were 'Midnight Anvil' and 'The Alder'. The former, which alludes directly to the forge of Heaney's *Door into the Dark*, was rejected because of that fact and because 'there was something too heroic in the phrase, something that might seem to be approving the manifest deadliness of the retaliatory attacks on Afghanistan and (later on) Iraq'. While 'Midnight Anvil' might have been too precariously political, 'The Alder', like 'Braird', was too pastoral: 'there was just too much comfort in the phrase' ('Planting the Alder'). Heaney concludes: 'The blow struck on the local anvil and the strike against the Twin Towers are the tuning forks for the poems that appear in the early pages of the book I would eventually call *District and Circle*.' While the background noise of *Electric Light* was the sizzle of raw electricity, in *District and Circle* it is the rumble of thunder. These repercussions resonate through one of the volume's most ominous poems, 'Anything Can Happen'. Commenting on the poem, first published in November 2001 as 'Horace and Thunder', the poet comes 'to a terrified awareness that the tallest things can be brought low', that Fortune is *rapax*, rapacious, a predator who 'makes the air gasp'. As in Hardy's 'Convergence of the Twain', one is struck by the awesome power of the gods, who, as the turnip snedder says in the book's opening poem 'Snedder': 'This is the way that God sees life ... from seedling-braird to snedder ... This is the turnip-cycle.' This is the heartless cycle of history.

The poems of *District and Circle* literally cover much of the same ground as *Death of a Naturalist*, Heaney's 'chosen region', 'but from new angles and frames of reference' and 'in defiance of the way things were going wrong among global powers and planetary conditions'. This region 'wasn't Derry and Antrim. Or Shankhill and Falls', and 'It had the virtue of unexpectedness.' Heaney consciously and unconsciously circles back through his past and poems in *District and Circle*, not to relive the past, but as in Yeats's later work, to forge, to hammer together, all of his work into a creative whole that includes the past, present and future. It is this desire for artistic wholeness that has informed the titles of his books. The many working titles suggest the master artisan labouring over not only the immediate and individual, but also over the immortal and universal.

District and Circle's closing poem 'The Blackbird of Glanmore', which occupies the same physical and emotional space as 'Mid-Term Break', returns us to the poet's past and provides a dramatic link with *Death of a Naturalist*. Behind the scenes we see a more literary and political subtext in 'Midnight Anvil' and 'An Advancement of Learning'. Some titles, like the poems themselves, 'slip' from the poet and into place as with *Door into the Dark, North* and *Station Island*. Other titles, as with *Wintering Out*, *Field Work, Seeing Things* and *The Spirit Level*, require more labour and are shaped by the poems around them. Then there are the titles that have been displaced by other poets' book titles as in *The Haw Lantern* and *Electric Light*. Buried among the palimpsest of Heaney's pages are working titles whose spirits hover over the published texts influencing them from beyond the book. For Heaney book titles are not labels stuck on when the work is done; they are quintessential components – sometimes the catalyst, sometimes the conclusion of the alchemy of literary production. The titles that work, work together to form Heaney's sacred book – the book of books perpetually renewed and transformed with each new tome.

NOTES

1. Charles Monteith, *My Best Advice!* (Dublin: Gong Publishing, 2000), p. 58. The book's subtitle reads: 'Over 100 famous Irish people share the best advice they ever received.' Seamus Heaney identified 'Polder' as the title in question. The author thanks Seamus Heaney for this and all other unattributed information regarding titles that appears in this essay.
2. For a detailed discussion of Heaney's material mysticism as it relates to literary production, see my '"Letter by Strange Letter": Yeats, Heaney, and the Aura of the Book', *New Hibernia Review* (Summer 1998), pp. 28–47.
3. Fax from Seamus Heaney to the author, 22 April 2004.
4. For more on Yeats's 'Great Book', see Hazard Adams, *The Book of Yeats's Poems* (Tallahassee: Florida State University Press, 1990), especially pp. 1–26.
5. Rand Brandes, 'Seamus Heaney: An Interview', *Salmagundi* (Fall 1998), p. 4.
6. Heaney writes: '"The Forge" was one of the first poems I wrote, post *Death of a Naturalist*, and the minute the first line came, I knew I had a title.'
7. 'Persephone' first appeared in a different form in the *Cambridge Review* (4 June 1966), p. 464.
8. Seamus Heaney, *A Lough Neagh Sequence* (Didsbury: Phoenix Pamphlet Poets Press, January 1969). The poem first appeared in *University Review* in 1967.
9. Heaney comments on the allusion to *Richard III* in an article about him in Patricia Beer, 'Seamus Heaney's Third Book of Poems', *Listener* (7 December 1972), p. 790.
10. 'For David Hammond and Michael Longley', dedicatory poem, *WO* 5.
11. Seamus Heaney, 'As We Roved Out', *Criterion* (1971), pp. 35–6.
12. See my 'The Manuscript Drafts of the Poem "North"', in *The Art of Seamus Heaney*, ed. Tony Curtis (Bridgend: Poetry Wales Press, 1985), pp. 52–62.
13. See my 'Worksheets for "Funeral Rites," "Punishment," "Act of Union" and "A Constable Calls"', *Quarto* (November 1975), pp. 3–17.
14. Seamus Heaney, *Hedge School, Sonnets from Glanmore* (Newark VT: Janus Press, 1979).
15. Ibid., p. 59.
16. Ibid., p. 60.
17. Seamus Heaney, 'Ulster Quatrains', *Recorder* 23 (1982).
18. See Rand Brandes, '"Inscribed in Sheets": Seamus Heaney's Scribal Matrix', in *Seamus Heaney: The Shaping Spirit*, ed. Catherine Malloy and Phyllis Carey (London: Associated University Presses, 1996), pp. 47–70.
19. Seamus Heaney, 'Lenten Stuff', *Erato* (Summer 1986), p. 1.
20. Seamus Heaney, 'Station Island', *Hudson Review* (Summer 1983), pp. 257–64.
21. Seamus Heaney, *Hailstones* (Dublin: Gallery Press, 1985).
22. Fax (22 April 2004) to author.
23. Seamus Heaney, 'Holdings', *Poetry Review* (Winter 1989/1990), pp. 4–5, and 'Resolutions', *Mica* (Winter 1992), pp. 31–2.
24. Seamus Heaney, *The Times Literary Supplement* (19–25 January 1990), p. 53.
25. Seamus Heaney, *The Tree Clock* (Belfast: Linen Hall Library, 1990), p. 12.
26. Fax (22 April 2004) to author.
27. Seamus Heaney, 'Weighing In', *The Times Literary Supplement* (17 January 1992), p. 28.

28. Seamus Heaney, 'Light Finally Enters the Black Hole', *Sunday Tribune* (4 September 1994), p. A9.
29. Seamus Heaney, *Diptych* (Goshen, IN: Goshen College, 1992).
30. Seamus Heaney, *College Green* (Autumn 1995), pp. 46–9.
31. Seamus Heaney, 'The Inner Zodiac', *Around the Globe* (Summer 2000), p. 29.
32. Seamus Heaney, *Crediting Poetry* (New York: Farrar, Straus and Giroux, 1996), p. 31. Brandes, 'Interview', p. 15.
33. Fax (22 April 2004) to the author. All further quotations are from this fax.

3

PATRICK CROTTY

The Context of Heaney's Reception

Intriguing issues relating to the workings of canonicity in contemporary writing surround Seamus Heaney's swift rise to international prominence in the 1970s and his increasing eminence in anglophone poetry worldwide in subsequent decades. In the poet's own generation, the congruence of wide popularity and critical acclaim has perhaps a readier parallel in mass culture (the Beatles and Bob Dylan) than in literature. Of twentieth-century poets about the scale of whose achievement there is something approaching consensus, only the ultra-canonical Yeats, Eliot and Auden have enjoyed the sort of High Street profile that brought Heaney's *Beowulf* and *District and Circle* into the hardback non-fiction best-seller lists in Britain. The contrast with the fortunes of the majority of leading figures in the modern pantheon is striking. For all the reverence their verse has received from critics and fellow-practitioners, writers even of the stature of Wallace Stevens and Elizabeth Bishop have remained more or less invisible to a non-specialist readership. And very few of the poets who have, like Heaney, made it into the Sunday supplements and the public consciousness have been given a welcome comparable to his in the academy. Robert Frost, Dylan Thomas, Ted Hughes and Sylvia Plath all won wide audiences for their work but Frost's academic reputation is mainly posthumous, Thomas's currently in abeyance, Hughes's uncertain and Plath's dependent on a handful of poems written at the end of her tragically abbreviated life. While not inconsiderable, the varieties of official recognition granted to Frost (who in his eighty-seventh year made a celebrated, wind-blown appearance at John F. Kennedy's inauguration) and Hughes (who accepted and invigorated the poet laureateship of England) look national rather than global when set against the example of a poet who has occupied simultaneously the Boylston Chair of Rhetoric and Oratory at Harvard and the Professorship of Poetry at Oxford, has been awarded innumerable honorary degrees, has performed at the ceremony marking the 2004 expansion of the European Union and has won the Nobel Prize for Literature. Even among the five English-language poetic beneficiaries of what Yeats called the bounty of Sweden, Heaney cuts a singular figure.[1] Neither the imperialist Rudyard Kipling nor his post-colonial polar twin Derek Walcott ever looked out on the world from an established canonical niche; austere and forbidding, the public personae cultivated by W. B. Yeats and T. S. Eliot were continuous with the stubbornly anti-democratic values promoted by their art. Heaney by contrast with Kipling and Walcott has had an easy relationship with the academy, at least in its official and literature-friendly aspects, and his warm and accessible demeanour in public not only accords with but, as it were, dramatises the egalitarian values of his poetry. His peculiar pre-eminence is manifested by the very existence of the volume for which this essay is written: no other living poet has been the subject of a *Cambridge Companion.*[2] The history of Seamus Heaney's 'reception' is to such a degree one of an accelerating succession of accolades that it makes the road from Mossbawn to Stockholm look straight and wide, at least in retrospect. This essay is less concerned with describing that road than with, first, exploring some of the questions raised by the extraordinarily rapid growth of the poet's reputation and, second, commenting upon the most vivid and/or influential critical responses to his work.

One of the first issues to arise out of a review of Heaney's career is the matter of his Irishness. The heady figurative and thematic discoveries of *Wintering Out* and *North* coincided so closely with and responded so eloquently to the newsworthy collapse of civil order in Northern Ireland that the poet's nationality has often been seen in the wider world as a key to his success, as a stroke of fortune that gave him an advantage over writers from less headline-dominating parts of the globe. The view from Ireland has always been different. Desmond Fennell's account of what he calls the Heaney Phenomenon in *Whatever You Say, Say Nothing: Why Seamus Heaney is No. 1* may be risible in literary critical terms, but his complaint that 'Ireland was not consulted on the matter'[3] of the poet's rise to fame reflects a fairly widespread Irish bewilderment in the earlier stages of the career at the scale of the international attention paid to Heaney's work relative to that of his immediate predecessors and contemporaries. It is customary when dealing with the emergence of a major poet from a small country to comment on the poetic hinterland from which he or she arose, usually in pitiful terms. Thus we speak about Yeats in the context of the brocaded Victorianism of Samuel Ferguson and his followers, or of Hugh MacDiarmid in the light of the inanities of the post-Burnsian lyric tradition in Scotland. Yet in 1966, the year of the appearance of *Death of a Naturalist*, Irish poetry seemed to its readers not only to be in a healthy state but to have entered a new era of vigour and professionalism. Austin Clarke was at the most prolific stage of a career that had started before the foundation of the southern state: his longest and most diverse volume, *Flight to Africa*, had been published to considerable domestic acclaim in 1963, and his ambitious verse narrative of mental breakdown and recovery, *Mnemosyne Lay in Dust*, had just appeared. Patrick Kavanagh – a crucial Heaney exemplar – had survived obscurity in the 1940s and notoriety in the 1950s to emerge into something akin to celebrity in the wake of the publication of his *Collected Poems* in 1964.

Yet though at home Clarke and Kavanagh were considered to be major poets, they attracted at best intermittent attention from Britain, the United States and beyond. Clarke had been championed by Donald Davie, who had taught for a time in Trinity College Dublin, and by Charles Tomlinson, the poet and academic who was the most vocal English advocate of poetic innovators from both sides of the Atlantic who could be accommodated neither in the narrative of Eliot/Pound modernism nor that of the Movement's reaction against it. Kavanagh appeared to have been influential on the early work of R. S. Thomas, and was admired by a group of quasi-bohemian London-based poets that included David Wright and John Heath-Stubbs. Otherwise he and Clarke were either ignored or condescended to: the briefly Dublin-domiciled John Berryman's sardonic reference to them in Dream Song 321 as 'those masters who can both read & write, / in the high Irish style'[4] catches the bemused attitude to post-Yeatsian Irish verse characteristic of residents of the more securely canonical echelons of Anglo-American poetry at mid-century. Louis MacNeice, who had died in 1963, enjoyed a high reputation in Britain; neither there nor in the Republic, however, was he considered a particularly Irish poet, though his legacy was about to be repatriated by a new generation of practitioners – Heaney's own – waiting in the wings in his native Belfast.

Already at centre stage in Irish poetry in 1966 were three poets born in the first decade after the constitutional settlement of 1922 who exhibited a brisk confidence in the contemporary resonance of their work and combined a sense of poetry's function as interpreter of national developments with an alertness to international contexts, both literary and political, as if in pro-active repudiation of the amateurishness and isolation of the milieu in which Clarke and Kavanagh had been forced to conduct the greater part of their careers. The debut collections of Richard Murphy (b. 1927), Thomas Kinsella (b. 1928) and John Montague (b. 1929) had all been published in the second half of the previous decade by Liam Miller's Dolmen Press. (Murphy had moved to Faber and Faber by 1963, while Kinsella and Montague would retain their link with Dolmen up until Miller's death in 1987.) With its handsome production values and key role in disseminating the fruits of Clarke's late rush of creativity alongside the work of this trio of ambitious and somewhat knowingly sophisticated young writers, Dolmen manifested a self-assurance that had been absent from Irish poetry publishing since the heyday of the Maunsel Press in the early part of the century; the reappearance of such confidence in the late 1950s and early 1960s can be seen in retrospect to have had much to do with the southern state's growing sense of poise and potential as it moved from the cultural and economic stagnation of the de Valera dispensation towards the relatively outward-looking and vibrant Lemass era.

Kinsella was much the most prominent and prolific of the younger Dolmen poets. His characteristic combination of gloom with a glittering elegance of expression, already in evidence in *Another September* (1958), was put to the service of a self-consciously post-holocaust imagination in the *Downstream* volume of 1962, where Irish historical experience is placed in a context of European catastrophe. His early style was to reach the apex of its development in the large-scale and elaborate meditations of *Nightwalker and Other Poems* (1968). *Downstream* and *Nightwalker* were accorded incomparably greater notice in the Republic's media than Heaney's 1960s volumes, *Death of a Naturalist* and *Door into the Dark* (the first of which was reviewed in the influential weekly *Hibernia* under the perhaps tellingly mistaken title *Death of a Nationalist*). Kinsella's work was exciting significant interest in Britain and the United States also, as attested by prizes, anthologisation and the poet's resignation from his post in the Civil Service in Dublin to take up employment for part of the year at the University of Southern Illinois. Around the time of the appearance of Heaney's first collection, then, an older contemporary was both at home and abroad commanding attention and respect of a kind that had hitherto eluded Irish-based poets in the post-Revival period. Though Kinsella's copious and diverse poetry has continued to develop in interesting and unpredictable ways up to the present,[5] there is a measure of consensus among his critics that his richest and most achieved work belongs to the 1970s, particularly to the collections *New Poems 1973* and *One and Other Poems* (1979), where he moves beyond the grandiosity of the earlier production to the chastened anti-lyrical style demanded by a series of ruminations on origins and memory in terms of myth, history, autobiography and Jungian psychology. It is one of the ironies of the canonical process that this most sustained and individual phase of Kinsella's career coincided with the partial eclipse of his reputation, a state of affairs to which the demands the mature poetry places upon the reader, the long-term consequences of the reaction to *Butcher's Dozen* (the poet's fiercely *engagé* verse-pamphlet on the Widgery Tribunal's vindication of the Bloody Sunday killings in Derry) and the rise of Seamus Heaney's critical stock may all be said to have contributed. (In relation to the last of these factors, admirers of

Kinsella and indeed of Heaney's gifted northern contemporaries might be forgiven for suspecting that international criticism can deal with only one groundbreaking Irish poet at a time.)

Though Montague and Murphy made rather less public impact than Kinsella, who along with Kavanagh and Clarke became in 1969 one of the first three Irish poets since Yeats to appear on the Republic's Leaving Certificate English syllabus, they shared his modernising and cosmopolitan impulse along with his aspiration towards a poetry of political commentary. Co-editor with Kinsella of the *Dolmen Miscellany* (1962), the volume that confirmed the arrival of the new generation, Montague was, like Heaney, an Ulster Catholic. His lean and at times spindly early lyrics are very different in manner from Heaney's 1960s work, but in exploring *inter alia* the world of the rural northern minority community, frequently from the perspective of childhood, they can be said to have opened up for poetry a territory that the younger poet would soon make his own. Montague was already by 1966 assembling the elements of his long historical meditation on the plight of his co-religionists in Ulster, *The Rough Field* (1972). Murphy, too, was moving from the discrete lyric and narrative poems of his slim Dolmen publications and prizewinning Faber collection, *Sailing to an Island* (1963), to a more sustained, overtly political mode. He had already published parts of *The Battle of Aughrim*, an historical tableau on the Williamite wars and their bitter Irish legacy that would receive wide attention in both Ireland and Britain on its appearance in book form in 1968: an edited televised version was the Irish entry for the Golden Harp Award, while an hour-long radio performance of the poem, with music by Seán Ó Riada and a cast of readers including C. Day Lewis and Ted Hughes, was twice broadcast on the BBC Third Programme. The title sequence of Kinsella's *Nightwalker* collection, a visionary denunciation of the venality of the independent Irish state, would first be published as a separate volume in the spring of 1967. The trajectory from self-contained reflective lyric to extended public sequence that characterised the 1960s work of these three still relatively young poets of the generation that preceded him may be said to have foreshadowed Heaney's progress from *Death of a Naturalist* to *North*. Indeed, the insistently first-person viewpoint and short-staved, short-lined versification of Part I of *North* may provide evidence of an ambiguity in Heaney's response to the ambitious example of his elders, as they can be interpreted as strategies for avoiding the diffusion of lyric intensity incurred by the shifting perspectives, ventriloquism and other 'modernist' procedures employed to varying degrees in *Nightwalker*, *The Battle of Aughrim* and *The Rough Field*: Kinsella, Murphy and Montague seem to have been equally present to their younger contemporary as guides to *what* and what *not* to do.

It takes time for developments "on the ground" to come to the attention of the wider community of poetry readers. General anthologies make a major contribution to establishing an audience for the art, but the fact that the most successful among them enjoy a long shelf-life means that prominent and influential anthological surveys are almost always to some degree out of date and consequently of limited utility as maps of the immediate environment. Thus though the advances made by Irish poetry in the decade leading up to *Death of a Naturalist* were registered outside the country through reviews, broadcasts and a variety of accolades, they remained almost invisible to the non-specialist and did not form part of any widely accepted vision of modern and contemporary verse. Even as late as 1972, the year of publication of *Wintering Out*, the two anthologies that offered readers on the European side of the Atlantic the readiest entry to twentieth-century poetry in English were the second edition of Kenneth Allott's *Penguin Book of Contemporary Verse* (1962) and the third edition of Michael Roberts's *Faber Book of Modern Verse* (1965), with its extensive Supplement by Donald Hall. A glance at the contents lists of these very different compilations illustrates the extent to which Irish poetry had dropped from the wider anglophone-world's sight since the death of Yeats. The Allott anthology strays from its characteristic British bias (or imperially stretches the boundaries of 'British') by including Yeats, Joyce and Kinsella alongside the briefly prominent W. R. Rodgers and the Irish-born but English-educated and domiciled Day Lewis and MacNeice. It finds no room for Clarke and Kavanagh. 'Those masters' are passed over also by the decidedly more internationalist and modernist Faber volume, where Day Lewis and MacNeice are the only Irish writers other than Yeats to feature. Apart from the Penguin selection's picking up on Kinsella's early eminence, both books entirely eschew Irish perspectives, whether northern or southern. (The treatment of Scottish and Welsh poetry is by contrast more or less in keeping with domestic understandings: even if Allott blimpishly excludes Hugh MacDiarmid, he includes Andrew Young, Edwin Muir, Norman Cameron, Norman MacCaig and W. S. Graham, from Scotland, and, from Wales, Vernon Watkins, R. S. Thomas, Dylan Thomas and Alun Lewis; Scottish poetry is represented in the Faber anthology by Muir, MacDiarmid, MacCaig and Graham, and Welsh by Watkins and the two Thomases.)

It seems clear then that when Robert Lowell, in a salute to *North* in the 1975 pre-Christmas Books of the Year column in the *Observer*, inaugurated the by now almost standard practice of describing Heaney as 'the best Irish poet since W. B. Yeats', he did so in the context of an international critical consensus that was resolutely ignorant of all that had happened in Irish poetry between the death of the older poet in 1939 and the debut of the younger one twenty-seven years later. The altered fortunes of Irish poetry in the present, when Heaney's compatriots of his own and subsequent generations feature in anthological and critical surveys alongside the once neglected Clarke and Kavanagh, are no doubt part of a wider cultural and political process of change, whereby the centralising certainties of the mid-century, ghosted by assumptions of the primacy of London and New York and by a hangover of imperial values, have given way to a view of the world alert to alterities of region, nation, class and gender. This process has gone hand-in-hand with the ending of the isolationism, cultural and otherwise, that marked Irish affairs for four decades or so after 1922.

In these new circumstances, post-Yeatsian Irish poetry has become for the first time notably influential on practice elsewhere, particularly Britain. While this is most obviously true of the work of Heaney and his fellow-northerners Michael Longley, Derek Mahon and Paul Muldoon, writers from both sides of the border enjoy generally easy relations with the rest of what has become in some respects a pan-archipelagic poetic economy. Indeed citation of the border can be confusing: Longley and Mahon began their careers as undergraduates in Dublin, where they were associated with Brendan Kennelly and Eavan Boland, and in a longer historical perspective they can be said to have contributed to a revitalisation of poetry in Ireland that began with Kinsella, Montague and Murphy and has continued in the work of northerners from Ciaran Carson to Leontia Flynn and southerners from Eiléan Ní Chuilleanáin and Paul Durcan to the much translated Irish-language poet Nuala Ní Dhomhnaill and beyond. Heaney has been a central figure in this revitalisation, and the fact that he has written by far the greater bulk of his poetry while domiciled in the Republic has doubtless helped drain a good deal of the utility from labels like 'northern' and 'southern'. (A good deal but not all: the suspicion of inherited attitudes to cultural identity shared by poets from both sides of the sectarian divide in Northern Ireland is not so marked in the work of their southern colleagues,[6] while Heaney's writing, in particular, as Bernard O'Donoghue has pointed out,[7] is strongly inflected by Ulster speech practices.)

Heaney may have been a central figure in all of this but he has not been the only figure. If the quantitative and qualitative surge in poetry in Ireland in the closing decades of the millennium is rather more deserving of the term 'renaissance' than the poetic aspect of the literary revival presided over by Yeats three-quarters of a century earlier, this later and greater regenerative movement cannot be said to have been presided over by anyone. And this brings us to a major question in relation to the reception of Heaney's work. Longley, Mahon and Muldoon are held in demonstrably high esteem by their peers in Ireland and elsewhere, and their work has been the object of sophisticated scholarly commentary. Why, then, are they so much less well known to the general public, and so much less widely read than Heaney? And why are there well over a score of critical monographs on Heaney, compared to a mere two on Muldoon and one each on Longley and Mahon?[8]

It is possible to have recourse to canonical conspiracy theories and speculation about astute career moves and the power of such institutions as Faber and Faber and Harvard University in response to these questions, but it is also legitimate to seek answers to them in the intrinsic qualities of the poetry. One has neither to endorse the Robert Lowell claim nor denigrate the achievement of Heaney's contemporaries to note the extraordinary breadth of appeal of his work, and its success in speaking simultaneously to specialist and non-specialist audiences. Heaney's expert auditors have included a conspicuously wide range of practising poets, from Lowell and Ted Hughes to Derek Walcott and Robert Pinsky, as well as leading academic critics like John Carey, Christopher Ricks and Helen Vendler. When I was a graduate student working on Scottish verse in the 1970s, I was struck (and, I confess, puzzled) by the emphatic preference of Hugh MacDiarmid and Norman MacCaig – poets of radically divergent aesthetic priorities from each other – for the work of Heaney over that of his Irish contemporaries and immediate predecessors, with which they clearly had a good deal of familiarity. Their enthusiasm was matched by people from what might be called the other end of the poetic scale, those who evinced no more than a low-level interest in poetry in general but who were already by the mid-1970s thronging Heaney's public readings in Ireland and Britain alike. Thirty years later the popular appetite for the work is, if anything, even greater: since the turn of the millennium books by Heaney have made up almost two-thirds of the total sales of contemporary poetry in the United Kingdom.[9]

Market statistics bear no necessary relation to aesthetic value, of course, and literary history is rich in examples of disjunction between contemporary taste and the judgement of posterity. Long experience of teaching Heaney's work, however, has made me extremely sceptical of reductive, non-literary explanations of his popularity, whether in terms of the influence of the mass media on perceptions of contemporary writing, or (the Fennell view) of the poetry's alleged feel-good evasion of politics. Students I have taught – whether primary school pupils in Munster or undergraduates in Britain, the United States and both sides of the Irish border – find an intimacy in Heaney's mode of address that brings them 'onside' in a way unparalleled by the work of other modern poets. I think this is partly a matter of the rootedness of the poetry (even at its most demanding) in English as it is spoken by ordinary people. The mimetic gift so lavishly deployed in *Death of a Naturalist* and never entirely absent from the subsequent collections must also be mentioned, as it lends an immediacy to the poems that draws in readers who are otherwise not particularly enthusiastic about poetry. Heaney's ability to evoke an action or sensation in a phrase constructed out of some of the most commonly used lexical resources is a very rare phenomenon in literature. (Something akin to it may be found in the early short stories of Ernest Hemingway.) This aspect of his work has led to a hostile typification of Heaney as a 'theory-allergic' writer who misrepresents the relationship between language and reality by writing as if *words* offered a sort of one-to-one replication of *things*.[10] Many of the poems from 'The Harvest Bow', through 'Hailstones', the 'Squarings' sequence and beyond, it might be countered, conduct a critique of the temptation towards a poetics of substance, revealing the poet's shrewd awareness of the problematic epistemological foundations of some of the most bravura effects of lyric art, both his own and others'. (The aesthetic impact of these events is in any event not entirely vulnerable to a theoretical penetration of their workings.) A third, less specifically linguistic factor contributing to the poems' success in winning the reader's trust is their uncommon alertness to the needs of those who encounter them, their unfussy incorporation of gloss in text. The opening section of 'Funeral Rites' provides a striking example of what might be called Heaney's authorial courtesy. Lines which offer themselves as descriptive information to readers unfamiliar with the 'waking' and 'removal' practices of Irish Catholic tradition will be read in terms of interpretation (and with a shock of recognition) by people of the same cultural background as the poet:

> I shouldered a kind of manhood
> stepping in to lift the coffins
> of dead relations.
> They had been laid out
>
> in tainted rooms,
> their eyelids glistening,
> their dough-white hands
> shackled in rosary beads.

And so on for another twenty-four further lines that subtly – and, as it were, incidentally – interstitch the Nordic details that give these verses their place in the larger figurative orchestration of Part I of *North*: the passage as a whole is a complex act of cultural negotiation which places the speaker simultaneously inside and outside the scene he evokes, giving due weight to the dignity and effectiveness of Irish Catholic funeral procedures, on the one hand, while acknowledging how strange they must seem to observers of different national or religious origin, on the other.

Comparison with the work of other twentieth-century poets can help highlight the sureness and distinctiveness of Heaney's artistic intelligence. Much has been written on connections between the Irish poet and a range of immediate predecessors, from Frost and Hughes to Herbert and Miłosz. I should like to cite the example of one poet on whom Heaney has published a characteristically generous essay, but in relation to whom he is rarely (if ever) discussed, in an effort to draw attention to the capacity for showing rather than merely stating that seems to me to account for much of the allure of his work. The vivid opening chapter of Edwin Muir's *An Autobiography* (1954) recounts the author's experience of growing up in the almost medieval simplicity of late-nineteenth-century Orkney. Some of the incidents narrated there also make their way into Muir's poems, where their colour and particularity generally fall victim to a tendency towards would-be universalising abstraction. Thus the seven-year-old Muir's terrified flight from his schoolmate Freddie Sinclair provides the subject of a few fascinating pages of the prose work but its attempted projection onto the plane of poetry leads only to the anodyne and rather obscure 'Ballad of Hector in Hades'. Muir's eagerness to find symbolic resonance in everything too often reduces his primary subject matter to a mere starting point for discursive mythopoeia; it can frequently seem that the poetry is so intent on the philosophical that it fails to register the sensory, empirical aspects of experience. Heaney's instinct, by contrast, particularly in the early work, is to dwell in the empirical, cautiously nudging symbolic significance from the objects of poetic attention by way either of implication or of colloquially grounded metaphor. Again the text (the thing in itself) and the gloss (the commentary) are one, or close to one. There are of course important differences between the poets. Muir had a more religious – or more conventionally religious – sensibility than Heaney, and his interest in dreams and psychoanalysis has no counterpart in the Irish poet's work. One of the persistent themes of Heaney's first two books, nonetheless, is connected to a staple concern of the Orcadian poet: the progression from a childhood world of immemorial custom to a chastened state of knowledge identified with modernity, sexuality and an awareness of time.

Their childhood perspectives, rural Irish settings and delight in evocatively tactile language continue to make Heaney's early poems appealing to many who do not put poetry at the centre of their lives. It is perhaps understandable that in the 1970s some readers and critics, brought up under the influence of Eliot and New Criticism to value 'difficulty' and allusiveness, should have been suspicious of a poetry so manifestly successful in arresting the attention of non-specialists. The poised existential ironies of Derek Mahon and brooding psychic explorations of Thomas Kinsella seemed self-evidently 'serious' in a way that was not true of the open-handed and at times rough-hewn lyrics of rustic life that appeared to a casual glance to be the stock-in-trade of *Death of a Naturalist* and *Door into the Dark*. Certainly my own memory of undergraduate poetry circles at University College Cork at the time suggests that we neither noticed the self-reflexive enactment of poetic metamorphosis embodied in 'Churning Day' (from the first volume) nor allowed the austere, tightly argued ontology of 'The Peninsula' (from the second) to shake our prejudice that what Heaney was offering was a homely County Derry version of pastoral; it was not until the appearance of the tartly challenging and disturbed *Wintering Out* in 1972 that we began to sense anything of the depth and scope of his talent. If we were in one way misreading the work, of course, we were in another way playing along with it – or being played along by it. The developmental narrative underlying Heaney's early books (and reinforced by the autobiographical commentaries in *Preoccupations*) involves a steady, organic growth in breadth and complexity from the most rudimentary beginnings. *Country boy explores poetic potential of own ordinary, inarticulate origins and in process discovers extraordinary powers of articulation* might be said to be the implicit story of the four collections from 1966 to 1975 that the poet would later describe as being essentially 'one book'.[11] To observe that the story has the qualities of myth as well as of history is not to cast doubt on the genuineness either of the exploration or of the discovery. For it to be a true story the first book needed to feature pieces of the simplicity of 'Digging' (that 'big coarse-grained navvy of a poem'[12]) and the awkwardness of 'An Advancement of Learning'. (The fact that *Opened Ground* accords *Death of a Naturalist* less than half the representation of *Door into the Dark* suggests that Heaney himself considers his debut to have contained a significant proportion of apprentice material.) It is much easier in 2008 than it was in 1971, now that we have had not only *Wintering Out* but the magisterial *Seeing Things*, the wryly summative *District and Circle*, and six other abundant and heterogeneous collections, to see the variously ruddy-cheeked and clumsy poems that accompany sophisticated lyrics like 'Blackberry-Picking' and 'Follower' as servants of one of the most urgently serious impulses in modern poetry. Time has in any case been kind to the early work, the best of which retains its vigour and freshness when retrospect has given a dandyishly literary appearance to some of the 1960s and 70s poems by Heaney's compatriots that seemed the stuff of ambitious authenticity back then.

Readers interested in tracing the growth of Heaney's reputation review by review should consult Michael J. Durkan and Rand Brandes's excellent reference guide,[13] where they will also find the statistical evidence of the poet's pre-eminence as a subject of academic enquiry. In the pages that follow I have space to do no more than comment on some of the more important monograph studies and bring my oar to bear on the ripples of dispraise that have troubled the stream of critical response to the poetry. The first book-length single study to appear on this side of the Atlantic was the short but lively *Seamus Heaney* by the English poet Blake Morrison.[14] It was published in 1982, the same year as the slim initial version (greatly expanded in three subsequent editions) of the Welsh poet Tony Curtis's edited collection *The Art of Seamus Heaney*. Morrison's perceptive account of the poetry from *Death of a Naturalist* to *Field Work* is notable, on the positive side, for its revisionist reading of the 1960s work in terms of its characteristically late modernist, textually self-aware exploration of the relationship between speechlessness and utterance (rather than in terms of its finding a language for the colourful violence of the natural world – the aspect of the poetry that had most excited Heaney's early reviewers). On the negative side, Morrison's clamorous assumption that Heaney belongs to an entity called 'British poetry' misconstrues the *oeuvre*'s cultural and literary contexts so insistently that one is tempted to surmise that it may have contributed an edge of intensity to the objection to being included in the *Penguin Book of Contemporary British Poetry* (also 1982, and co-edited by Morrison) that prompted the poet to publish *An Open Letter* in 1983. Other significant monographs include Elmer Andrews's *The Poetry of Seamus Heaney: All the Realms of Whisper* (1988), a meticulous and perceptive study that is at its most individual in its argument for the primacy of the auditory, the passive and the sub-rational as modes of cognition in Heaney's work. Henry Hart's *Seamus Heaney: Poet of Contrary Progressions* (1992) is theoretically informed and original, if hermeneutically somewhat overcharged. The book's interpretation of the career trajectory as a matter of deepening mysticism and of a post-colonially driven, deconstructive response to the binarisms of the imperial English canon imputes a more systematic (and metaphysical) character to the corpus than that diverse and exploratory body of lyrics can easily bear, though the approach has the virtue of facilitating some interesting individual readings. Hart's commentaries, like those of a number of other North American scholars, are hampered by a lack of inwardness with the historical contexts of the poetry, particularly where the nuances of political and religious division in Northern Ireland are concerned. Michael Parker's *Seamus Heaney: The Making of the Poet* (1993), while critically a good deal less sophisticated than Hart's book, contains invaluable contextualising detail, including information on the poet's early life and career unavailable elsewhere. If John Wilson Foster's *The Achievement of Seamus Heaney* (1995) is, at a mere fifty-nine pages, much the briefest of the major studies, it is also one of the most ambitious. Foster writes with brisk authority on the Irish, British and wider Western contexts of the work, offering a judiciously illustrated argument that Heaney's verse and criticism, taken together, mark a highly serious and at least partly successful attempt to restore poetry to the cultural eminence it had enjoyed from classical antiquity to the end of the Romantic era. Eloquence and compression are characteristics also of Andrew Murphy's *Seamus Heaney* (1996), a contribution to the British Council sponsored Writers and Their Work series. While self-confessedly focusing on the Irish aspects of Heaney's primary materials (literary, linguistic, historical and political), Murphy weaves a subtle commentary on critical reaction to the work into his account of the career. (His handling of the controversy surrounding *North* is a model of dispassionate shrewdness.) Pertinently to the topic of the present essay, if not altogether persuasively, he surmises in a postscript that the poetry's ongoing engagement with a range of English writers from the Elizabethans to Hardy and Hughes may be a key to its popularity in Britain.

Three monograph studies distinguished by their combination of depth, critical flair and textual responsiveness may be described as indispensable to the serious student of Heaney. These are Bernard O'Donoghue's *Seamus Heaney and the Language of Poetry* (1994), Helen Vendler's *Seamus Heaney* (1998) and Neil Corcoran's *The Poetry of Seamus Heaney: A Critical Study* (1998). It is perhaps paradoxical that in limiting its enquiry to linguistic matters O'Donoghue's book should demonstrate more decisively than most both the formal and attitudinal plenitude of the Heaney canon and the complexity of its negotiations with such identity categories as Ireland, Ulster, Britain and England. Though the study is underpinned by a grasp of linguistics and a thorough knowledge of English and Gaelic metrics, its arguments are conducted in an almost cheerfully intimate and accessible style. O'Donoghue is particularly insightful in his weighing of the cultural freight of individual words and phrases in the poems, whether the opening lines of 'Bone Dreams', with their glancing allusion to the Sutton Hoo Burial, or the biblical 'numbered heads' at the end of the first section of 'Seeing Things' (the fact that he is an Irish-speaking scholar of Middle English contributes significantly to his pre-eminence as interpreter of the relationship between text and intertext in the poetry). O'Donoghue's book is notable, among other things, for identifying the centre of gravity of the career in the collections from *Station Island* onwards; it nevertheless has many interesting observations to make about the early work, not least among them that the opaque, cultivatedly unmelodious language of *Death of a Naturalist* is to a degree foreign to Heaney's nature and that an underlying urge towards the *claritas* and airiness of *Seeing Things* is evident in the verse from the beginning. O'Donoghue also engages more thoroughly than any other commentator with the responses of earlier critics, and his friendly, respectful disagreement with Henry Hart's rather programmatic account of the poet's development runs through his book like a musical motif.

Helen Vendler is the pre-eminent formalist poetry critic of her time, the author of classic studies of George Herbert, John Keats, Wallace Stevens, Yeats's poetic forms and Shakespeare's sonnets. Given that her time is one in which the academic study of literature has taken on a strongly anti-aesthetic bias and concerned itself, sometimes to the exclusion of other considerations, with 'unmasking' the imperialistic, patriarchal or otherwise reprehensible value systems inscribed in novels, poems and plays, the conventional description of her as a practitioner of New Criticism is less than adequate. Rather Vendler is an embattled defender of the aesthetic, a dauntless creditor of poetry (to adapt the title of Heaney's Nobel lecture) in an era when many of her colleagues across the English-speaking world draw their salaries and win renown for *dis*crediting it. As a poet whose work is to an unusual degree responsive to the pressure of history and politics, Heaney might seem an unlikely subject for a critic so definitively anxious to vindicate the autonomy of the verbal icon. And indeed, though Vendler repeatedly acknowledges Heaney's sense of the social responsibilities of poetry in her book, she can be less than surefooted in writing of the matrix out of which the work emerged. She inveighs against the tyranny of theme in discussions of contemporary verse, arguing instead for the necessity of approaching poems as 'provisional symbolic structures'.[15] Her suggestion that the import of Part I of *North* is that the post-1969 Troubles in Northern Ireland were cultural rather than political in origin, however, not only unwittingly imputes a reductive banality to the sequence but counters her general point about the irrelevance of abstracted subject matter by raising the question as to how a series of poems with such a glib 'truth' to communicate could be taken seriously.[16] *North* is, of course, more profound, more alert and more inconclusive in its meditation on the violence of the early 1970s than Vendler's typification allows. A number of hostile critics, it seems fair to say, have reacted to the sequence as if it constituted some sort of programme for government. To object to their procedures by insisting that the 'content' of poetry is different from the content of purely discursive modes of writing is one thing; to rule the ideational machinery of a poetic work out of court as an object of critical attention, however, quite another. Indeed, much of the authority of Heaney's poetry derives from his successful quest for avenues of aesthetic approach to ethical and political concerns, which, though they both pre-exist and in important senses (and of necessity) remain untouched by his treatment of them, are nevertheless absorbed into its textures. If the intellectual grounds of Vendler's fencing off of the aesthetic from the political are less stable than she claims, though, there is no doubting the extraordinary acuity of perception of which she is capable in relation both to the dynamic architecture of the individual poems she chooses to write about and to the dialogue initiated by those poems with the historical range of the English-language tradition. She also exhibits a perhaps uniquely subtle appreciation of the complex structure of reverberations that characterises the *oeuvre* as a whole. A 'Second Thoughts' section appended to each chapter examines Heaney's characteristic tendency from very early in his career to view from a new vantage point material already explored in previous work (what we might call, courtesy of the collection published eight years after the appearance of Vendler's study, his habit of circling his district). Her observations on the way 'Damson' re-imagines 'Sunlight' are particularly suggestive. The book, in fact, abounds with insights, for example on the connection between the communal perspective of the rural poems of the 1960s, on the one hand, and the impersonality of the bog body symbol of the poetry of the 1970s, on the other. Vendler is particularly instructive in relation to the contribution of form to effect (not least where the 'square' twelve-liners of *Seeing Things* are concerned) and provides an invigorating commentary on the long debate with the sonnet and its inherited privileges that runs from 'Requiem for the Croppies' through 'Clearances' to 'At the Wellhead'. Some of the freshest discussions in her study concern areas of the poet's output that might be thought of as comparatively inaccessible and atypical – the acerbic satires of 'Sweeney Redivivus', for instance, or the cerebral parables of *The Haw Lantern*.

O'Donoghue's focus on questions of language and Vendler's eclectic modus operandi mean that neither of these writers offers a fully comprehensive critical account of the Heaney corpus, obligatory reading though their books will long remain for those wishing to explore the poetry in depth. I hope it is fair to the many gifted and energetic commentators on Heaney's work to observe that one study stands out from all the others by virtue of its scope, scholarship, seamless transitions between text and context and sustained elegance of style. The first version of Neil Corcoran's book appeared in 1986 under the misleadingly humble rubric of the Faber Student Guides series, twelve years before the rewritten, updated and much longer second edition with which I am concerned here. Though Corcoran takes what might seem a rather predictably chronological approach to the work, offering eight volume-by-volume chapters on the poetry, along with a ninth on the criticism and a biographical appendix, the strong narrative line is inflected throughout by his interrogative intelligence. His exegeses are thorough and in many cases ('The Mud Vision', for example, or 'Two Lorries') groundbreaking. Corcoran brings a sensibility steeped in modern poetry to bear on Heaney's output, and his citations of other poets, from David Jones to

Philippe Jaccottet, are consistently apposite and enlightening. One of the most attractive things about his treatment of the writing is his willingness to come to evaluative conclusions, as when, after an exhilarating and exhaustive discussion of the 'Squarings' sequence, he declares that work 'the most purely pleasurable and unexacerbated of Heaney's poems'.[17] Corcoran is also ready to temper approbation with reproval: in his chapter on the criticism he links what strikes him as an example of unconscious sexism in the essay on *Hero and Leander* in *The Redress of Poetry* to what Patricia Coughlan has seen as the problematic gender politics of the bog poems.[18] He is particularly persuasive on the symbiotic relationship between the prose and the poetry. He observes that the 'finest moments' in the former occur 'when the pressure of a patiently attentive, slowly cumulative close reading ... prompts, or permits itself, an entirely appropriate act of celebration or rapture',[19] and goes on to demonstrate how some of these moments in turn facilitate a breakthrough in Heaney's own verse (the continuity between the reading of Elizabeth Bishop's 'Sestina' in *The Redress of Poetry* and the writing of 'Two Lorries' providing a particularly vivid case in point).

Some of the most searching or otherwise interesting responses to Heaney take the form of essays or book chapters, and given that scholars and critics are unlikely to devote a monograph to a body of work with which they feel no great affinity, it is unsurprising to find that these briefer treatments include a greater proportion of dissenting voices than the roster of book-length studies. Other than Desmond Fennell's choleric pamphlet, the two most insistent short works of dis-appreciation to appear to date are undoubtedly the late James Simmons's 'The Trouble with Seamus', a contribution to Andrews's *Seamus Heaney*, and David Lloyd's '"Pap for the Dispossessed": Seamus Heaney and the Poetics of Identity', which was published in a periodical in 1985 before its absorption into the author's *Anomalous States: Irish Writing and the Post-Colonial Moment* eight years later. Simmons's essay is written in a no-nonsense, hail-fellow-well-met style appropriate to its suspicion of modernism, ruralism and people disinclined to support the Royal Ulster Constabulary. Though Heaney is charged with artistic shortcomings ('Bogland' is characterised by 'wild ... slovenly use of language', the poetry as a whole is 'brilliant, amusing, hypnotic, obscure, excessive, seductive, ridiculous and not central', etc.[20]), the main criticism laid against him is political, namely a failure to repudiate the prejudices of his tribe. The poet, we are told, is in thrall to the values of de Valera, identifies with paramilitary nationalism and sports a religious sensibility 'clogged with the fag-end of Catholicism':[21] Simmons throws accusations about in a manner akin to his nationalist opposite number Desmond Fennell, albeit with greater jollity. Lloyd's procedures might appear to be at the furthest possible remove from those of Simmons, given that '"Pap for the Dispossessed"' is committed to a rarefied, thoroughly intellectualised and abstract prose. Appearances can be deceptive, however, and there is in fact little to choose between the two essays in terms of the gap between textual engagement and indictment that opens up in both. Lloyd, too, is ultimately concerned with politics (albeit of the Marxist rather than liberal unionist variety), and he seeks to prove that Heaney's reputation is based on his poetry's fitting the requirements of an obfuscatory late-capitalist vision of culture derived from an imperial, Arnoldian model that has only been reinforced by the hapless regionalists and revivalists who have attempted over the decades to repudiate it. He begins with an extended analysis of the contradictions in nineteenth-century Irish cultural nationalism but the relevance of this formidably brilliant disquisition to Heaney (a poet demonstrably less exercised by questions of national identity than Lloyd claims) remains a matter of assertion rather than illustration in the series of condemnatory and astigmatic readings of poems and passages which constitutes the second section of his essay. I have space to mention only one of these, an account of 'The Tollund Man' in which Lloyd startlingly fails to notice that his sense of the insufficiency of mere 'aesthetic performance',[22] like his incredulity at the prospect of the eponymous bog body's making germinate the scattered flesh of victims of modern violence, accords with rather than counters the implicit argument of the poem. The combination of censoriousness of tone and hermeneutic ineptness that characterises the second section of '"Pap for the Dispossessed"' serves as a painful reminder that critics who wish to read 'against the grain' ought first to invest some effort in identifying it.

Whatever else can be said about Edna Longley, a dominant and sometimes controversial presence in Irish poetry criticism over the last three decades, no one could accuse her of not looking closely at the poems she writes about. 'The Tollund Man' is the subject of a reading of exemplary subtlety in her '*North*: "Inner Emigré" or "Artful Voyeur"? *North*' (first published in the 1982 edition of the Curtis collection), an essay that goes on to use its admiring account of this and other tentatively speculative lyrics from *Wintering Out* as the basis of an exacting critique of Part I of *North*, seen by contrast as a work of willed systematisation and historically problematic mythmaking. Whereas Longley laments what she sees as the too-directly political and nationalist stance of *North*, Seamus Deane in 'Seamus Heaney: The Timorous and the Bold', a magniloquent, if in some respects curiously reserved chapter in his *Celtic Revivals* (1985), applauds the growing realisation he finds in *North* and *Field Work* that poetry can achieve authenticity only by recognising the implication of lyrical subjectivity in its own historical moment and taking on the burden of politics. (Deane interestingly politicises the much-commented-upon quality of guilt in Heaney's poetry, arguing that it is the communally typical guilt of the northern victim of Unionist and British oppression.)

In singling out four pieces for comment I have run the risk of misrepresenting the character of the voluminous middle-length secondary material on Heaney, most of which is warmly appreciative, and some of which, like a number of the monograph studies that go unmentioned here, is content to be straightforwardly explanatory. Major essays include Stan Smith's illuminating investigation of the semiotics of the poetry, 'The Distance Between: Seamus Heaney', and Douglas Dunn's probing, sceptical, ultimately celebratory examination of *Seeing Things*.[23] It is in their seriousness and variety – rather than their mere existence – that the best responses to Heaney attest to the depth of interest of his work. We might say of that work, as Heaney himself said of Yeats's in his Nobel lecture, that it succeeds in doing 'what the necessary poetry always does, which is to touch the base of our sympathetic nature while taking on at the same time the unsympathetic reality of the world to which that nature is constantly exposed'.[24] There is every indication that it will go on being 'received' for many years to come.

NOTES

1. I exclude Joseph Brodsky as a writer whose main achievement is in Russian.
2. There is a *Cambridge Companion to Margaret Atwood*, but Atwood is primarily a novelist.
3. Desmond Fennell, *Whatever You Say, Say Nothing: Why Seamus Heaney is No. 1* (Dublin: ELO Publications, 1991), p. 18.
4. John Berryman, 'Dream Song 321', in *His Toy, His Dream, His Rest* (London: Faber and Faber, 1969), p. 253.
5. Thomas Kinsella's *Marginal Economy* (2006), *Man of War* (2007) and *Belief and Unbelief* (2007) are the most recent additions to the 'Peppercanister' series of poems inaugurated in 1972 by *Butcher's Dozen*.
6. The fact that John Montague is an exception to this 'rule' is a reminder of the dangers of generalisation.
7. Bernard O'Donoghue, *Seamus Heaney and the Language of Poetry* (Hemel Hempstead: Harvester Wheatsheaf, 1994), *passim*, but see particularly Chapter 2 'Phonetics and Feeling'. *Beowulf*, published five years after O'Donoghue's study, is in linguistic terms the most sustainedly 'northern' of all Heaney's volumes.
8. See Tim Kendall, *Paul Muldoon* (Bridgend: Seren, 1996); Clair Wills, *Reading Paul Muldoon* (Newcastle-upon-Tyne: Blooodaxe, 1999); Fran Brearton, *Reading Michael Longley* (Newcastle-upon-Tyne: Blooodaxe, 2006); and Hugh Haughton, *The Poetry of Derek Mahon* (Oxford: Oxford University Press, 2007).
9. See Adam Newey, review of *Electric Light*, *New Statesman* (16 April 2001).
10. See Terry Eagleton, 'Hasped and Hooped and Hirpling', review of *Beowulf*, *London Review of Books* (11 November 1999), p. 15.

11. 'I'm certain that up to *North*, that was one book; in a way it grows together and goes together' (John Haffenden, 'Meeting Seamus Heaney: An Interview', in *Viewpoints: Poets in Conversation* [London: Faber and Faber, 1981], p. 64).
12. Seamus Heaney, 'Feeling into Words', *P* 43.
13. Michael J. Durkan and Rand Brandes, *Seamus Heaney: A Reference Guide* (New York: G. K. Hall, 1996). See also Elmer Andrews's *The Poetry of Seamus Heaney*, Critical Guides Icon (Cambridge: Icon Books, 1998) for an overview, with commentary and extensive quotation, of the critical response to the poetry up as far as *The Spirit Level.*
14. An earlier monograph had already appeared in the United States: Robert Buttel's *Seamus Heaney* (Lewisburg, PA: Bucknell University Press, 1975) offers a critically unadventurous account of the first three collections.
15. Helen Vendler, *Seamus Heaney* (London: HarperCollins, 1998), p. 9.
16. Ibid., p. 51.
17. Neil Corcoran, *The Poetry of Seamus Heaney: A Critical Study* (London: Faber and Faber, 1998), p. 185.
18. Ibid., p. 215. See Patricia Coughlan, '"Bog Queens": The Representation of Women in the Poetry of John Montague and Seamus Heaney', in *Gender in Irish Writing*, ed. Toni O'Brien Johnson and David Cairns (Milton Keynes: Open University Press, 1991), pp. 88–111, for an exacting feminist reading of 'the poetry of Montague and Heaney as a whole' as 'insistently and damagingly gendered' (pp. 107–8). See also Catherine Byron, *Out of Step: Pursuing Seamus Heaney to Purgatory* (Bristol: Loxwood Stoneleigh, 1992), for a less theoritical, if in some respects more nuanced investigation of Heaney's gender politics.
19. Corcoran, *Poetry*, p. 231.
20. James Simmons, 'The Trouble with Seamus', in *Seamus Heaney: A Collection of Critical Essays*, ed. Elmer Andrews (Basingstoke: Macmillan, 1992), pp. 48, 55.
21. Ibid., p. 52.
22. David Lloyd, *Anomalous States: Irish Writing and the Post-Colonial Moment* (Dublin: Lilliput Press, 1993), p. 28.
23. Stan Smith, 'The Distance Between: Seamus Heaney', in *The Chosen Ground: Essays on the Contemporary Poetry of Northern Ireland*, ed. Neil Corcoran (Bridgend: Seren, 1992), pp. 35–61; Douglas Dunn, 'Quotidian Miracles: *Seeing Things*', in *The Art of Seamus Heaney*, ed. Tony Curtis, 3rd edn (Bridgend: Seren, 1994), pp. 207–23.
24. Seamus Heaney, 'Crediting Poetry', *RP* 466–7.

4

DENNIS O'DRISCOLL

Heaney in Public

Writers, according to Seamus Heaney, 'live precisely at the intersection of the public and the private'.[1] One of the most direct statements of a public nature in his own poetry occurs in his pamphlet, *An Open Letter*. This Burns-stanza poem was written as a polite protest – jocose but entirely in earnest – at finding himself categorised as 'British' in the *Penguin Book of Contemporary British Poetry*, an influential anthology in which his work was accorded pride of place. Pride of place of a different kind provoked this normally celebratory poet into refusing to raise his glass, as he insisted, 'My passport's green. / No glass of ours was ever raised / To toast *The Queen*' (*OL* 9).

An Open Letter was published by the Field Day Theatre Company (of which Heaney was a director) in Derry, a city with nomenclatural problems of its own. Ideal as a platform for a public statement of this kind, Field Day proposed – through plays, pamphlets and anthologies – a re-examination of fundamental assumptions about culture and identity in Ireland. What Seamus Heaney wrote of *The Field Day Anthology of Irish Writing* applied to the work of the Company as a whole – it aimed 'to reveal and confirm the existence of a continuous tradition, contributed to by all groups, sects and parties active in the island's history, one in which a more generous and hospitable notion of Ireland's cultural achievements will be evident'.[2] Read in this spirit, *An Open Letter* avoids narrow nationalism by the very tone it adopts – temperate and tolerant rather than grimly chauvinistic. While an Ulster Unionist's reading is likely to be coloured by Heaney's choice of passport, the poet himself – in the last of his Oxford lectures – preferred to envisage the poem conferring dual citizenship:

> I wrote about the colour of the passport ... not in order to expunge the British connection in Britain's Ireland but to maintain the right to diversity *within* the border, to be understood as having full freedom to the enjoyment of an Irish name and identity within that northern jurisdiction ... There is nothing extraordinary about the challenge to be in two minds. If, for example, there was

> something exacerbating, there was still nothing deleterious to my sense of Irishness in the fact that I grew up in the minority in Northern Ireland and was educated within the dominant British culture. My identity was emphasized rather than eroded by being maintained in such circumstances. (*RP* 201–2)

Field Day is of course best remembered for its theatre productions, including *The Cure at Troy* – Seamus Heaney's version of Sophocles's *Philoctetes* – and, above all, *Translations* by Brian Friel. An appropriately theatrical air infuses *An Open Letter*, too – not least when Heaney, rehearsing his own reluctance to demur at the Penguin anthology's title, draws on J. M. Synge's *Playboy of the Western World*:

> For weeks and months I've messed about,
> Unclear, embarrassed and in doubt,
> Footered, havered, spraughled, wrought
> Like Shauneen Keogh,
> Wondering should I write it out
> Or let it go. (*OL* 8)

Playful in every sense, *An Open Letter* engages in gestures reminiscent of the 'anglings, aimings, feints and squints … Test-outs and pull-backs, re-envisagings' Heaney describes in 'Squarings' as he recalls childhood games of marbles (*ST* 57). Recognising that the editors of the Penguin anthology, Blake Morrison and Andrew Motion, are enthusiastic advocates of his work, he ruefully speaks of biting 'hands that led me to the limelight / In the Penguin book' (*OL* 13); but he does so with such good grace and good humour that one might suspect a kind of stage-bite to be the worst injury likely to be inflicted by the poem. However, if diplomacy is judged on its results, it becomes clear that Heaney's presence in the literary world is sufficiently weighty for even his lightest gesture – a flick of the nib like a flash of teeth – to succeed in delivering its aims. As conclusive evidence of this, one notes that Heaney and his fellow-poets from Ireland, north and south, have ceased to be automatically classified as British by editors and critics; recent anthologies from major United Kingdom publishing houses bear titles and subtitles which take account of Heaney's protest. *The Firebox*, Sean O'Brien's anthology from Picador in 1998, was subtitled *Poetry in Britain and Ireland after 1945*, while the same year saw publication of *The Penguin Book of Poetry from Britain and Ireland since 1945*, edited by Simon Armitage and Robert Crawford.

That Seamus Heaney regarded *An Open Letter* as more than a *jeu d'esprit* is obvious from another open letter he wrote in 1983, one published in the 'Letters to the Editor' page of the *Irish Times*. On the eve of a constitutional referendum in the Irish Republic, which its supporters urged on the electorate as a means of copper-fastening an existing legislative ban on abortion, Seamus Heaney – writing from his Dublin home – alluded to *An Open Letter*:

> Recently some poems of mine were included in an anthology entitled *The Penguin Book of Contemporary British Poetry*. I have since felt it necessary to demur at the adjective 'British' ... If the proposed amendment to the Constitution is passed, a significant number of people from this State are likely to be even more embarrassed to be called Irish. Their Constitution will have infringed their intellectual, emotional and moral identity. And, since abortion is already outlawed, I do not believe that this affront to their inner freedom is necessary.[3]

The letter to the newspaper illustrates an important component of Heaney's diplomatic prowess, his even-handedness – in this instance, his willingness to be 'in two minds' does not exclude the repudiation of a certain kind of Irishness: intrusive rather than inclusive. Almost twenty years later, in another letter of protest in the *Irish Times*, he again held the balance between what he called 'every party and every denomination'.[4] Expressing dismay that the Duchess of Abercorn – 'a passionate advocate of the value of creative writing in primary education' – had been forced by Republican protests to cancel a visit to a Catholic school in County Tyrone, Heaney praised the 'cross-community, cross-border' dimension of her work. His hard-won eschewal of tribal positions and reflex reactions won the respect of the notoriously censorious Donald Davie who remarked that Heaney's 'refusal to endorse unequivocally one or the other bigoted faction in his native Ulster has been, not a shucking off of responsibility, but on the contrary (implausible as this must seem to the hard-liners on both sides) an admirably tenacious and costly assertion of just such responsibility'.[5] For Davie, Heaney is a poet 'in the public eye' whose feet are planted on ancient ground; a poet whose engagement with contemporary issues is deepened by his rootedness in a living pastoral tradition:

> Heaney, I
> Appeal to you who are more in the public eye
> Than us old codgers: isn't it the case
> The Muse must look disaster in the face?

With a taxonomic flourish worthy of W. H. Auden, Heaney has made a distinction between civic poetry, public poetry and political poetry, categorising Auden's work as 'civic', Yeats's as 'public' more than political and reserving the 'political' tag for poets like Bertolt Brecht, Adrienne Rich, Pablo Neruda and Allen Ginsberg who share 'a specifically political understanding of the world'.[6] Clearly, Heaney too – in his own public role – aspires towards a Yeatsian inclusiveness, free of factionalism, and he ultimately directs his work towards Evgeny Baratynsky's 'reader in posterity'. It is because he is an inclusive, non-factional poet of second thoughts, of two minds, of the 'in-between' and undogmatic, that he is so trusted whenever he adopts a firm stance on a public issue; Christopher Ricks, as early as 1979, described him as 'the most trusted poet of our islands'.[7] His vociferous support for civil rights in Northern Ireland, his long commitment to the anti-apartheid movement and his more recent role as United Nations 'goodwill ambassador' are activities one expects of a spokesman for the 'Republic of Conscience'. This enlightened country (significantly a republic), mapped by Heaney for an Amnesty International commission, challenged him 'to consider myself a representative / and to speak on their behalf in my own tongue' (*HL* 13).

The fact that he always speaks in his 'own tongue' is a further reason why Heaney is trusted by his readers. His language is so personal, so individual, so inimitable, so far removed from any official idiolect used by politicians or businessmen that it can never be confused with a media-speak of borrowed opinions, received assumptions or stock responses. Every idea is examined afresh, as every word is coined anew; he is a subscriber to no one's manifesto, political or literary. Relevant too is the texture of the language he uses: dense and rooted in an age when – influenced by CNN, MTV and similar global media – English has simultaneously internationalised and atrophied. At the same time, with the conviction of a poet who takes it for granted that 'no poetry worth its salt is unconcerned with the world it answers for and sometimes answers to',[8] he has looked to the ethical example of East European poets like Osip Mandelstam and Czesław Miłosz, examining their lives and exploring their ideas as well as savouring their works. He strives to achieve the balance they maintained between guarding private integrity and engaging subtly with public issues. As he declared with the ring of a solemn undertaking, 'In order to be the power it should be, poetry has to establish a public force, yet it must never barter its private rights in exchange for a public hearing.'[9]

Donald Davie, with some justification, characterised himself as a pasticheur of late Augustan styles. But Heaney – notwithstanding 'Sweeney Redivivus' and parts of *The Haw Lantern* – was not a pasticheur of mid-twentieth-century, mid-European styles to any prolonged extent; his general eschewal of irony or satire, traditional tools of the public poet, places him at an immediate remove from East European poets such as Miroslav Holub and Zbigniew Herbert to whom he has devoted critical attention. True, one can find in Heaney's collections some of the verbal economy associated with the East Europeans whom he read most avidly ('Sunlight, turfsmoke, seagulls, boatslip, diesel'). True, too, that the parable poems in *The Haw Lantern* bear some resemblance to certain works of Herbert and Miłosz; but direct poem-by-poem comparison would be difficult to sustain. In any event, it was Richard Wilbur's poem 'Shame', fused with his own memories of arriving at an Orcadian airfield, that 'induced' the writing of 'From the Republic of Conscience';[10] and Heaney's allegorical poem bears a closer consistency in pace and tone to 'Shame' than to the work of, say, Marin Sorescu, Wislawa Szymborska or the East Europeans already mentioned. Moreover, the heart of *The Haw Lantern* lies in 'Clearances', the sonnets for his mother; and such is the natural density and rhythmical richness of his language that his literary temperament is incapable of total surrender, unless as an experiment with contrarieties undertaken by a poet of constantly evolving style, to the ascetic aesthetic, the 'wire-sculpture' bareness of a Vasko Popa or János Pilinszky.

Immensely affirmative though he may be in much of his critical writing, a poet of Heaney's idealism, for whom poetry exerts 'a binding force, a religious claim' and is no mere tenure-track career option or postmodernist plaything,[11] might not altogether baulk at endorsement of Mandelstam's fiery declamation, 'I divide all of world literature into authorised and unauthorised works. The former are all trash; the latter – stolen air.'[12] Among Heaney's 'assumptions' regarding contemporary Irish, British and American poetry is that it is 'somehow otiose in comparison with what it should or might be', and that it has 'failed to live up to E. M. Forster's imperative "Only connect," connect the prose and the passion, the world of sensibility with the world of telegrams and anger. Connect the literary action with an original justifying vision and with the political contingencies of the times.'[13] Against those perceived inadequacies in the body poetic, Heaney posits the example of Robert Lowell. Depicting him as a poet whose 'voice is not just representative of his own sensibility and of nothing else', Heaney's observations have an obvious bearing on Lowell's overtly public poems: 'Inauguration Day: January 1953', 'For the Union Dead', 'Fall 1961', 'July in Washington', 'Waking Early Sunday Morning' and numerous late sonnets. But *Life Studies*, too (usually shelved under 'confessional'), he reclassifies as 'a public book' which 'profiles its figures against public reality'. Employing words equally relevant to himself, Heaney adds that, despite having had 'no public career apart from poetry', Lowell 'nevertheless brought the career of poetry into profile within his society and having done so rebuked current assumptions that the poetic enterprise is too pure or too exquisite to survive the impurities and coarseness of the historical moment'.[14] This was an important awareness for Heaney to carry into his own dark historical moment in Ulster – random bombings, 'dirty protests', hunger strikes – as he progressed and processed towards the public and private interweavings of 'Station Island'.

A prolific translator, Seamus Heaney opts for broad fidelity to the original texts over Lowellesque 'imitation' and regards as a worrying 'indulgence' the modern practice whereby a poem is 'smashed and grabbed rather than rendered up'.[15] Yet his most faithful translations often resonate with contemporaneous public significance. In the essay 'Earning a Rhyme', he describes how he had followed – one might say *imitated* – Lowell's methods in his initial draft of *Sweeney Astray* but then found a stricter translation more coherent and more convincing (*FK* 59–66). Faithfulness did not, however, degenerate into blandness and he brought to his vigorous translation some public aspirations not unlike those quoted earlier concerning *An Open Letter*:

> Part of my intention of doing *Sweeney* was in the deepest (and least, I hope, offensive) sense political. I wanted the Unionist population to feel that they could adhere to it, that something could be shared. For example, names and landscapes. And that's why I changed all of the place names into their modern equivalents.[16]

Again and again in his translations, one finds Heaney's imaginative grip on a text being tightened and his focus sharpened by some public event from which the translation derives added plangency. The preface to his *Beowulf* suggests that 'The Geat woman who cries out in dread as the flames consume the body of her dead lord could come straight from a late-twentieth-century news report, from Rwanda or Kosovo' (*B* xxi). Commenting on the political conditions that prevailed as his translation of Sophocles's *Antigone* (*The Burial at Thebes*) was under way, he noted that 'Early in 2003, the situation that pertains in Sophocles's play was being re-enacted in our own world. Just as Creon forced the citizens of Thebes into an either/or situation in relation to Antigone, the Bush administration in the White House was using the same tactic to forward its argument for war in Iraq.'[17] When Heaney's version of the *Antigone* chorus which warns against overstepping 'what the city allows' appeared in the *New Yorker* in March 2003 (under the non-committal title 'Sophoclean'), it was clear that it could be read as a veiled admonition to President Bush; indeed, Heaney himself – perhaps recalling Robert Lowell's much-publicised letter of protest to President Lyndon B. Johnson during the Vietnam War – stated before a public reading of the poem that 'Sophoclean' could have been alternatively titled 'Letter to George W. [Bush]'.[18]

Heaney's response to the 11 September 2001 terrorist attacks on America, 'Horace and the Thunder' – published, within months of the bombings, in both the *Irish Times* and *The Times Literary Supplement* and later renamed 'Anything Can Happen' – was a version of a Horace Ode (1.34). While taking some liberties with the original Latin, in order to respond more acutely to the facts of the Twin Towers tragedy, he believed 'the poem still does justice to the sense and emotional import of the original while being true enough to what has happened in our time'.[19] The work of a poet negotiating between two languages and 'two minds', Heaney's translations inhabit two eras: he permits them to speak for themselves as great autonomous classical texts and to speak across time to some of the central public issues of 'our time'. To the translations already mentioned, one could also add earlier examples such as the 'Ugulino' section of Dante's *Inferno*, which dates from the 'dirty protests' by Irish Republican Army inmates of the Maze Prison, a poem which he later described as having 'an oblique applicability (in its ferocity of emotion and in its narrative about a divided city) to the Northern Irish situation'.[20] The section about the police widow and hunger-striker's father inserted in *The Cure at Troy* (a work largely faithful to Sophocles in other respects) represents one of Heaney's most public pronouncements and probably his most frequently cited. This declaration from the Chorus ('No poem or play or song / Can fully right a wrong / Inflicted and endured') may echo Yeats's assertion that a poet has 'no gift to set a statesman right';[21] but it has itself proved that a gifted poet can inspire even a politician without being narrowly partisan:

History says, *Don't hope*
On this side of the grave.
But then, once in a lifetime
The longed-for tidal wave
Of justice can rise up,
And hope and history rhyme ...[22]

The fact that the Sinn Fein leader Gerry Adams used *Hope and History* as the title of one of his books, even after US President Bill Clinton had opted for *Between Hope and History*, and Nadine Gordimer, the novelist and anti-apartheid activist, had added her voice to the chorus of publications with *Living in Hope and History*, indicates how extensively those lines permeated the consciousness of public life. The practice of ventriloquising a public voice through the voices of the poets he translates was acknowledged by Heaney himself when he remarked that he 'wrote in a couple of extra choruses' in *The Cure at Troy* because 'the Greek chorus allows you to lay down the law, to speak with a public voice. Things you might not get away with in your own voice, in *propria persona*, become definite and allowable pronouncements on the lips of the chorus.'[23] 'Mycenae Lookout' – neither translation nor imitation, but rather a dramatised sequence of original poems – again uses a classical text to comment indirectly, but unmistakably, on the Troubles. The discreet but observant watchman from the *Agamemnon* of Aeschylus steps out of the wings and takes centre stage to deliver four searing monologues, soaked in blood and betrayal, until the limpid outpourings of the fifth and final section ('fresh water / in the bountiful round mouths of iron pumps / and gushing taps': *SL* 37) shimmer with tentative hope. As the watchman's tongue is loosened, the poet's own tongue is ungoverned, enabling him to look back in apoplectic anger at the calamitous years of the Troubles.

While much of Heaney's poetry bears out his claim in 'Station Island' to be a man with 'no mettle for the angry role' (*SI* 65), the pent-up anger to which a public poem like 'Mycenae Lookout' gives vent is analogous to the private anger charted elsewhere in *The Spirit Level*, in the poem 'Weighing In'. 'Is it any wonder,' Heaney (having grown up in a land of borders and divisions) had asked in 'Terminus', that 'when I thought / I would have second thoughts?' (*HL* 4). There are times, however, as 'Weighing In' avers, when the imperative to speak out and indeed lash out is greater than the need to hedge one's bets and qualify one's position in the interests of balancing one's poetry books:

> Two sides to every question, yes, yes, yes ...
> But every now and then, just weighing in
> Is what it must come down to, and without
> Any self-exculpation or self-pity ... (*SL* 18)

Anger is palpable too in 'The Flight Path' (*SL* 22–6) when Heaney, red-eyed from transatlantic travel but wide-eyed with pleasure on the train to Belfast ('Plain, simple / Exhilaration at being back'), is confronted by a prominent Republican activist whose crude demand, 'When, for fuck's sake, are you going to write / Something for us?', is countered by Heaney's firm and forthright response, 'If I do write something, / Whatever it is, I'll be writing for myself.' But Heaney had discovered, as far back as *North*, that everything he wrote would be fine-combed for its relevance to the Troubles. Some critics accused *North* of aestheticising, mythologising and glamorising the Ulster violence; poems like 'Punishment' and 'Kinship' were assumed to reveal a questionable personal ambivalence towards paramilitary activity. Even the otherwise admiring Blake Morrison, in an early study of the poet, perpetrated the opinion – based on a constrictingly narrow reading of certain lines – that *North* sometimes 'grants sectarian killing in Northern Ireland a historical respectability which it is not usually granted in day-to-day journalism: precedent becomes, if not a justification, then at least an "explanation"'.[24]

Caught in verbal crossfire between the Republican bully, seeking public support for his cause, and the critic convinced that a modicum of support may already have been unwittingly conceded, Heaney continued speaking for himself – a private poet with a public platform, a public poet whose utterances were tested against private experience. However different their basic premises, the commissioning Republican and the decommissioning critic are both tacitly acknowledging the power of poetry – poetry as propaganda in one case, as disinterested truth in the other. In a gloss on the episode with the impatient and importunate Republican of 'The Flight Path', Heaney offered a compelling summary of his position as a poet on whom competing demands for public poetry are made:

> I'm not in favour of stand-off. I'm in favour of tension and connection. The very fact that you have a figure on a train coming to you – either in the poem or in life – or you have various prophets in your own country telling you what you should be doing, is just a signal of how carefully and deeply the mystery of poetry has to be guarded. It *is* very potent.[25]

During an 'outraged moment' of extreme violence in Ulster (a graveyard shooting, a brutal murder of two plainclothes soldiers), Heaney again defied those who had portrayed him as a 'smiling public man', given to anodyne and evasive political utterances. At a *Sunday Times* reception in his honour, he risked further biting of 'hands that led me to the limelight' with some highly critical reflections on the British media's coverage of Northern Irish affairs. Finding 'the self-respect of the Irish people' eroded by the indifference and insensitivity of the British Government and media, he decided – as in *An Open Letter* – that 'therefore it is time to break / Old inclinations not to speak':

> Detachment has kept many poets from engaging in direct political poetry or even from political journalism, since they fear that at best they would only be exploiting an internationally chic, politically sexy platform, and at worst would be giving consolation and corroboration to terrorist factions, especially if they happened to voice complaints against conditions upon which those factions peremptorily base their right to act.
>
> Yet the caution rightly induced by detachment has its limits.[26]

One of the earliest occasions where Heaney had found caution and detachment inappropriate was the aftermath of the Civil Rights Movement march in October 1968. His front-page *Listener* article – something of an open letter – explained why balance ('Two years ago, in an article on Belfast, I tried to present both sides as more or less blameworthy') had perforce given way to 'weighing in' ('it seems now that the Catholic minority in Northern Ireland at large, if it is to retain any self-respect, will have to risk the charge of wrecking the new moderation and seek justice more vociferously').[27] The same civil rights march provoked 'Craig's Dragoons', a sardonic ballad written from a Unionist perspective (exasperation overwhelmed even-handedness in this instance), which was Heaney's contribution to a radio programme introduced by the composer Sean O'Riada: 'We've gerrymandered Derry but Croppy won't lie down, / He calls himself a citizen and wants votes in the town.'[28] Another angry work of Heaney's which has been allowed very restricted circulation is 'The Road to Derry', three of the original four stanzas of which were published on the front page of the *Derry Journal* on the twenty-fifth anniversary of Bloody Sunday. Written in 1972 at the request of the singer Luke Kelly, but never actually recorded by him, it is poised between poem and song, combining elements of the Gaelic lament and the broadsheet ballad (another form of open letter):

> My heart besieged by anger, my mind a gap of danger,
> I walked among their old haunts, the home ground where they bled;
> And in the dirt lay justice like an acorn in the winter
> Till its oak would sprout in Derry where the thirteen men lay dead.[29]

Neil Corcoran has pointed to the similarities between the endings of 'The Road to Derry' and 'Requiem for the Croppies' ('in August the barley grew up out of the grave'; *DD* 24).[30] But, whereas one assumes that aesthetic standards (the poem is not particularly good), as well as the fear that it would be used as a hymn in Republican martyrology, discouraged Heaney from including the former in a collection, the latter was published in *Door into the Dark* and widely admired and anthologised. Both 'Requiem for the Croppies' and 'The Road to Derry', as public poems, inevitably altered as the political situation altered. When the singer Christy Moore wanted to record 'The Road to Derry', after its 1997 publication, Heaney refused on the grounds that its moment had passed, that it would be 'irresponsible' to declaim and disseminate the song at such a safe distance from the carnage of Bloody Sunday. Having recounted his exchange with the singer, he told an interviewer, 'It's one thing to launch into the dangerous waters of the moment, but a very different thing to punt the currents later on.'[31] In the same interview, he spoke of the subsequent fate of 'Requiem for the Croppies':

> My poem about the croppies was particularly pleasing to me because it was a sonnet. It was an example, if you like, of an official English-poetry form, but one that incorporated what had been sub-cultural material during my growing-up – ballads about '98, and so on. This was matter of deep political relevance, and it was important that it be acknowledged. At the same time, I have to admit that the poem's meaning changed over the years. By the mid-Seventies, to recite 'Requiem for the Croppies' in Ireland in public would have been taken as a gesture of solidarity with the Provisionals.[32]

Only a poet with a keen awareness of his public role would need to be as sensitive to the political ramifications of his work as Heaney or indeed Yeats ('Did that play of mine send out / Certain men the English shot?'). Heaney has stated that 'the audience for poetry is usually smallish; the potential public for it is very large. Some people get an audience and then get what Wordsworth called "a public".'[33] He cites Robert Frost as an example of a poet with a public, Gerard Manley Hopkins and Wallace Stevens as poets with an audience. The size of Heaney's public may be gauged from an Arts Council of England study published in 2000, estimating that his books accounted for 63.8% of British sales volume in the 'contemporary poets' category in 1998/1999.[34] Even the Sophoclean *The Burial at Thebes* entered Ireland's best-seller list for a couple of weeks after its publication in the spring of 2004. The trust engendered by Heaney's work, among readers normally wary of poetry, includes trusting him to reach out and enlighten rather than to reach down and patronise when it comes to great classical texts in translation or original poems containing arcane allusions.

Heaney's poetry has grown in density over the years (literary and mythological references are more frequent), yet his public remains a steadfast one, finding its own spirit level in the work. Neither the creature of his audience nor yet indifferent to it, his intimacy with his primary readership – his highly attentive and alert Irish one – allows him to precisely calibrate the tone and content of his poems without being overly self-conscious about using native locutions or locations. Whereas, for Donald Davie, Heaney is 'an Irishman writing in the first place for the Irish', Desmond Fennell – as much controversialist as critic in his long essay, 'Whatever You Say, Say Nothing' – is so determined to attribute the poet's reputation to international networking ('Ireland was not consulted on the matter') that he glibly underestimates the risks taken and the originality achieved by Heaney in presenting his language on its own local terms: 'The poems with difficult words and Irish allusions ... challenge [academics] engagingly as literary interpreters – justifying them by giving them work to do.'[35] As was demonstrated by the avalanche of 'Letters to the Editor' in the *Irish Times*, arising from the publication there of a distillation of Fennell's essay, poetry remains a prominent art in Ireland and a jury of readers is always ready to volunteer a verdict when a writer's reputation goes on trial.

Heaney recognises the unique nature of the society in which he lives, observing that 'one of the binds as well as one of the bonuses for poets in Ireland' lies in the fact that 'every poem is either enlisted or unmasked for its clandestine political affiliations'.[36] Asked by an *Irish Times* journalist whether he envies 'the quiet lives of the poets in America or Britain', he responded:

> Well, I don't actually, no. The Americans are at bay in prosperity and freedom, in a way ... the poet in America for a long time has had great difficulty in escaping from the arena of the first-person singular. In England, I think the poet has great difficulty in escaping from the civility of the literary tradition itself. In Ireland, you cannot divorce the literary from the historical, from the political, from the usual life. You may pretend, like Joyce, that you are going to

> pursue aesthetic matters, but that is in fact a weapon to deal with these other contingencies.[37]

The circuit on which a Heaney poem may run, from the personal to the historical to the political to the communal, is encapsulated in Sven Birkerts's remark that 'Although his lines are seldom political in any overt sense, they retain an implicit – I would even say organic – sense of communal connectedness.'[38] This observation astutely captures the way in which Heaney's finest work, because it is so securely rooted in time and place, can be effortlessly and indeed unconsciously political; or, as is the case with his elegies, it is political mainly by implication. Conversely, the poems ('Whatever You Say Say Nothing', for instance) which are explicitly political or topical in theme are less frequently successful, and several such poems remain uncollected.

Eavan Boland has described her native Dublin, Heaney's adopted city, as presenting 'a very powerful and intense and abrasive atmosphere for poets, and anyone who has lived there knows that it is as far as a poet can get from a flattering environment!'[39] True to this description, a few years after *Irish Times* readers had been informed by Desmond Fennell that Heaney's 'good but minor poetry ... says nothing of general relevance', Eamon Dunphy, another controversialist turned temporary poetry critic, offered readers of Ireland's *Sunday Independent* the benefit of a pageful of Heaney's alleged shortcomings: 'I don't think Seamus Heaney's poetry is very good. His prose is even worse: oblique, tortured, pretentious.'[40] Further mailbags from the public, arguing the merits or demerits of Ireland's freshly garlanded Nobel laureate, followed. So much for the notion of a writer whose advancement from rural lamplight to Nobel limelight has been an unimpeded odyssey. As the poet himself, echoing Ted Hughes, remarked more realistically, 'The beginning of praise is the beginning of execration.'[41]

If the taunts of Fennell (who veers close to championing the idea of poetry as propaganda) and Dunphy (who jeers at Heaney as an 'essentially obscure and dull' writer) are not supported by evidence of serious engagement with poetry, other critics of Heaney's *oeuvre* (who have included friends, contemporaries and former students) are deeply involved in the art as distinguished critics and practitioners. Although widely (and, in my opinion, rightly) regarded as Heaney's finest and most original collection, *North* was greeted with a virtually unanimous vote of no confidence in his native Ulster: Edna Longley and Ciaran Carson were fierce in their criticism of the collection, while Paul Muldoon did not venture beyond its dedicatory section when selecting work for his anthology, *The Faber Book of Contemporary Irish Poetry* (1986). An essay by James Simmons, entitled with characteristic combativeness 'The Trouble with Seamus', lays a long list of unsubstantiated charges – including 'violent nationalism' and 'reactionary politics' – at Heaney's door, contending that he is a poet without 'moral centre' who 'may turn out to be an almost total irrelevance like W. R. Rodgers, who also had a marvellous verbal gift'.[42]

With so much 'friendly fire' to contend with over the years, and a constant volley of other voices – whether, for instance, a feminist objecting to his alleged stereotyping of women, a poet-critic suggesting that he should be more industrious in generating love poems, or a prominent older poet urging him to 'Join Our Century before it's too late'[43] – Heaney, as a writer with a large public, is subjected to a critical interrogation which is far wider and more intense than that experienced by most poets. It is a measure of his importance as a poet that he draws such a diversity of critical attention and quite proper that the major claims made for his *oeuvre* should be thoroughly appraised and closely audited. But whether the experience of being publicly rebuked by colleagues whom he had befriended and championed has had direct consequences for the subsequent direction of his work is something about which one can only speculate. One might ask whether the plain-spoken locutions and contemporary settings of *Field Work* were a reaction to the criticism in Ulster of the mythic aspects of *North*'s highly wrought poetry – or did *Field Work* follow naturally from the more direct writing in Part II of *North*? Did the criticism from Ulster colleagues have positive consequences, insofar as it liberated Heaney from any constraining literary debts or group loyalties?

Heaney's reflections in verse on public events (from the IRA ceasefire of 1994 to the expansion of the European Union ten years later) have made him Ireland's unofficial poet laureate, and his popularity has not been earned at the cost of cheap controversy or artistic compromise. While primarily an inward artist, he grappled with public issues even before the Troubles flared ('Docker' appeared in 1966 in *Death of a Naturalist*); and he came to regard 'a poem of political protest' as 'not only an honourable, but a necessary thing', eventually regretting not having risked 'an intervention' at the time of the IRA hunger strikes: 'It was a moment for poetry to strike through social and political concerns, and to say this was an *awesome* sacrifice.'[44] His responses to political events in America, Iraq and – through the innovative, journal-like 'Known World' – the former Yugoslavia are testimony that the public dimension of his art extends beyond Ireland; and he would surely dissent both from W. H. Auden's hypothesis that 'if not a poem had been written, not a picture painted, not a bar of music composed, the history of man would be materially unchanged' and from Conor Cruise O'Brien's worst fears about the 'unhealthy intersection' of art and politics.[45] But Heaney is in fact less manifestly public in his poetic preoccupations than contemporaries such as Paul Durcan, Tony Harrison, Adrian Mitchell or Adrienne Rich; he prefers to 'speak in' than to speak out and sees poetry as something which is subtle in its effects: 'I can't think of a case where poems changed the world, but what they do is they change people's understanding of what's going on in the world.'[46] Always preserving an untrammelled inner space for the 'lyric impulse', he told his friend Seamus Deane, 'The quick and the purity of the inward act has to be preserved at all costs, however essential the outward structures may be for communication, community and universal significance.'[47]

Denis Donoghue, considering the ways in which a public catastrophe may impinge on the imagination of a poet (the Irish Civil War on Yeats, the Second World War on Eliot), rightly concluded that a fitting artistic response does not always prove imaginatively possible: 'There is sometimes a level of impingement which issues in a kind of brute silence rather than in a high degree of articulation.'[48] Donoghue might well have cited Heaney's 'Land of the Unspoken', whose 'unspoken assumptions have the force / of revelation' (*HL* 19). Imbued with 'negative capability' – with doubts, not dogmas – Heaney finds the unheard melodies of silence counter-pointing the siren songs of speech; the dread that (like the speaker in 'The Stone Verdict') he will say too much vies with scruples about negligently holding his silence. Nonetheless, there is in Ireland a large expectation – and not just among habitual readers of the poet's work – that, in times of public crisis or exultation, Heaney will prove capable (whether in poetry or prose) of capturing the public mood, eloquently articulating communal feelings, rising to an occasion with a cadenced, felicitous, elevated language. Irish newspapers have featured mini-essays from Heaney in response to major occurrences such as the ceasefire of 1994, the Omagh bombings and the 'Good Friday' agreement in 1998. Breaking the shocked and helpless silence felt in Ireland, immediately after the Omagh atrocity, he quoted a bereaved friend as having once told him, 'What is spoken may not altogether assuage loss, but it mirrors it and, while this may not be immediately helpful, it is appropriate.'[49]

An occasion when an individual loss led to two responses by Heaney – one spontaneous, the other reflective; one in public prose, the other in private verse; both deeply felt and adapted to its respective medium – was the sectarian murder in May 1997 of Sean Brown, a Gaelic Athletic Association official from Heaney's home village of Bellaghy. Heaney, who would later write 'The Augean Stables' – one of the 'Sonnets from Hellas' – in Brown's memory, initially responded to the death with an open letter, a handwritten condemnation reproduced on the front page of the *Irish News* of 15 May 1997. Although in Greece at the time, on a private holiday (completing an earlier journey, interrupted by the Nobel Prize announcement in 1995), he took considerable pains – some of the alterations he made to his fax can be deciphered in the newspaper – to draft and despatch the fax from his holiday venue: a moving instance of his faith in Wilfred Owen's 'reciprocity of tears' and a practical manifestation of the integrity he once defined in his essay 'What Makes a Good Poet?':

> there is something to be learned from the example of all good poets including Owen and W. B. Yeats, and of course the great Wordsworth, namely, that it is the poet's job to be sensitive to the tensions and strains which run through the life of the times. What distinguishes the good poet is the ability to trace these tensions home through the fault lines of his or her own sensibility, and to be true to the workings of his or her own spirit while remaining alert to the workings of the world. This is what we might call artistic integrity, and is a *sine qua non.*[50]

NOTES

1. Seamus Heaney, 'Foreword', in *Lifelines*, ed. Niall MacMonagle (Dublin: Town House, 1992), p. xii.
2. Seamus Heaney, 'A Field Day for the Irish', *The Times* (5 December 1988), p. 18.
3. Seamus Heaney, 'Letters to the Editor', *Irish Times* (3 September 1983).
4. Ibid. (22 January 2000), p. 17.
5. Donald Davie, 'Responsibilities of *Station Island*', *Salmagundi* no. 80 (Fall 1988), pp. 64–5.
6. Seamus Heaney quoted in Henri Cole, 'The Art of Poetry LXXV', *Paris Review* no. 144 (Fall 1997), p. 104.
7. Christopher Ricks, 'The Mouth, the Meal and the Book', in *Seamus Heaney*, ed. Michael Allen (London: Macmillan, 1997), p. 97.
8. Seamus Heaney, 'The Peace of the Word', *The Sunday Times 'Culture' Supplement* (17 January 1999), p. 11.
9. Seamus Heaney, 'Current Unstated Assumptions about Poetry', *Critical Inquiry* (Summer 1981), p. 650.
10. See John Brown, *In the Chair: Interviews with Poets from the North of Ireland* (Co. Clare: Salmon, 2002), p. 84.
11. Heaney, 'Current Unstated Assumptions', p. 650.
12. Osip Mandelstam, *The Collected Critical Prose and Letters*, tr. Jane Gary Harris and Constance Link, ed. Jane Gary Harris (London: Collins Harvill, 1991), p. 316.
13. Heaney, 'Current Unstated Assumptions', p. 646.
14. Ibid., p. 649.
15. Seamus Heaney, 'Como Conversazione: On Translation', *Paris Review* no. 155 (Summer 2000), pp. 294–5.
16. Heaney quoted in Marilynn J. Richtarik, *Acting Between the Lines: The Field Day Theatre Company and Irish Cultural Politics 1980–1984* (Washington DC: Catholic University of America Press, 2001), p. 150.
17. Seamus Heaney, programme note for *The Burial at Thebes*, Abbey Theatre, Dublin, 5 April 2004, n.p.

18. Heaney, reading at 'Poetry Now' festival, Pavilion Theatre, Dun Laoghaire, 27 March 2004.
19. Seamus Heaney, 'Reality and Justice: On Translating Horace, *Odes*, 1, 34', *Translation Ireland* (Spring 2002), p. 10.
20. Heaney, interviewed by Rand Brandes, *Salmagundi* no. 80 (Fall 1988), p. 12.
21. W. B. Yeats, 'On being asked for a War Poem', *Yeats's Poems*, ed. and annotated by A. N. Jeffares (London: Macmillan, 1989), p. 259.
22. Seamus Heaney, *The Cure at Troy: A Version of Sophocles' 'Philoctetes'* (London: Faber and Faber, 1990), p. 77.
23. Heaney quoted in Seamus Heaney and Robert Hass, *Sounding Lines: The Art of Translating Poetry* (Berkeley, CA: Doreen B. Townsend Center for the Humanities, 2000), p. 23.
24. Blake Morrison, *Seamus Heaney* (London and New York: Methuen, 1982), p. 68.
25. Heaney interviewed by Theo Dorgan, *RTE Radio 1* (Dublin), 8 May 1996.
26. Seamus Heaney, 'Anglo-Irish Occasions', *London Review of Books* (5 May 1988), p. 9.
27. Seamus Heaney, *Listener* 80.2065 (24 October 1968), p. 522.
28. See Karl Miller, 'Opinion', *Review* nos. 27–8 (Autumn–Winter 1971–2), pp. 47–8.
29. Seamus Heaney, 'The Road to Derry', *Derry Journal* (31 January 1997), p. 3.
30. Neil Corcoran, *The Poetry of Seamus Heaney: A Critical Study* (London: Faber and Faber, 1998), p. 249.
31. *Seamus Heaney in Conversation with Karl Miller* (London: Between the Lines, 2000), p. 24.
32. Ibid., pp. 19–20.
33. Heaney interviewed by Myles Dungan, *RTE Radio 1* (Dublin), 13 April 2004.
34. Ann Bridgwood and John Hampson (eds.), *Rhyme and Reason: Developing Contemporary Poetry* (London: Arts Council of England, 2000), p. 23.
35. Davie, 'Responsibilities', p. 64; Desmond Fennell, 'Whatever You Say, Say Nothing: Why Seamus Heaney is No. 1', *Stand* 32:4 (Autumn 1991), pp. 48, 50.
36. Heaney quoted in Cole, 'Art of Poetry' , p. 106.
37. Heaney quoted in Deaglán de Bréadún, 'Comfortable Image Belies the Serious Poet', *Irish Times* (13 September 1984), p. 13.
38. Sven Birkerts, *Readings* (St Paul: Graywolf Press, 1999), p. 140.
39. Eavan Boland interviewed by Patty O'Connell, *Poets & Writers Magazine*, (November/December 1994), p. 40.
40. Eamon Dunphy, 'Stand in Line or Be Called a Philistine', *Sunday Independent* (8 October 1995), p. 14.
41. Heaney interviewed by David Hanly, *RTE Radio 1* (Dublin), 9 October 1995.
42. James Simmons, 'The Trouble with Seamus', in *Seamus Heaney: A Collection of Critical Essays*, ed. Elmer Andrews (London: Macmillan, 1992), pp. 39–66.
43. See Patricia Coughlan, '"Bog Queens": The Representation of Women in the Poetry of John Montague and Seamus Heaney', in *Seamus Heaney*, ed. Allen pp. 185–205; Andrew Waterman, 'Ulsterectomy', *Hibernia* (26 April 1979), pp. 16–17; and Peter Porter, 'Privileges of an Irish Poet', *Sunday Telegraph* (30 August 1998), p. 13.
44. *Heaney in Conversation with Miller*, p. 23.
45. W.H. Auden, 'The Public v. The Late Mr William Butler Yeats', *The Complete Works of W.H. Auden: Prose, Volume II, 1939–1948*, ed. Edward Mendelson

(London: Faber and Faber, 2002), p. 7; Conor Cruise O'Brien, 'An Unhealthy Intersection', *New Review* 2:16 (July 1975), pp. 3–8.

46. Heaney quoted in Christy Zempter, 'Heaney: Power of Poetry Lies in Effect on Individual', *This Week Newspapers* (15 April 2004).
47. Heaney quoted in 'Unhappy and at Home', interview by Seamus Deane, (*The Crane Bag Book of Irish Studies 1977–1981*, ed. Mark Patrick Hederman and Richard Kearney [Dublin: Blackwater Press, 1982], p. 70).
48. Denis Donoghue interviewed by Myles Dungan, *RTE Radio 1* (Dublin), 23 February 2004.
49. Seamus Heaney, 'The Reciprocity of Tears', *Irish Times* (22 August 1998), p. 7.
50. Seamus Heaney, 'What Makes a Good Poet?', *Portal* no. 2 (July 2000), p. 5.

5

FRAN BREARTON

Heaney and the Feminine

In the 1960s, and at a formative point in Seamus Heaney's career, the influence of Robert Graves – as both poet and critic – was profoundly felt. His images and ideas echo through Heaney's early writings (as do those of another Gravesian acolyte of the 1950s and 1960s, Ted Hughes) and a glance at Graves's 1960s love poems is to see the source for some of Heaney's emerging 'word-hoard'. More than this, Heaney formulates his own emergence as a poet, and his views on poetic craft, in Gravesian terms, and his early 1970s essays are indebted to Graves's 1960s Oxford poetry lectures. In an oft-quoted passage from the 1972 essay 'Belfast' Heaney writes:

> I have always listened for poems, they come sometimes like bodies out of a bog ... surfacing with a touch of mystery. They certainly involve craft and determination, but chance and instinct have a role in the thing too. I think the process is a kind of somnambulist encounter between masculine will and intelligence and feminine clusters of image and emotion.
>
> I suppose the feminine element for me involves the matter of Ireland, and the masculine strain is drawn from the involvement with English literature. (*P* 34)

Leaving the Ireland–England politics aside for the moment, this is an endorsement of a Gravesian aesthetic. The first poetry collection by Graves that Heaney acquired was the uncompromisingly titled 1964 volume *Man Does, Woman Is*, a title that Graves glosses in terms strikingly similar to those found later in Heaney's criticism: 'Ideally women *are*, meaning that they possess innate magic ... but theirs is not doing in the male sense. Whenever men achieve something magically apt and right and surprising, their *duende* has always, it seems been inspired by women.'[1] For Graves, as for Heaney, the distinction between men and women (or in Heaney's more diplomatic terms 'masculine' and 'feminine') is also implicated in an understanding of poetic technique. 'Would-be poets', Graves argues, merely 'experiment in loveless Apollonian techniques', whereas true poets 'who serve the Muse wait for the inspired lightning flash of two or three words that initiate composition and dictate the rhythmic norm of their verse'.[2] He then quotes in illustration of the principle his own poem 'Dance of Words', from *Man Does, Woman Is*: 'To make them move, you should start from lightning / And not forecast the rhythm: rely on chance / Or so-called chance for its bright emergence ...'[3]

In the passage from 'Belfast' quoted above Heaney affirms a belief in feminine 'mystery', of that 'chance / Or so-called chance' of the muse poet's inspiration. (Heaney goes on to talk of 'the lure of the native experience' – feminine seductiveness – as against 'the marks of English influence' – masculine will.) He also implicitly echoes the idea that 'man does, woman is': Heaney's pro-active 'craft and determination', 'will and intelligence' are Graves's 'Apollonian techniques'; the 'mystery', 'image and emotion', his Muse-inspired 'lightning flash'. The argument validates, while it seemingly negates, the poet's control, the 'somnambulist' nature of the encounter a deceptive denial of 'will and intelligence' even as female agency is, in these terms, disallowed. The argument is developed by Heaney in 'Feeling into Words' (1974), with 'craft' something learned, a 'capable verbal athletic display', and therefore by implication masculine, and 'technique' the 'discovery of ways to ... raid the inarticulate' another version of feminine 'mystery' (*P* 47). Like Graves, he cites Alun Lewis as a poet who had a 'real technique' (in Graves's phrase, an understanding of 'the lost rudiments of poetry'[4]); like Graves, he quotes one of his own poems – 'The Diviner' – in illustration, with its self-reflexive epiphanic (accidental) 'gift' of discovery; he then quotes in full, as a clincher to the argument, Graves's 'Dance of Words'. In 'Feeling into Words', he also offers, in miniature, the thesis of Graves's *The White Goddess*, which argues that after a struggle for supremacy, the ancient religion of the goddess was hidden from view, and 'patrilinear' substituted for 'matrilinear institutions'.[5] For Heaney, that prehistorical struggle is brought back to life in the context of the violence in Northern Ireland: it is a violence with a 'religious intensity ... a struggle between the cults and devotees of a god and goddess'; a female 'sovereignty' has been 'temporarily usurped or infringed by a new male cult' (*P* 57).

As Grevel Lindop notes, the 1960s brought to the Western world 'new religions, new psychotherapies, new sexual freedoms ... Occultism, paganism and a kind of feminism were in the air.'[6] Robert Graves probably has a lot to answer for here. The same might be said of D. H. Lawrence, whose earth mothers and renderings of a primitivist female sexuality took on a new lease of life after the *Lady Chatterley's Lover* trial in 1960; or of Ted Hughes, who read *The White Goddess* in 1951 and never fully recovered from his absorption of its dubious gender politics and imaginative power. Heaney's 'feminine principle' is usually discussed first and foremost in the contexts of the Irish Republican tradition and Irish Catholicism, to which I will return. The influence of Joyce is unmissable too ('To ourselves ... new paganism ... *omphalos*'[7]). Nevertheless, to begin with the influence of Graves is also to note that Heaney's version of the 'feminine' cannot be fully understood without reference to the broader climate of the 1960s from which it is in part derived. His terms may be less stark than Graves's; but perhaps they are, in their way, no less uncompromising, and equally indebted to some of the more controversial aspects of Jungian (archetypal) thought.[8]

Heaney, in other words, like other male poets before him, genders the very writing of poetry and the nature of 'inspiration' in ways which, in the aftermath of deconstruction and second-wave feminism, seem now rather dated. Take the following observation about form and language from 1974:

> I am setting up two modes and calling them masculine and feminine – but without the Victorian sexist overtones to be found in Hopkins's and Yeats's employment of the terms. In the masculine mode, the language functions as a form of address, of assertion or command, and the poetic effort has to do with conscious quelling and control of the materials, a labour of shaping; words are not music before they are anything else, nor are they drowsy from their slumber in the unconscious, but athletic, capable, displaying the muscle of sense. Whereas in the feminine mode the language functions more as evocation than as address, and the poetic effort is not so much a labour of design as it is an act of divination and revelation; words in the feminine mode behave *with the lover's come-hither instead of the athlete's display*, they constitute a poetry that is delicious as texture before it is recognised as architectonic. ('The Fire i' the Flint', *P* 88; my italics)

There are three things in this passage of particular note. First, Heaney's attribution of particular qualities to the 'feminine' and the 'masculine' is, even for its time, unusually phallocentric,[9] and it may be seen to carry political implications for an understanding of the roles played by men and women – too transparently to require further explication here. Second, a parallel is drawn between the authoritative ordering structure of the masculine, and the nature of poetic form: the poet's shaping of his material is a 'conscious quelling and control', one, moreover, predicated in sexual terms, since that 'quelling' is a response to the 'lover's come-hither'. Third, the masculine is overtly performative, since it is a 'display'; the feminine is essentialist, something innate to be divined and revealed through its marriage with the 'muscle of sense'.

Heaney's 'sexual linguistics' here are by no means unique, and following Gilbert and Gubar's pioneering study, *No Man's Land: The Place of the Woman Writer in the Twentieth Century*, cannot (his own disclaimer of 'without the Victorian sexist overtones' aside) be seen as entirely remote from a tradition of male-authored 'linguistic misogyny'. Heaney's two modes here, as with his 'masculine strain ... drawn from the involvement with English literature' and 'feminine element' from Ireland, bear some resemblance, although the historical context has changed, to Ong's '*patrius sermo*' ('father speech') learned through male classical education, as against the '*materna lingua*' ('mother tongue') which is modified by the male author.[10] In 'The Ministry of Fear', its other more obvious political and aesthetic agendas aside, one might argue that the 'hobnailed boots ... walking ... all over the fine / Lawns of elocution' (*N* 64) do not so much assert the 'matter of Ireland' against 'English literature', but simply bring one version of *patrius sermo* into conflict with another. That is, Heaney, like others before him, posits a marriage between masculine and feminine elements within the language, but, metaphorically speaking, it's always the man (or the male poet) who goes out to work.

Gilbert and Gubar observe that 'masculine linguistic fantasies fall into four categories', some of which may overlap:

> (1) a mystification (and corollary appropriation) of the powers of the *materna lingua* itself; (2) a revision of the *materna lingua* which would assert (male) power over it; (3) a recuperation (or a wish for recuperation) of what are seen as the lost powers of the *patrius sermo*; (4) a transformation of the *materna lingua* into a powerful new kind of *patrius sermo*.[11]

In a sense, all four may be seen at work in different ways in Heaney – the 'matter of Ireland' is also a feminine 'mystery' which inspires the poet; the feminised 'subculture' is brought 'to cultural power' by finding its voice through the male poet; the Irish tradition is asserted against the English one; 'the English lyric' is reinvented in an Irish-English style and idiom.[12] Instances of such linguistic fantasies abound in his 1970s poems. In 'Broagh', that 'last / *gh* the strangers found / difficult to manage' (*WO* 27) encompasses the historical 'unmanageability' of the Irish, resistant to the definitions or constraints imposed on them by an imperial power; it renders the *materna lingua* of the local placename a mystery; in being 'difficult to manage' the 'last / *gh*' is also implicitly feminised (a sense reinforced by the poem's fluidity of imagery); the mystery also becomes a form of resistance, full of a 'come-hither' that cannot easily be quelled or contained – except by the familiar voice of the poet who thereby appropriates its powers. In *North* the linguistic self-consciousness of the poems plays 'masculine' and 'feminine' modes of language against each other, as in 'Ocean's Love to Ireland', where the vowel sounds, sibilance and compounds of the 'feminine' – 'Rush-light, mushroom-flesh' – sink under the consonantal weight of the 'Iambic drums / Of English' which 'beat the woods'. At the same time, the poem plays 'iambic drums' against trochaic ones (a characteristic rhythmical quarrel in Heaney) before the poet reasserts the iambic as his own by the close of the poem: 'The ground possessed and repossessed' (*N* 46–7).

Some of the complications and overlaps in Heaney's sexual linguistics are related to the nature of the language question in Ireland more generally. But there is one point to note about Heaney's 'feminine mode' in relation to language, which is that the feminine never really finds its own voice: it is evoked, addressed, uncovered (sometimes covered) and revealed only by its masculine opposite. As Judith Butler notes in her discussion of the dialectic of Same and Other, that dialectic is 'a false binary, the illusion of a symmetrical difference which consolidates the metaphysical economy of phallogocentrism, the economy of the same'. Consequently, 'the Other as well as the Same are marked as masculine; the Other is but the negative elaboration of the masculine subject with the result that the female sex is unrepresentable'.[13] Or, in Cixous's phrase, 'the same is what rules, names, defines, and assigns "its" other'.[14] The observation may be pertinent to the question of 'voice' in Heaney's poems, since on the rare occasions when he has adopted a female persona, he has not done so with any notable degree of success. For a poet of his superb technical accomplishment and tonal sensitivity, the problem is revealing. Neil Corcoran voiced his unease with what he sees partly as a 'failure of empathy' in the monologues 'The Wife's Tale' and 'Undine': 'When Heaney speaks as a woman in these poems ... it still seems very much his own voice doing the talking.'[15] A poem such as 'Undine' contains also its elements of male sexual fantasy, contributing to its tonal problems: 'I swallowed his trench / Gratefully, dispersing myself for love / Down in his roots' (*DD* 26); the female persona in the service of male fantasy is also apparent in 'Bog Queen': 'My body was Braille / for the creeping influences' (*N* 32). In the controversial 'Punishment', one criticism might be that while the poem professes empathy ('I can feel the tug / of the halter'), it slips rapidly into objectification ('I can see her drowned / body'). More recently, 'Cassandra', from *The Spirit Level*, obliquely returns to some of the problems of 'Punishment': 'No such thing / as innocent / bystanding'. Yet it does so, once again, from the view of the 'Watchman', Heaney's imagination drawn to the silenced (eternal) female victim:

> Her soiled vest,
> her little breasts,
> her clipped, devast-
> ated, scabbed
> punk head,
> the char-eyed

famine gawk –
she looked
camp-fucked

and simple. (*SL* 30–1)

Heaney's 'dialectic', in other words, as the tonal problems of some of these poems imply, cannot 'voice' its Other; yet at the same time, his aesthetic is predicated on same/other thinking. From his criticism, in particular his 1970s essays, the following 'binaries' may be either directly extrapolated or inferred: Masculine/Feminine; England/Ireland; Active/Passive; (Protestant/Catholic); History/Mystery; Craft/Instinct; Sense/Sensibility; Structure/Sound; Consonants/Vowels; (Male poet/Female poet). They find their parallel in the 'word-hoard', Heaney's own *Spiritus Mundi*, of the poems: wells, rivers, fluidity, passivity – woman; shaft; spade, solidity, activity – man. That is, his 'binaries' are deeply embedded in his aesthetic practice.

As with his gendering of language, the other 'binaries' of Heaney's criticism might all too easily collapse under the weight of their inherent political contradictions (such as the implied association of England, Protestantism and male poet – i.e. Heaney). But they may also be seen as false binaries that ultimately serve to affirm 'Man' not 'Woman'. In a context in which the influence of French feminist thinking has profoundly affected the way we read texts, Heaney seems to come gift-wrapped for critics such as Hélène Cixous and Luce Irigaray, and ripe for deconstruction. It may be something of an historical irony, although not a coincidence, given the climate of the time, that the essays in which Heaney's binary masculine and feminine modes are so explicitly affirmed predate by only a year Cixous's seminal exposé of this mode of thinking in *The Newly Born Woman* (although another decade was to pass before her text appeared in English translation). Famously, Cixous begins 'Sorties' thus:

> Where is she?
> Activity/Passivity
> Sun/Moon
> Culture/Nature
> Day/Night
>
> Father/Mother
> Head/Heart
> Intelligible/Palpable
> Logos/Pathos.
> Form, convex, step, advance, semen, progress.
> Matter, concave, ground – where steps are taken, holding- and dumping-ground.

> Man
> ———
> Woman
>
> Always the same metaphor; we follow it, it carries us, beneath all its figures, wherever discourse is organized.[16]

For Cixous, 'Woman' is seen as 'Night to his Day – that has forever been the fantasy. Black to his white. Shut out of his system's space, she is the repressed that ensures the system's functioning.'[17] What she identifies as the 'metaphor' of male-centred discourse here is at the heart of Heaney's imagery to an extent that is almost uncanny: the feminine, for Heaney, is associated with 'the matter of Ireland'; the maternal centre is the ground that 'holds / and spreads'; it is also that 'wet centre', the 'Inwards and downwards' concave bog-hole of the landscape; the male poet 'cannot be weaned / Off the earth's long contour, her river-veins'; the 'palpable' is that from which the 'unsaid' can be gleaned.[18]

To accept Cixous's contention that this metaphor leaves woman as absent ('Where is she?') is not thereby necessarily to denigrate Heaney's poetry. (Indeed, the controversy generated by some of his 1970s poems in terms of their politics and/or gender politics is also testament to their imaginative power.) It is, however, to recognise the underlying perceptions of gender that contribute towards his aesthetic 'system's functioning', and to recognise that the system poses problems for the feminist reader. For Patricia Coughlan, whose essay 'Bog Queens' is the first sustained feminist critique of Heaney's poetry, and of the 'centrality of the feminine' in his work, Heaney is 'dismayingly reliant upon old, familiar and familiarly oppressive allocations of gender positions'. This is something which must, she argues, inflect any celebration of his poetry as possessing 'universality of utterance and ... utopian insight'. It is hard to gainsay Coughlan's critique of one particular aspect of Heaney's poems (although this is by no means the whole story) – that is, his representation of women as archetypal figures who assist the male figure to self-discovery.[19] Heaney's women are not women as such, but closer to a Jungian *anima*: 'a man's image of a woman', as Storr describes it, a 'personification of male erotic desire' who also possesses 'age-old wisdom'.[20] Coughlan's conclusions regarding the 'absence of woman as speaking subjects', and her contention that Heaney's poetry as a whole is 'insistently and damagingly gendered' in this regard are also persuasive.[21] Her essay remains the vital starting point for any exploration of those subjects. Further, it remains the case that, even in a sceptical postmodern critical climate, Heaney is more than usually subject to praise in terms of his 'universality' and political inclusiveness, and Coughlan's caution regarding the questions gender might raise in relation to such praise also has a more general application.

The two passages quoted above in which Heaney most explicitly genders language and form do not make their way into his *Finders Keepers: Selected Prose 1971–2001*, nor do those terms appear in his later criticism. That may be one consequence of a changing critical climate, and, as with 'Cassandra', suggests a responsiveness in Heaney to a context far removed from the one in which he began to write. Nevertheless, the binary (and essentialist) thinking still affects Heaney's criticism, suggesting it is integral to his perception of literature, culture and politics. Two examples serve to illustrate the point. In a more recent essay, 'Through-Other Places, Through-Other Times', when discussing W. R. Rodgers, Heaney suggests that Rodgers 'associates something original in himself with the lyrical element in the Irish countryside that had ... the native tint of wonder in it [and] ... something vestigially Catholic too'. '[E]qually present', though, he argues, 'was the Scottish inheritance, everything from the Adamnation of the Lowland Covenanters to the Unionist determination that marked the solemn leaguing and covenanting of the Ulster Volunteers in 1912' (*FK* 397–8). As in earlier essays, it is as if a Jungian *animus* and *anima*, or, put another way 'will' *versus* 'emotion' are displaced onto the 'two traditions' of Ulster. Since Heaney rarely writes about women poets, or female selfhood, choosing to define himself against, or in relation to, other male writers – Wordsworth, Joyce, Yeats, Eliot, Hughes – his criticism functions effectively in terms of the insight it offers into his own aesthetic, and as, perhaps, with most poet-critics, his analytical approach is best suited to those subjects with whom Heaney as poet identifies. But it is worth noting that, as with Robert Graves, his is also a version of the feminine which has problematical consequences for reading a female poet, evidenced when the critical method is applied to Sylvia Plath. Plath fails, for Heaney, on terms which her own poetry undermines, and like that last '*gh*' she seems a little difficult to manage. In 'The Indefatigable Hoof-taps: Sylvia Plath', Heaney reads Plath's progress as a poet through a passage from Wordsworth's *Prelude* ('There was a Boy; ye knew him well'). Her breakthrough into the *Ariel* poems is for Heaney indicative of the attainment of a 'somnambulist poetic certitude'; yet what 'may finally limit' the work, he suggests, 'is its dominant theme of self-discovery and self-definition'. The point is expanded as follows:

> I do not suggest that the self is not the proper arena of poetry. But I believe that the greatest work occurs when a certain self-forgetfulness is attained, or at least a fullness of self-possession denied to Sylvia Plath. Her use of myth, for example, tends to confine the widest suggestions of the original to particular applications within her own life ... In 'Lady Lazarus' ... the cultural resonance of the original story is harnessed to a vehemently self-justifying purpose, so that the supra-personal dimensions of knowledge – to which myth typically gives access – are slighted in favour of the intense personal need of the poet. (*GT* 168)

Critical opinion on Plath's 'Lady Lazarus', of course, often divides readers. Yet one might as easily argue the opposite: that 'self-forgetfulness' is a luxury denied the female poet struggling to express female subjectivity; that the supposedly broader 'cultural resonance' of the biblical story is suppressed precisely because of its association with a patriarchal Christian religion; and that myths cannot tell essential truths, or allow access to 'supra-personal dimensions of knowledge', but are always appropriated, adapted and modified according to the needs of a particular time, place or person (one of which may be, of course, the need to sublimate 'intense personal need' into the illusion of the 'supra-personal'). Perhaps more appositely than intended, Heaney's closing quotation is from the 1802 Preface to *Lyrical Ballads*, in which Wordsworth explains how we discover through the process of writing 'what is really important to men' (*GT* 169).

None of this is to forget that Heaney's conceptions of 'masculine' and 'feminine' emerge from a time in the late 1960s and early 1970s when what have now become literary-critical (if not scientific or anthropological) commonplaces – that gender is socially constructed; that male constructions of the 'feminine' serve the needs of masculinity but in doing so deny the truths of female experience – were as yet largely unheard of in the academy; and at a time when essentialism was not on the critical blacklist. The 1960s 'kind of feminism' to which Lindop refers is also less than familiar to a twenty-first-century readership. Unlikely as it might seem, Graves has been praised for his feminist poetics, for his advocacy of the all-powerful goddess – even though the all-powerful goddess is, in Graves's terms, a myth which serves not women but the male poet. More recent feminist criticism has questioned whether female subjectivity can ever be realised through archetypal thinking, however powerful the 'feminine' archetype might be, although the question remains open.[22] Yet in view of those debates, it may seem surprising that (with some notable exceptions) a positive response to, even celebration of, Heaney's 'feminine principle' has continued for the last thirty years – and on the part of some of his female critics. In the late 1980s, Jacqueline McCurry praised the unifying 'female thematic elements' in Heaney's poetic; Carlanda Green uncritically described Heaney's 'faith in the creative aspect of the Earth Mother' as signalling his (political) optimism: the 'female principle' is 'the regenerative, spiritual principle of life'; it is also 'timeless'.[23] More recently, one of the most influential American critics of modern poetry, Helen Vendler, has reacted against those 'feminists' who 'have detected "patriarchal" attitudes' in the poems. She writes:

> The terms of reproof against Heaney have been almost entirely thematic ... I myself regard thematic arguments about poetry as beside the point. Lyric poetry

> neither stands nor falls on its themes; it stands or falls on the accuracy of language with which it reports the author's emotional responses to the life around him.[24]

Vendler's conception of the lyric poem here is, essentially, a Romantic one, an echo of Wordsworth's Preface to the *Lyrical Ballads*, and of what Heaney calls his own (Wordsworthian inspired) 'myth of poetry' – although Heaney himself has subsequently moved away from a position as extreme as Vendler's.[25] I have suggested above that 'the accuracy of language' in Heaney is not separable from the politics of gender, or from politics per se; nor, we might suggest, can an 'emotional response' exist in isolation from social and cultural conditions – and conditioning. (If language accurately reports Heaney's 'emotional responses', how is 'accuracy' to be measured?) Theodor Adorno offers one possible corrective to this perspective when he points out that:

> the lyric work is always the subjective expression of social antagonism. But since the objective world that produces the lyric is an inherently antagonistic world, the concept of the lyric is not simply that of the expression of a subjectivity to which language grants objectivity ... [P]oetic subjectivity is itself indebted to privilege: the pressures of the struggle for survival allow only a few human beings to grasp the universal through immersion in the self or to develop as autonomous subjects capable of freely expressing themselves.[26]

Lyric poetry does not, as Vendler points out, stand or fall only on its thematic elements; yet neither does it stand or fall regardless of them. (As with 'Undine', a felt unease with the thematic aspects of the poem may be seen as implicated in its unease tonally, formally and linguistically.) The debate in these terms is not so much about Heaney's gender politics, but about profoundly different conceptions of what constitutes the lyric poem. Nevertheless, the influence of a 'romantic' reading of Heaney – which is also the way Heaney sometimes himself asks to be read – may be one reason why his 'politics' have been critiqued with some selectivity. Indeed, Vendler herself praises poems for their thematic elements when those elements may be read as politically or ethically commendable in relation to Irish history.[27]

A related issue in terms of the positive reading of Heaney's 'feminine' may thus also be the dominant interest in the national, rather than gender politics of the poems. The politics of gender in Ireland, and in Northern Ireland, have themselves tended to be sidelined by the politics of place; the cause of women has been subordinated to the cause of national politics, a situation only gradually being redressed. In a sense, that position can be seen as replicated in miniature in the critical response to Heaney's work, in which a hierarchical reading might simply place England/Ireland and the politics of place at the top of the list without necessarily subjecting the other binaries implied to the same level of scrutiny. That said, while I have been suggesting that some of Heaney's critical writings are very much of their time, and by no means unique in their gender politics, it is also the case that the 'feminine' in Heaney cannot be understood apart from Irish national and cultural contexts, any more than those contexts can be separated from his gender politics. His 'timeless' feminine takes on contextual specificity in two significant ways: first, in so far as it resonates within the framework of Catholicism; second, in its association with the Irish Republican tradition.

In Attwater's *Catholic Encyclopaedic Dictionary* (1949) the definition of 'Man' is, in its entirety, as follows:

> Man: A rational creature composed of a body and a soul. The soul, a spiritual substance, is united to the body as its substantial form. Man's last end is happiness.

The first part of the much more lengthy definition of 'Woman' affirms that:

> Woman has a double life-task: as an individual, her moral perfection; as a member of society, in union with man to represent and develop humanity in all its aspects. As individuals, man and woman are morally equals. Since humanity is composed of male and female, each requires the other for its social complement; each has qualities lacking in the other. Since the completely developed feminine personality is found in motherhood (not necessarily restricted to its physiological aspect) all activities impairing woman's chief social duty, maternal influence whether in the spiritual or material sphere, are to be avoided. Christianity, in raising marriage to the dignity of a sacrament, raised women from varying degrees of degradation to moral equality with man, and it taught the nobility of freely chosen virginity. This elevation of woman centres in the Blessed Virgin Mary: respect for women rises and falls with that for her.[28]

While modes of expression may have changed in the decades following the Second Vatican Council, these definitions remain at the heart of Catholic doctrine as it was consolidated at the first Vatican Council set up in 1869 (a consolidation whose rigidities are perhaps not disconnected from the decline of papal political power in the nineteenth century, and the loss of the papal states), and are part of the context for any evocation of Heaney's own Catholicism. Nor are they entirely remote from other 'definitions' – such as those of Jung, or Graves – already discussed. It is something of a commonplace, perhaps, to note that for Heaney, the 'feminine' in his poetry may be seen as, among other things, reflective of the beliefs and culture of his Catholic background – but it is important to note precisely what those beliefs entail. They are not simply a celebration of motherhood and virginity, they are also about complementarity, about essentialist differences – beyond the biological – between the sexes, and about, once again, the construction of the 'other' whose 'double life-task' keeps the (patriarchal) system functioning. The Second Vatican Council, while it acknowledged that 'women claim for themselves an equity with men before the law and in fact', gave at best only qualified support for that claim, continuing to affirm, somewhat contradictorily, that 'children ... need the care of their mother at home' and that 'This domestic role of hers must be safely preserved, though the legitimate social progress of women should not be underrated on that account.'[29] Heaney's celebrations, and commemorations, of maternal figures – in some of the outstanding lyric poems of his career – tend to leave Catholicism's gender roles untroubled even though his is by no means an untroubled relationship with Catholicism per se. To do so may be necessary for the poise and tonal quietude established in the poems. In the maternal elegies at the heart of *The Haw Lantern*, 'Clearances', the beauty of the poems is implicated in the mother's silence; in her silent communion with her son while peeling potatoes ('I was all hers'); and in her innate resistance to that learned *patrius sermo*. Instead, it is 'the wrong / Grammar that kept us allied and at bay'. In sonnet 5, folding the sheets becomes a metaphor for that relationship, as the poet first 'pulled against her', and then is drawn closer to 'end up hand to hand', an eternal umbilical cord, as well as an essential difference, at work. Heaney's maternal figures are likely to be found pumping, ironing, cooking, cleaning and nurturing, their 'chief social duty' unquestioningly that enjoined upon them by the Church, and here transformed by the poet into an aesthetic as well as social 'ideal'. In 'Clearances', the mother-figure is a kind of essential feminine protected and preserved by the poet ('The space we stood around had been emptied / Into us to keep'); she may also be read as the symbol of a prelinguistic order, as the mother-country, a pastoral ideal (seeded by man); as a life-giving force; even perhaps the absent focus of desire ('utterly empty, utterly a source'; *HL* 24–32). As Cixous writes:

> Man's dream: I love her – absent, hence desirable, a dependent nonentity, hence adorable. Because she isn't there where she is. As long as she isn't where she is. How he looks at her then! When her eyes are closed, when he completely understands her, when he catches on and she is no more than this shape made for him: a body caught in his gaze.[30]

The counter-force to this tranquil feminine is the Gravesian-style muse or goddess who inspires fear as well as devotion, the woman who, as Coughlan notes, 'dooms, destroys, puzzles and encompasses the man, but also assists him to his self-discovery'. 'For their own sake,' says Cixous of men, 'they need to be afraid of us', a point exemplified by Heaney when he asserts that 'Fear is the emotion the Muse thrives on.' Or, as Graves says of his white goddess, her nests are 'littered with the jaw-bones and entrails of poets'.[31] That fear in Heaney's poems fills precisely the 'need' identified by Cixous, in as much as it serves his emergent sense of self: 'This terror, cold, wet-furred ...' ('An Advancement of Learning', *DN* 19). It is also, as in 'Kinship', sometimes explicitly associated with the goddess/muse and with the conjunction of femininity, sex and death: 'the goddess swallows / our love and terror' (*N* 45). Juliette Wood draws attention to the extent to which the existence of the 'Celtic Goddess' has been 'subject to back projection of twentieth-century ideas'; she also points out that 'popular feminist ideas' about a 'strong but loving matriarchal goddess' may be 'more adequately described as mythology about the Celts rather than Celtic mythology'.[32] That 'back projection' has some relevance to Heaney, in whose writing the goddess figure works on two levels: political and personal. The 'feminine' archetype is implicated in Celtic mythology's relation to Irish nationalism, as in Heaney's early explication of the conflict in Ireland as a struggle 'between the cults and devotees of a god and goddess'. Consequently, his use of the sovereignty goddess myth as a means of addressing the 'Troubles', and his association of woman, land and national spirit, have been much discussed and critiqued – by Edna Longley, Patricia Coughlan and others. The politics of poems such as 'Act of Union', with its metaphorical rape of Ireland by England, have been scrutinised to a degree that needs no repetition here.[33] The mythologising carries obvious links to Irish literary and cultural history, and to the gender roles of 'feminised' Celt and 'masculine' Teuton ascribed to Ireland and England in the late nineteenth century; it also shares the problems of such ascriptions in so far as women themselves are concerned. But the 'muse' who is, as Graves called her, the 'perpetual Other Woman' is manifest for Heaney as a feminised landscape (in contrast to Graves, who sees the muse as embodied, at different times, in actual women);[34] consequently feminisation contributes in a different way to his aesthetic 'system's functioning'. Although it is to take images out of context, in his criticism and poetry we see the landscape penetrated by the (phallic) pump; the pump is also the navel of the earth from which the poet draws nourishment. Digging deeper into the ground simulates the sexual act, as in 'Kinship': 'the soft lips of the growth / muttered and split ... the shaft wettish / as I sank it upright' (*N* 40). Thus, in displacing his 'other woman' onto the landscape, are the principles of the Catholic sacrament of marriage and the poet's desire for a Jungian '*femme inspiratrice*', a Gravesian Muse, equally satisfied.[35]

In the short poem 'Smoke', from *The Flower Master*, Medbh McGuckian, describing 'That snake of orange motion to the hills', observes that:

> They seem so sure what they can do.
> I am unable even

To contain myself, I run
Till the fawn smoke settles on the earth.[36]

The 'snake of orange motion' is an image of the 'whins on fire along the road'; more obliquely, it is also the (male) Orange Order on their annual 12 July parade out of Belfast, with their political certainties. The poem is also about writing poetry, and about poetic form and tradition. Perhaps it is not stretching a point too far to suggest that the 'They' who 'seem so sure', in contrast to the uncontained female poet who breaks the boundaries of the line-ends, are also the (privileged) male poetic voices by which McGuckian has always been surrounded – Heaney, Muldoon and Carson among them. Yet in apparently expressing self-doubt, McGuckian both differentiates herself from certainties that, the poem implies, are rigid, even complacent, and she simultaneously exposes the *un*certainties that lie beneath the surface of that outward display of confident brotherhood: they only '*seem* so sure what they can do' (my emphasis).

Perhaps the more interesting question, then, is not whether or how Heaney's conceptions of the 'feminine' serve the interests of politics, or reflect a particular cultural context for women in twentieth-century (Catholic) Ireland, or misrepresent real women, but the extent to which the construction of masculinity in the poems, predicated on the alterity of the feminine, serves the poet's own lyric subjectivity. It is easy to see the masculine persona as self-serving in unproblematic ways, as seeming 'so sure' what he can do. But if we can learn anything from the association of Heaney with such figures as Jung and Graves, as well as from gender theory, it may be the recognition that while whatever is meant by the 'feminine' serves masculinity, masculinity may itself be in psychological and historical crisis. 'Heaney and the Masculine' might therefore have been a more revealing – and more appropriate – title for this essay, since it is the subject as occluded in Heaney criticism as the *animus* is in Jung's psychology, even as it is central to his construction of a poetic voice. Partly that may be a broader problem in criticism of Irish literature more generally, where masculinity, particularly in the context of the Northern Irish Troubles, is a subject that has not yet received the level of attention it deserves.

In other words, while the 'feminine' in Heaney, in its multiple guises, serves to bolster a 'masculine' persona, that it is required to do so may be more indicative of an unease, or split, within that masculine stance than anything else. Nor is it difficult to see where the psychological triggers for a masculine anxiety might lie. First, the male poet as ordering and controlling in formal terms is yet subject to external ordering and controlling forces in his political environment. Second, the Northern Irish Troubles themselves demand a masculinist (wartime) solidarity with which the poet, speaking for his 'subculture', wishes to be identified, yet from which he wishes to distinguish himself – in the interests of aesthetic integrity and individuality. Related to this, Heaney's breaking of the line of patriarchal inheritance (writing not digging) brings its own pressures to bear on the poet.

The collision of ideologies in 'The Toome Road', which is also a collision of versions of masculinity, symbolises the first of these. The 'armoured cars / In convoy, warbling along on powerful tyres' begin a (rhythmical) duel in the poem, as once again iambic stresses play against the poet's own (often trochaic) assertions: 'I had rights-of-way, fields, cattle in my keeping' (*FW* 15). The poem's conclusion, with its 'invisible, untoppled omphalos', affirms both national identity and masculinity: the British 'soldiers standing up in turrets' are, in a sense, emasculated – their 'guns' are 'dormant' – whereas the omphalos 'stands vibrant'. The terms repeat themselves in *Beowulf*. For Helen Phillips, it is Heaney's 'treatment of the females in *Beowulf* that is most disappointing'. She argues that 'Forces from his own earlier writing seem to shackle what he can achieve, diverting what the poem presents into pre-shaped patterns that deprive the reader of important meanings that the female characters possess.'[37] Equally pertinent here, however, is the extent to which the enterprise pits the might of the Anglo-Saxon against the might of the Irish poet: 'I took it on,' Heaney says, 'because deep down in my ear, and in my very body almost, across my shoulders, I could feel the yoke of the Anglo-Saxon line and I loved the sense of shouldering it up and shouldering it back.'[38] The project can thus be seen as continuous with those 'hobnailed boots' as a counter to the (linguistic and political) 'yoke' which oppresses the poet.

Such hyper-masculine assertions are complicated by that second anxiety, the conflict between individual and collective identity, between inheritance and discontinuity. The sense of the poet as both of and apart from his community is pervasive in Heaney's poetry, particularly at the height of the Troubles. In 'Casualty',

> The common funeral
> Unrolled its swaddling band,
> Lapping, tightening
> Till we were braced and bound
> Like brothers in a ring. (*FW* 22)

Yet the poet also identifies with his subject, who 'would not be held / At home by his own crowd', retreating from the collective mourning with 'I missed his funeral' (*FW* 22–3). The split self recurs often in the poems, a self that professes to be liberated and constrained simultaneously: 'subjugated, yes, and obedient ... arraigned yet free'; 'manoeuvrable / yet outmanoeuvred'.[39] The split may also be related to Heaney's desire both to claim a (male) inheritance, and to distance himself from it. Talking of the farming community in which he grew up, he observes that: 'Work meant hauling stuff, the spuds, the hay, the cows and so on. If you come from that background, and then get translated from it into that area where you are working at poetry, there's something in your primal being that needs to justify it to yourself.'[40] Put more bluntly, this perhaps suggests a need to 'justify' poetry as a suitably manly activity. In this, of course, Heaney is far from alone. Glover and Kaplan note, for example, that in the nineteenth century, 'one crucial move in [Thomas] Carlyle's creation of a distinctive literary persona was his alignment of the writer's work with the simple dignity of his father's daily labour as a stonemason', thereby 'reclaim[ing] the world of literature for men', creating a 'kind of brotherhood, united in devotion to their calling', a 'kinship between men'.[41]

In the poem in which the question of paternal inheritance is first addressed, 'Digging', male selfhood is destabilised only to reassert and reclaim the world of letters for men. In one sense, 'Digging' is about the end of the line, not its beginning; Heaney, by marking himself out as a poet, is affirming a break with the past. But that break is what the poem is designed to repress. 'I've no spade to follow men like them,' he avers; but the poem ultimately claims the opposite. Its closing image – 'Between my finger and my thumb / The squat pen rests. / I'll dig with it' (*DN* 14) – thus sits on a contradictory fence somewhere between the suggestion of generational continuity, one man seeding the next, and a private, solitary metaphorical masturbation. What drives the need to affirm continuity where there is none may be precisely that anxiety, the need to 'justify' the poet's role as something other than a self-indulgence which, in Heaney's terms, is implicitly feminised. As Cixous observes of literary history more generally, 'It all comes back to man – to *his* torment, his desire to be (at) the origin. Back to the father.'[42] Her point is that women's suffering is elided; but the word 'torment' in relation to male writers is revealing too. At the point of being unmanned, Heaney habitually reasserts masculinity: in crossing the bridge in 'An Advancement of Learning' and thereby affirming individual strength; in understanding the 'exact / and tribal ... revenge' in 'Punishment' (*N* 38) and allying himself with a male social grouping; or, in 'Digging', in the implied association of pen, gun and penis. That he does so suggests a dominant paternal presence, and as he has said, 'My father is dead since 1986 but there's still a strong inclination when we assemble to speak his words and speak through him like our eternal father, *through Him with Him and in Him*';[43] it is also redolent of some anxiety about that presence, and about his own role in the continuation of a patriarchal line.

Heaney himself has noted that 'The sureness of a literary voice may derive from a set of convictions and attitudes which include some that are dismaying.'[44] Perhaps, ironically enough, Heaney's gender politics prove less 'dismaying', even for the feminist reader, with the recognition that his voice is rather more uncertain than it sometimes purports to be. Heaney habitually, if not consciously, defines his lyric voice in terms of sameness (heredity; the male community) and difference (the poet at one remove from his community, the insider and outsider). The more overt Same/Other of his feminine/masculine binaries thus serves, in one sense, to elide, or disguise, inherent contradictions in his 'masculine' persona. Rather than writing 'out of the *anima* of his personality', as Douglas Dunn once said Michael Longley does,[45] Heaney tends instead to write *to* it, as if it is external to, and does not thereby problematise the self. But that externality is also a fiction, a created rather than absolute 'other' which he simultaneously 'rules, names, defines'. As 'District and Circle' suggests, with its walk down 'a corridor ... To where I knew I was always going to find / My watcher on the tiles, cap by his side' (*DC* 17), Heaney's poetic journeys sometimes have foreknowledge of their destination inscribed in their beginning. That surety brings its own rewards. Yet in terms of Heaney's gender politics, what can seem, if not dismaying, then at least disappointing, is his reluctance to take what Cixous calls 'the risk of *other*, of difference ... delighting to increase through the unknown that is there to discover, to respect, to favor, to cherish'.[46]

NOTES

1. Robert Graves, *Poetic Craft and Principle* (London: Cassell, 1967), pp. 114–15.
2. Robert Graves, *Mammon and the Black Goddess* (London: Cassell, 1965), p. 147.
3. Robert Graves, *The Complete Poems*, ed. Beryl Graves and Dunstan Ward (London: Penguin, 2003), p. 542.
4. Robert Graves, *The White Goddess* (1948), 4th edn (London: Faber, 1999), p. 17.
5. Ibid., p. 6.
6. Grevel Lindop, Introduction to Graves, *White Goddess*, p. xvii.
7. James Joyce, *Ulysses*, ed. Richard Ellmann (London: Penguin, 1986), p. 7.
8. For Jung, as Anthony Stevens notes, masculine and feminine are the 'two great archetypal principles': the mother is 'Mother Nature, Goddess of Fertility'; the father 'Ruler, Elder, King and Lawgiver'. The archetypes find their echo in Graves's symbolic marriage in *The White Goddess* of a Sun-god with a reigning Moon-goddess, and in Heaney's delineation of a cultic struggle. Jung, pre-empting Graves's own practice, also claimed as important for man 'a wife to create his home' and 'a *femme inspiratrice* ... to ... inspire his greatest works' (Anthony Stevens, *Jung* [Oxford: Oxford University Press, 1994], pp. 68–71).
9. George Mosse does note, however, in his 1996 study *The Image of Man*, that 'the manly ideal' is remarkably resilient, even post-1918, and does not begin to break

down until the 1950s. See David Glover and Cora Caplan, *Genders* (London: Routledge, 2000), p. 61.

10. Sandra M. Gilbert and Susan Gubar, *No Man's Land: The Place of the Woman Writer in the Twentieth Century: Vol. I The War of the Words* (New Haven: Yale University Press, 1987), in particular Chapter 5 'Sexual Linguistics', and the discussion of Ong, pp. 252–3.
11. Ibid., p. 153.
12. See Heaney interview with Mike Murphy, *Reading the Future: Irish Writers in Conversation with Mike Murphy* (Dublin: Lilliput Press, 2000), p. 84.
13. Judith Butler, *Gender Trouble: Feminism and the Subversion of Identity*, 2nd edn (London: Routledge, 1999), pp. 131–2.
14. Hélène Cixous, 'Sorties', in Hélène Cixous and Catherine Clément, *The Newly Born Woman*, tr. Betsy Wing (London: Tauris & Co., 1996), p. 71.
15. Neil Corcoran, *Seamus Heaney* (London: Faber, 1986), p. 57.
16. Cixous, 'Sorties', p. 63.
17. Ibid., p. 67.
18. See 'Bogland' (*DD* 41–2); 'Kinship' (*N* 43); 'Antaeus' (*N* 12); 'The Harvest Bow' (*FW* 58).
19. Patricia Coughlan, '"Bog Queens": The Representation of Women in the Poetry of John Montague and Seamus Heaney', *Gender in Irish Writing*, ed. Toni O'Brien Johnson and David Cairns (Milton Keynes: Open University Press, 1991), pp. 88, 90, 108.
20. Anthony Storr, *Jung* (London: Fontana, 1973), pp. 50–1.
21. Coughlan, 'Bog Queens', p. 108.
22. Diane Purkiss notes that 'valorizations of a feminine maternal body and personality which is and has always been nurturative and non-violent, have much in common with the ideology of gender which feminism sets out to oppose, an ideology in which the subordination of women was predicated on biological determinism' ('Women's Rewriting of Myths', *The Feminist Companion to Mythology*, ed. Carolyne Larrington [London: Pandora Press, 1992], p. 447).
23. Jacqueline McCurry, 'The Female in Seamus Heaney's Prose Poetics and the Poetry of *The Haw Lantern*', *Eire-Ireland* 23:4 (Winter 1988); Carlanda Green, 'The Feminine Principle in Seamus Heaney's Poetry', in *Seamus Heaney: Modern Critical Views*, ed. Harold Bloom (New Haven, New York and Philadelphia: Chelsea House Publishers, 1986), pp. 149, 150–1.
24. Helen Vendler, *Seamus Heaney* (London: HarperCollins, 1998), p. 6.
25. Heaney affirms the influence of Wordsworth's Preface in forming his original 'myth of poetry' (interview with Murphy, *Reading the Future*, p. 87). But when pushed on the subject of Vendler's approach in an interview with Karl Miller, he does concede, diplomatically, that thematic arguments cannot be entirely beside the point: see *Seamus Heaney in Conversation with Karl Miller* (London: Between the Lines, 2000), pp. 19, 50–1.
26. Theodor Adorno, 'On Lyric Poetry and Society', in *Modern Literary Theory: A Reader*, ed. Philip Rice and Patricia Waugh, 4th edn (London: Arnold, 2001), p. 114.
27. See for example Vendler's interpretation of Heaney's 'archaeological myth' in *North*, which she praises as questioning, and thereby subverting, what she sees as

Ireland's tendency towards 'a generalized cultural approval of violence' (*Seamus Heaney*, p. 51).

28. Donald Attwater (ed.), *The Catholic Encyclopaedic Dictionary* (1931) (London: Cassell, 1949).
29. 'The Church Today', *Documents of Vatican II* (1963–5), ed. Walter M. Abbott (London: Geoffrey Chapman, 1966), pp. 207, 257.
30. Cixous, 'Sorties', p. 67.
31. Coughlan, 'Bog Queens', p. 99; Cixous, 'Sorties', p. 69; Seamus Heaney quoted in Dick Davis, 'Door into the Dark', in *The Art of Seamus Heaney*, ed. Tony Curtis, 4th edn (Bridgend: Seren, 2001), p. 29; Graves, *White Goddess*, p. 22.
32. Juliette Wood, 'Celtic Goddesses: Myth and Mythology', *Feminist Companion to Mythology*, ed. Larrington, pp. 122, 134.
33. See Edna Longley, 'Inner Emigré or Artful Voyeur: Seamus Heaney's *North*', in *Poetry in the Wars* (Newcastle: Bloodaxe, 1986); Coughlan, 'Bog Queens'.
34. Graves, *Mammon*, p. 151.
35. See note 8. Where Graves lives out that Jungian belief literally, through marriage and his various muses, Heaney does so symbolically.
36. Medbh McGuckian, 'Smoke', *The Flower Master and Other Poems* (1982) (Oldcastle: Gallery, 1993), p. 11.
37. Helen Phillips, 'Seamus Heaney's *Beowulf*', *Art of Seamus Heaney*, ed. Curtis, p. 275.
38. Heaney interview with Murphy, *Reading the Future*, p. 94.
39. 'From the Frontier of Writing' and 'Wolfe Tone' (*HL* 44, 6).
40. Heaney interview with Murphy, *Reading the Future*, p. 91.
41. Glover and Caplan, *Genders*, p. 76.
42. Cixous, 'Sorties', p. 65.
43. Heaney interview with Murphy, *Reading the Future*, p. 90.
44. *Heaney in Conversation with Karl Miller*, p. 51.
45. Douglas Dunn, 'The Poetry of the Troubles', review of Michael Longley, *Selected Poems 1963–1980*, *Times Literary Supplement* (31 July 1981), p. 886.
46. Cixous, 'Sorties', p. 78.

6

JUSTIN QUINN

Heaney and Eastern Europe

The poetry of Eastern Europe had a deep and wide-ranging influence on anglophone poetry for a good deal of the Cold War, and the division of the world by two superpowers necessarily created interest among poets about the status of their opposite numbers. The differences across the divide were profound: to varying degrees, the states of the Soviet bloc did not tolerate dissent, and many poets died or spent a long time in jail as a result of this. Poets of the Western world, on the other hand, could enjoy a middle-class lifestyle by teaching literature at university (either as professors of creative writing or academic critics). However, they were haunted by the Russian poet Osip Mandelstam's aperçu that 'Poetry is respected only in this country – people are killed for it';[1] the corollary of this was that although Western poets could write and publish what they wanted, readers did not care as much about what they wrote as, say, Russian readers did about their poets. A story is told that during a public reading Boris Pasternak forgot the lines of a poem, and the audience were able to complete it; a similar situation is difficult to imagine in any English-speaking country during the same period. Such is the background to Seamus Heaney's statement in 1986 that 'poets in English have felt compelled to turn their gaze East and have been encouraged to concede that the locus of greatness is shifting away from their language' (*GT* 38).

Only now that the dust has settled are critics beginning to document these Cold War poetic transactions.[2] A key element of this critical work is to examine the influence of the East on the poetry and criticism of Seamus Heaney. His position as one of the most important and publicly acclaimed poets in the anglophone world made his advocacy of these poets extremely significant. He wrote about Russian poets including Osip Mandelstam (1891–1938) and Joseph Brodsky (1940–96), Polish poets including Czesław Miłosz (1911–2004) and Zbigniew Herbert (1924–98), and the Czech poet Miroslav Holub (1923–98). Most of these were viewed as 'poets under pressure', which meant that they suffered under political regimes and that this conditioned the poetry they wrote as well as its reception.

Heaney's engagement with these Slavic poets was, paradoxically, both profound and superficial.

It was profound because these poets provided him with new ways to respond to the pressures of politics on poetry. Heaney came to maturity in Northern Ireland at the time of the outbreak of the Troubles, and his *oeuvre* can be profitably read as a series of changing responses to the difficulties of that situation. During one of the most intense periods of the Troubles in the early to mid-1970s, Heaney's interest in Eastern European poets, especially Mandelstam, likewise intensified. A poem such as 'Exposure', which was written during this period, evokes the figure of Mandelstam in a prison camp as moral exemplar. Heaney imagines 'a hero / On some muddy compound, / His gift like a slingstone / Whirled for the desperate' (*N* 72). By not following this example, Heaney reckons, he has missed, 'The once-in-a-lifetime portent, / The comet's pulsing rose' (*N* 73), though what exactly that might be is left unclear. The Mandelstam figure joins the other figures in Heaney's poetry who step forward to reproach him, among other things, for leaving Northern Ireland in 1972. More generally, given the differences between the USSR (Union of Soviet Socialist Republics) and Ireland in this period, the figure is a means of exploring what his own role should be. This aspect of Heaney's approach has been amply discussed by critics. Going further, we see that several of these poets meditated deeply on the issue of empire, and they often did so through the example of Rome. It was a means not merely to elucidate the contemporary situation, but to deal with the subject of European history in their poetry, and the historical fates of their particular countries. Heaney was born as a subject of possibly the most important empire since that of Rome, and his study of the Slavic poets often suggested tones or imagistic turns for dealing with this theme. They helped him avoid some of the traps that lie in wait for the post-colonial writer.

On the other hand, his engagement with Slavic poets was superficial because Heaney has neither reading nor speaking proficiency in any Slavic language, and this fact should not be passed over too quickly. An important consequence of this is that his relationship with this poetry is signally different from his relationship with languages he has translated, including Irish (both older and more modern) and Old English. The cultural significance of translating from these two languages is clear: Heaney claims them both as part of his heritage as an Irish poet writing in English. More importantly perhaps, there was a deep investment in his transmission of the poetry from one language to another; above all this is a question of the linguistic imagination being put to a hard task, and reaping significant rewards. Whereas with Slavic poetry he could only speculate as to how it sounded in the original, and thus remarks of this tenor are not uncommon: 'A Russian poet once told me that the Mandelstam stanza has the resonant impact of late Yeats' (*GT* 79). Such a statement would be odd in a critic of, say, prose fiction, but in the case of Heaney, who in his own work (as a poet, critic and translator) is so close to the grain of etymology and its implications for national fates, it is facile. That he is hermetically sealed from the original texts of Slavic poetry in the twentieth century is a fact that his own criticism glosses over by fantasising identification with anglophone touchstones. Previous critics, even those familiar with Slavic languages, have not confronted this fact, and yet to do so opens more avenues than it closes. I will investigate one of these here, and I will also elucidate the strong influences the Slavic poets have exerted as exemplars, both morally and in their treatment of the subject of empire.

In his essay 'The Impact of Translation', Heaney wrote eloquently of his shock on discovering the work of Miłosz. The poem 'Incantation' was read out to him by one of Miłosz's main English translators:

> My first experience of these lines, spoken in the upstairs study of a silent house, empty that afternoon except for ourselves, was altogether thrilling ... It proclaimed in argent speech truths we had assumed to be previous to poetry, so richly established outside its formal citadel that they could never be admitted undisguised or untransmuted through the eye of the lyric needle. (*GT* 36–7)

For a poet who had matured under the aegis of New Criticism, with its emphasis on irony, obliquity and restraint, Miłosz's didacticism came as a bolt from the blue. Heaney quickly moves to generalise:

> It is therefore typical of work by many other poets, particularly in the Soviet republics and the Warsaw Pact countries, whose poetry not only witnesses the poet's refusal to lose his or her cultural memory but also testifies thereby to the continuing efficacy of poetry itself as a necessary and fundamental human act ... They are the ones who toed the line, not just the verse line but the line where courage is tested, where to stand by what you write is to have to stand your ground and take the consequences. (*GT* 38, 39)

This is where Heaney's admiration for Slavic poets begins, and his praise of Brodsky and Herbert is voiced in similar terms (although he correctly makes no mention of such refusals or political testing in his essay on Miroslav Holub, who held an important academic position in Czechoslovakia even during the period of normalisation after the Comintern invasion of 1968). It follows that Western poets (described by Heaney as 'a procession of ironists and dandies and reflexive talents'; *GT* 40) have stopped confronting fundamental truths. Because the poets of the East have been forced by history to confront these, they speak with unshakeable moral, and (by Heaney's implication) therefore artistic, authority.

This stance has drawn much criticism. For instance Thomas Docherty in a review of *The Government of the Tongue* stated that 'there is at work what might be termed an "imperialism of thought," in which the critic reduces the potential anarchic confusion produced by obscure "foreign" writing through a reduction of that alterity to identity, through the production of "conscience" in Heaney's terms'.[3] Exactly such a reduction from 'alterity to identity' can be seen in Heaney's equation of Mandelstam and late Yeats above. However, when Docherty goes on to posit the 'radical incomprehensibility' of Slavic poetry, we see that his alterity is just as bizarre as Heaney's easy identifications. It is as though Russian, Polish and Czech are dialects of Etruscan, since it seems to be impossible to learn one of these languages and the ways of its attendant world. Neil Corcoran is more balanced in his criticism:

> In relation to the work of his East European contemporaries, however, Heaney is too abject. Their significance, he says, compels modern poets in English to recognize that the 'locus of greatness is shifting away from their language.' There is something too eagerly penitential in this, and also, in the context of exemplary witness to suffering, something almost vulgarly prone to think in terms of competitive 'greatness'.[4]

A further aspect of this abjectness is the subordination of aesthetic considerations to moral values. The work of Miroslav Holub and the later poetry of Zbigniew Herbert, so bare of pun, metaphor and rich linguistic ambiguity, is praised extravagantly by Heaney, and it is fair to suppose that his response was significantly conditioned by the Iron Curtain billowing grimly in the background. It is of note then that Heaney used the publication of *Finders Keepers: Selected Prose 1971–2001* (2002) to exclude the essays that make such 'abject' points. It is as though Heaney himself has listened hard to the critics, or at least to Corcoran, and realised that the overstatements and enthusiasms of the 1980s did not deserve a prominent position in his critical work. We see the gradual reinstatement of aesthetic, as opposed to ethical, criteria: thus Mandelstam remains not through an account of how awful Stalin's Russia was, but through Heaney's exposition of the Russian's brilliant essay on Dante, which is a counterweight to Eliot's interpretation of the Italian poet.

One of the central ideas of that essay is the idea of *reversibilità*. In standard accounts of metaphor, there is an object and another to which it is likened (the tenor and the vehicle); for Mandelstam's Dante, there is no distinction between the tenor and vehicle. On the face of it, this appears to be a technical remark about a poetic device, but the implications are significant. If you employ *reversibilità*, the language with which you describe an object can easily become the generator, or even the subject, of the poem itself. By such an account, poems do not make propositions about objects or states of affairs (or indeed about how dreadful totalitarian regimes are), they take delight in the fabric of language itself, a fabric that can be turned now that way, now this. Mandelstam goes on to remark: 'Here I would like to point out one of the remarkable peculiarities of Dante's psyche: he was terrified of the direct answer, perhaps conditioned by the political situation in that extremely dangerous, enigmatic and criminal century.'[5] It is only fair to remark here that the change in Heaney's critical prerogatives lagged far behind his intuitions as a poet. The type of radical ambiguity that Mandelstam indicates here as the core of Dante's art (and by implication, of poetry in general), was at the centre of Heaney's own poetry from the outset. Whereas he might write essays in admiration of Eastern European poets such as Herbert and Holub who have no apprehension of such *reversibilità*, he did not try to bring such models to bear on his own poetry. This fruitful duplicity of speech in Heaney was due, in social terms, to the circumspection which people from Northern Ireland often employ when talking about politics (as exemplified by Heaney's poem 'Whatever You Say, Say Nothing' in *North*), and, in literary critical terms, it is due to Heaney's education in New Criticism. In this matter, Mandelstam's example then was less an influence than a confirmation.

But in the case of Mandelstam's treatment of empire, and more particularly of the legacy of the Roman Empire, it is possible to talk of influence as opposed to confirmation.[6] The Polish poet and critic Jerzy Jarniewicz, discussing Heaney's poems from *The Haw Lantern*, remarks:

> It has been justly observed by many commentators that Heaney's parabolic poetics derives from Eastern European tradition in which this particular mode was a medium for talking about the communal experience of the occupied nations without exposing the text to the interrogating eye of a censor; ancient Rome or Greece proved especially helpful in the writers' efforts to smuggle a critical thought.[7]

Such use of allegory was widespread among the poets of the former Comintern countries, and indeed it was one of the main attractions for Western readers. No matter how obscure a poem might seem, there was the frisson of seeing it as an encrypted defiance of state power. There is an important distinction to be made here: such an allegorical use of ancient Rome was of no interest to Mandelstam, and as a consequence played a different role in Heaney's engagement with the Russian poet. Perhaps the reason for this is that Mandelstam had come to poetic maturity before the left-wing totalitarian regime had installed itself in Russia, unlike later poets such as Herbert and Holub. Mandelstam – who described Stalin in one poem as 'the Kremlin mountaineer' whose fingers were 'fat as grubs' and for whom 'every killing is a treat'[8] – had little use for such allegorical niceties. *Reversibilità*, yes; but not simplistic political codes.

Mandelstam's understanding was historical rather than allegorical: Rome was the source of European culture, and throughout his life he was drawn to those parts of Russia that were most influenced by its empire. (Russia, with its Cyrillic letters and Orthodox Church, which so often seems beyond the pale of Europe, represents a Roman legacy from Byzantium that is just as valid as the Latin legacy of Western Europe.) In her memoir, his widow Nadezhda stated that:

> The ancient link between these areas (particularly Armenia) with Greece and Rome seemed to him a token of the unity of the world (or, rather, European) culture ... His conviction that culture, like grace, is bestowed by a process of continuity led M[andelstam] to see the Mediterranean as a 'holy land.' This explains the constant references to Rome and Italy in his verse. Rome is man's place in the universe, and his every footstep there resounds like a deed.[9]

The identification is borne out by the title of Mandelstam's second collection *Tristia* (1922), which recalls Ovid; and when visiting the area around the Black Sea, Mandelstam was acutely aware that the Roman poet was a previous inhabitant. In a poem of 1914, Mandelstam went as far as declaring, echoing the French sixteenth-century poet Joachim Du Bellay, that 'Nature is the same as Rome, and mirrored there / We can see the forms of civic power displayed';[10] and in another poem from the same year the city is associated with 'a freedom dwelt in by the spirit, / The destiny that chosen souls attain'.[11] A poem of 1915 describes the motion of the Roman plebs through the city in the following terms:

> The bushes moved against them like a wall,
> And then a sudden rush of warriors' tents;
> They break away in sacred turbulence.
> The fleece crests, a great wave poised to fall.[12]

It is worth remarking here on Joseph Brodsky's error about Mandelstam's poetry. Brodsky said that 'Toward the twenties, the Roman themes gradually overtake the Greek and biblical references, largely because of the poet's growing identification with the archetypal predicament of a "poet versus an empire."'[13] In fact, Rome is present as a theme as early as 1912, and is especially strong in the period 1913–15, and so predates the Bolshevik terror. There is no doubt that Mandelstam was preoccupied with the relations between the poet and his empire, but this did not lead Mandelstam to the kind of allegorical doublespeak of a poet like Holub. Brodsky perhaps shifted the dates in his mind in order to make the contrast between art and empire starker. This was one of his own recurring themes, as for instance in 'Torso', here in Howard Moss's translation:

> If suddenly you walk on grass turned stone
> and think its marble handsomer than green,
> or see at play a nymph and faun that seem
> happier in bronze than in any dream,
> let your walking stick fall from your weary hand,
> you're in The Empire, friend.[14]

The speaker's attitude to the way imperial art improves nature is not clear, although the final affirmation here is rather grim. More important is the way the poem makes the gaze of empire coincident with that of art: it continues by imagining the thousand years of imperial rule, and how a torso ages within that epoch. Without solving them, the poem raises questions about the complicity of art with worldly dominion, and it eschews the reductive iconography of the artist, or poet, 'under pressure'.

It is perhaps because the stories of Russian poets' travails with the Communist regime are so alluring that critics have not commented upon this preoccupation with empire which finds a full resonance in Heaney's work of the late 1980s and early 1990s. In *Seeing Things*, the figure in the compound no longer holds an important place in Heaney's imagination. A more complex set of relations replaces him, as Heaney explores the role of art not merely as resistance, but as complicit with empire. In 'The Tower', Yeats proposes that the successful poet gives men images by which they live – it being irrelevant whether those images accurately reflect the real world or not. Heaney's imagination is moving in a similar direction:

> Beneath the ocean of itself, the crowd
> In Roman theatres could hear another
> Stronger groundswell coming through ...
>
> How airy and how earthed it felt up there,
> Bare to the world, light-headed, volatile
> And carried like the rests in tides or music. (*ST* 58)

In the first tercet, Heaney makes Rome permeable to the wider natural horizon, much as Mandelstam did in showing how 'civic forms' are visible in nature; an important aspect of this is that the Roman crowd are thus put in touch with the earth. In an early poem Heaney favours Antaeus, the Greek mythological figure who is strengthened by contact with the earth, and throughout the rest of his poetry such contact is seen as an unalloyed good. Also of note is that such a transaction is effected by art: the crowd are in a theatre listening to the performance of dramatic poetry.[15]

This is more than a mere convergence of imagery (the Roman crowd, the waves, as well as the musical notation that was an important leitmotif for Mandelstam). In his later poetry, Mandelstam became increasingly preoccupied with poetry's obligation to be autochthonous, to be of its country's soil. In Heaney's 'Squarings', from where this poem is taken, Roman polity becomes a mediating element between the earth and dramatic art, and such a connection is creative of society. Or, as Heaney has it in the next part of 'Squarings', the earth turns into an ocarina which has 'stops to play / The music of the arbitrary on' (*ST* 59). A later part of the sequence is set in Red Square, but here it is Boris Pasternak, a much more accommodating figure than Mandelstam, who is alluded to:

> The big cleared space in front was dizzying.
> I looked across a heave and sweep of cobbles
> Like the ones that beamed up in my dream of flying
>
> Above the old cart road, with all the air
> Fanning off beneath my neck and breastbone.
> (The cloud-roamer, was it, Stalin called Pasternak?)
>
> Terrible history and protected joys!
> Plosive horse-dung on 1940s' roads.
> The newsreel bomb-hits, as harmless as dust-puffs. (*ST* 76)

Here we see how proximity to one of the great sources of political power, the Kremlin, sponsors Heaney's poetic flight of fancy. The expanse of Red Square (a space that is representative of the polity in a way that the Roman theatre mentioned earlier is) literally sends Heaney into transports. The parenthesis, with Stalin's sobriquet for Pasternak, intimates Heaney's knowledge of this tricky patronage. (In comparison with Mandelstam, the tactful Pasternak enjoyed greater privilege under Stalin.) But what is most engaging about this passage is Heaney's reluctance to lead such concerns back into the usual polemics of the 'poet under pressure', preferring to find an image to express the troubled relation between the huge military violence which a figure like Stalin could unleash and the previous ecstatic flight (viz., the effect of those 'bomb-hits' of the last line, which are made innocuous by the aesthetic distance of the camera).

For all his fascination with Mandelstam, Heaney is aware that his own situation is closer to that of Pasternak – that is, he is more likely to be found with heads of state than in a prison compound; and indeed censurable complicity is one of Heaney's central themes. This has perhaps been more help than hindrance for him in dealing with the subject of the British Empire, where his own privilege contrasts with the 'wretched of the earth', Frantz

Fanon's sobriquet for colonised peoples. Granted, a poem like 'The Toome Road' from *Field Work* figures British soldiers as Roman charioteers who are ignorant of the cultural heritage that Heaney possesses: 'O charioteers, above your dormant guns, / It stands here still, stands vibrant as you pass, / The invisible, untoppled omphalos' (*FW* 15). This is the equivalent of shaking one's fist at the giant once his back is turned; if it were Mandelstam, the stone of the *omphalos* would be slotted into the sling and hurled straight at his face. That Heaney is acutely aware of such a difference is borne out by the first poem in the same collection. Heaney goes with a friend to eat oysters, and it strikes him that this is something of an imperial luxury: 'Over the Alps, packed deep in hay and snow, / The Romans hauled their oysters south to Rome: / I saw damp panniers disgorge / The frond-lipped, brine-stung / Glut of privilege' ('Oysters'; *FW* 11). He indulges in the pleasure knowingly and 'deliberately' in the hope that the taste, as he says (in a borrowing from Richard Wilbur), 'Might quicken me all into verb, pure verb'.[16] One of the traps for the post-colonial writer is eloquent complaint about, in essence, being on the losing side; 'The Toome Road' has something of this. But in 'Oysters' Heaney's indulgence in imperial privilege makes him a more Virgilian figure, that is, more complicit with imperial power. In an earlier poem 'Act of Union', Heaney conflates two voices: first, that of the male in sexual congress, and second, that of a colonising monarch, and then takes them for his own (*N* 49–50). In a later poem 'A Royal Prospect', the lovers (who we know, extra-poetically, to be from Irish Catholic backgrounds) are figured as 'two royal favourites, / Unhindered and resented and bright-eyed' (*ST* 41). The poem concludes by turning an interrogative eye on the two lovers: 'pleas will be allowed / Against every right and title vested in them / (And in a court where mere innocuousness / Has never gained approval or acquittal)' (*ST* 41). This is not the complaint of the colonised, but a poet contending with the 'Glut of privilege'; or as Brodsky might say: 'You're in The Empire, friend.'

It is helpful here to contrast Heaney's use of the East with that of Michael Longley. Heaney works primarily by analogy: as Docherty remarked, he looks for identifications rather than differences. Occasionally this can lead to infelicitous observations, such as the equation of Mandelstam with late Yeats, but more often it provides him with profitable ways to reassess the relations between his poetic gift and political situations. Such reassessments are often the subject of his critical prose, but more importantly they are the thematic mainstay of the poems: to put it bluntly, he will make a poem out of the idea that poetry should be independent of politics, but paradoxically those politics are an integral part of Heaney's poems as a kind of provocation. Eastern European poets provided instructive examples for his ongoing meditations, but his poetry is not *about* European history beyond that of Britain and Ireland. Jarniewicz remarks that it is strange that one searches 'in vain for any direct reflection of the most important events of the twentieth century in the work of a poet so obsessed by history'.[17]

In contrast, Michael Longley's *Gorse Fires* (1991) marks the beginning of a preoccupation with Eastern Europe, as in 'Ghetto', which has the poet imagining the children who died in the Holocaust. One of the central themes of the book is the difficulty of homecoming, and the last poem narrates Odysseus' troubled return to his home and his murder of the suitors in his house. Here the violence would appear fitting, but in 'Ghetto' which precedes this by a few pages, we have only lament and consolation. In Part V, he imagines the people starving in the ghetto and:

> Who are turning like a thick slice of potato-bread
> This page, which is everything I know about potatoes,
> My delivery of Irish Peace, Beauty of Hebron, Home
> Guard, Arran Banners, Kerr's Pinks, resistant to eelworm,
> Resignation, common scab, terror, frost, potato-blight.[18]

The last threat here makes clear the historical parallel between the Irish Famine and the Holocaust. The names of the potato types bring together, among other things, Ireland, Jewry and the defence of Britain. By uselessly imagining the consolation of the potatoes, he makes the genocide more poignant, and the very names of the potatoes themselves offer the hope of a cure of history. It isn't that 'Ghetto' uses the Holocaust as a vehicle to talk about Ireland as the tales from the *Odyssey* obviously do: the Second World War is an important theme in the book in general – at once as a crisis of the British empire and an important event in Longley's own life (his father fought in it). Longley's poetry is *about* the history of Eastern Europe in the twentieth century in a way that Heaney's poetry when he uses figures like Mandelstam in 'Exposure' simply isn't. 'Ghetto' is part of the larger drama of Europe which the book is concerned with, and in personal ways with Longley's own family history.

Nevertheless it should not be forgotten that the analogies Heaney finds in the East are varied and nuanced. While he is occasionally concerned with the martyrology of the 'poet under pressure', in other poems his engagement is more complex in its explorations of the liaisons and ligatures between political and poetic power. It develops in unexpected ways and does not leave us merely staring at a figure in a prison compound, whose poetry is 'a slingstone / Whirled for the desperate' (*N* 72). Mandelstam, as he stood in the compound, was thinking about other places – for instance, Roman scenes – and the richness of Heaney's imaginative engagement with the poets of Eastern

Europe can only be grasped if one follows Heaney following them to places that lead far from Russia.

The final point I wish to deal with here is translation. As I remarked earlier, Heaney knows these Eastern European poets only through translation. I am not competent to judge the translations of Mandelstam into English, but it is worth considering Brodsky's comments about these:

> In the available versions, one encounters an absolutely impersonal product, a sort of common denominator of modern verbal art. If they were simply bad translations, they wouldn't be so bad. For bad translations, precisely because of their badness, stimulate the reader's imagination and provoke a desire to break through or abstract oneself from the text: they spur one's intuition. In the cases at hand this possibility is practically ruled out: these versions bear the imprint of self-assured, insufferable stylistic provincialism; the only optimistic remark one can make regarding them is that such low-quality art is an unquestionable sign of a culture extremely distant from decadence ... 'OK,' a young American poet or reader of poetry may conclude after perusing these volumes, 'the same thing goes on over there in Russia.'[19]

Brodsky does not identify the translators, but in 1977, when these comments were published, Robert Tracy had not yet published his versions of Mandelstam's *Stone*, and the translation available most widely was the Penguin edition by Clarence Brown and W. S. Merwin (which was the edition in which Heaney first encountered the Russian poet[20]). Brown is a scholar of Russian literature and Merwin is an American poet. Their translations made no attempt to replicate the formal aspects of Mandelstam's poetry (a failing which Brodsky said was 'to lie about what the poet has lived and died for'[21]). Most disturbing of all is the idea of the linguistic loop: at the very point when the reader (whether American or Irish) thinks that he is being brought beyond the borders of his own language, he walks unknowingly straight into a mirror.

The case of Miłosz is not so clear. His poetry ranges from formal to free verse to prose, and while his translators have for the most part avoided the formal poetry, they have not done so exclusively. It is also worth noting who those translators are: Robert Pinsky and Robert Hass, who can be numbered with Merwin as three of the most important American poets of the last half-century. None knows the language he translates from, and where Merwin had the assistance of a scholar, Pinsky and Hass worked in collaboration with the author. I have argued that Heaney's engagement with Eastern Europe poetry is profound on the level of theme, and superficial on the level of language; this then is inverted in Heaney's engagement with American poets. Though he has spent many years working in the United States, Heaney has never been drawn to the themes that animate American poetry (a good counter example here would be Thom Gunn, who writes about American experience). However, as a reader of Mandelstam, Miłosz and Brodsky (among whose translators number Richard Wilbur and Anthony Hecht), Heaney has of necessity absorbed the idiom of the generation of American poets after Lowell and Bishop, a generation about which he has little to say in his criticism.

Perhaps the most important book in this respect is *Seeing Things*. The long sequence, 'Squarings', in forty-eight parts, was a new development for Heaney. The idiom becomes looser, and yet at the same time more philosophical; he is less insistent on closing each part of the sequence with a tight formulation (one of them, xxii, even ends with a jokey note to himself). Even while it contains elements that display the direct influence of Miłosz (for instance, that the roots of true poetic language are in childhood), the sequence ranges with less design than Miłosz could; its poetic wandering and relaxed delivery are much in the manner of Robert Hass. Obviously, provenance here is a complex issue (for instance, Charles Altieri has shown how much Miłosz influenced Hass[22]), but this is the very type of overlap that is so beneficial for poets and so richly exceeds the usual characterisation of the poetic relations between the East and West in this period. A further example is Brodsky, a poet who was deeply influenced by among others W.H. Auden and W.B. Yeats: it is possible to say that such a poet is translated *back* into English by the likes of Wilbur and Hecht, poets who have been influenced by the very same tradition (even while one deplores the quality of Brodsky's poems in English – whether originals or translations by himself).

The most recent episode in Seamus Heaney's relationship with the East was the publication of his translations, with Stanisław Barańczak, of Jan Kochanowski's *Treny*, or *Laments* as they have translated it (1995).[23] The work of this Polish poet of the Renaissance could not be further from the polemics of the poet under pressure that animated Heaney's imagination, and the imaginations of many others, through the 1970s and early 1980s. In part this was an attempt to see what was said beyond the borders of the European tradition, to encounter something Other, or at least to rediscover aspects of the European tradition that had been lost to the West. With the fall of the Iron Curtain, and the return of the awareness that, say, Vienna is farther east than Prague, Heaney and Barańczak's translation of *Treny* can stand as a symbol for the reinstatement of the poetry of the East within the European poetic tradition proper, by which I mean that that tradition does not properly exist without the East. Kochanowski's sequence laments the death of his young daughter, and in the third threnody, he imagines their reunion:

> What can I do, then? what else do, except
> Follow whatever way your light foot stepped?

There, Heaven grant it, at my journey's end,
Your slender arms will reach and gird me round.

And in the original:

Nie lza, nie lza, jedno się za tobą gotować,
A stopeczkami twymi ciebie naszladować.
Tam cię ujźrzę, da Pan Bóg, a ty więc drogimi
Rzuć się ojcu do szyje ręcznykami swymi![24]

It is noteworthy that the edition is bilingual, and also that Heaney replicates the rhyme structure of the originals; for rhyme schemes, as I quoted Brodsky above, are what poets live and die for. It also indicates that Heaney looks to the East for lessons in art and not just in politics. Heaney's engagement with poets from Eastern Europe has been extremely varied from the 1970s to the present, but it has never been merely a niche interest of his; rather, their examples helped him at crucial junctures in his career, as he reacted to, and indeed helped create, cultural politics in Ireland during the last three decades.

NOTES

I would like to acknowledge the assistance of Dennis O'Driscoll and David Wheatley in locating several sources for this essay, as well as Jerzy Jarniewicz for comments on the final version.

1. Mandelstam quoted by Nadezhda Mandelstam, *Hope against Hope: A Memoir*, tr. Max Hayward (London: Harvill, 1971), p. 159.
2. For instance, Charles Altieri, 'Polish Envy: American Poets' Polonising in the 1970s and '80s', *Metre* 15 (Spring 2004), and Clare Cavanagh, 'The Unacknowledged Legislator's Dream: Zbigniew Herbert and Anglo American Poetry', *Indiana Slavic Studies* 9 (1998).
3. Thomas Docherty, 'The Sign of the Cross: Review of *The Government of the Tongue*', reprinted in *Seamus Heaney*, ed. Michael Allen (London: Macmillan, 1997), p. 150.
4. Neil Corcoran, *The Poetry of Seamus Heaney: A Critical Study* (London: Faber and Faber, 1998), p. 212.
5. Osip Mandelstam, *The Collected Critical Prose and Letters*, tr. Jane Gary Harris and Constance Link, ed. Jane Gary Harris (London: Collins Harvill, 1991), p. 416.
6. There isn't space here to examine a further important aspect of this relationship: Mandelstam was deeply preoccupied with Dante, and Heaney's reading of Mandelstam coincided with his own interest in the Italian poet.
7. Jerzy Jarniewicz, *The Bottomless Centre: The Uses of History in the Poetry of Seamus Heaney* (Łódź: Wydawnictwo uniwersytetu łódzkiego, 2002), p. 103.
8. Mandelstam quoted in N. Mandelstam, *Hope against Hope*, p. 13.
9. Ibid., pp. 250, 249.
10. 'Qui voudra voir tout ce qu'ont peu nature, / L'art et le ciel (Rome) te vienne voir' (Joachim Du Bellay, *Les Antiquités de Rome*, ed. Françoise Joukovsky [Paris: Flammarion, 1994], p 29).

11. Osip Mandelstam, *Stone*, tr. Robert Tracy (London: Collins Harvill, 1991), pp. 175, 187.
12. Ibid., p. 205.
13. Joseph Brodsky, *Less than One* (London: Penguin, 1987), p. 128.
14. Joseph Brodsky, *Collected Poems in English*, ed. Ann Kjellberg (New York: Farrar, Straus and Giroux, 2000), p. 78.
15. Another convergence of imagery, although this time with a Greek motif, is to be found between Mandelstam's 'Sleeplessness. Homer ...' (*Stone*, p. 203), and the sixth sonnet of 'Glanmore Revisited' in *Seeing Things*.
16. See 'A Fire-Truck' from Richard Wilbur's *Advice to a Prophet and Other Poems* (1961), where he observes the truck 'Blurring to sheer verb'. (*New and Collected Poems* [London: Faber and Faber, 1989], p. 207).
17. Jarniewicz, *Bottomless Centre*, p. 11.
18. Michael Longley, *Gorse Fires* (London: Secker & Warburg, 1991), p. 42.
19. Brodsky, *Less than One*, p. 142.
20. Seamus Heaney, 'The Poet as Witness and Victim', *Irish Times* (6 April 1991).
21. Brodsky, *Less than One*, p. 140.
22. Altieri, 'Polish Envy'.
23. Also worth passing mention here is Heaney's version of Leoš Janáček's song cycle *Diary of One Who Vanished* (1999).
24. Jan Kochanowski, *Laments*, tr. Seamus Heaney and Stanisław Barańczak (London: Faber and Faber, 1995), pp. 6–7.

7

BERNARD O'DONOGHUE

Heaney's Classics and the Bucolic

In the best recent book on Irish literature and Greek tragedy, Marianne McDonald observes that in many ways Ireland 'is constructing its identity through the representations offered by Greek tragedy'.[1] It is clear that this remark applies to Seamus Heaney at least as much as to any other writer in the modern Irish tradition, and his use of Greek tragedy has received a good deal of comment. In this chapter I want to consider, in dealing with Heaney's relationship with classical literature, two sustained, and recently reinforced, elements in his poetry, and the relations between them.[2] The first is the use of the pastoral in his writing, whatever term we choose to describe it: pastoral, anti-pastoral, bucolic, eclogue, Doric. The second is to see this in the context of his turning to the classics in his writing generally, and his purposes in doing so. I want to suggest that there is surprisingly little difference in the use he makes of tragedy and of other classical genres: all genres (and the pastoral is the most prominent) turn tragic in his hands, largely as a consequence of the public circumstances of his lifetime.

The Latin and Greek classics have been a constant presence in Heaney's poetry throughout his writing lifetime: Hercules and Antaeus, Sophocles' *Philoctetes* and *Antigone*, Aeschylus' *Agamemnon*, the Virgilian Golden Bough, Narcissus, Hermes, more recently Horace.[3] As a poet of the modernist tradition Heaney has a gift for incorporating a classical mythological figure into his own world; for example, the poet remembers his father's advice to his daughter when she was going by ferry to England: 'look for a man with an ashplant on the boat' (*ST* 85). She would be safe next to a cattle-dealer like himself; but of course this character is also Hermes, the figure of 'The Stone Verdict' (*HL* 17). The list of Heaney's classical usages is very extensive.[4]

As a starting point, I want here to bring these two things – the country writing, and the classics – together in the volume where Heaney uses the eclogue form most insistently and repeatedly, *Electric Light* (2001). First I will review the insistent presence of eclogues in that volume, and I will end by trying to reach some conclusions about their use and function in Heaney's writing generally. Using in my title the term 'bucolic', rather than the more general term 'pastoral', draws initial attention to *Electric Light*. *Bucolica* was Virgil's term for these country poems, from the Greek *boukolika*, 'songs about herdsmen' ('eclogues' means 'selections'); but of course 'bucolic' in modern usage is also a wider term, to embrace country concerns in all senses. Though the eclogue is the recurrent form in *Electric Light*, it is a rather more narrowing term than I want to use. What I want to argue is that, while we would expect the bearing of classical tragedy on the modern era to be an unconsoling one, we might look to the bucolic poems for comfort. This is not the case in practice; it is increasingly characteristic of Heaney's use of the pastoral to show it to be as devastated by violence and pity as tragedy. (This subversion of pastoral can itself be part of the form; perhaps the most familiar instance in English is by a poet well known to Heaney, in Donne's 'Twicknam Garden': 'And that this place may thoroughly be thought / True Paradise, I have the serpent brought.'[5])

First of all though, we might quickly recall the prehistory of the pastoral/ bucolic in Heaney's writing. I won't spend too long on this because it is familiar territory, dealt with comprehensively in all the earlier criticism of Heaney. To start with the most obvious and literal pastoral inspiration for the poet, *Death of a Naturalist* broke on the world in 1966 with a powerful impact that was largely linked to its nature as country poetry: tadpoles and blackberries and digging and thatching (in Virgil's *oeuvre*, this is more the matter of the *Georgics*, a work which remains to be treated by Heaney and which might indeed be even more in his element).[6] The early agricultural subjects seemed natural enough; Heaney had grown up on a farm and often returned to it. And Irish farming, as Heaney often reminds us, had been transplanted into poetry in English with great success by Patrick Kavanagh. Heaney recalls Kavanagh's authority in this matter in a wonderful passage in the poem 'The Loose Box' in *Electric Light*:

> On an old recording Patrick Kavanagh states
> That there's health and worth in any talk about
> The properties of land. Sandy, glarry,
> Mossy, heavy, cold, the actual soil
> Almost doesn't matter; the main thing is
> An inner restitution, a purchase come by
> By pacing it in words that make you feel
> You've found your feet in what 'surefooted' means
> And in the ground of your own understanding –
> Like Heracles stepping in and standing under
> Atlas's sky-lintel, as earthed and heady
> As I am when I talk about the loose box. (*EL* 14)

We might bear this passage in mind before making too absolute a divide between Heaney's early and late bucolics: sandy, glarry, mossy, heavy, cold – nothing could better represent the language and spirit of the early pastoral volumes than this run of trochaic adjectives in this late poem. But the location of them in the experience of Heracles – standing 'in the ground of your own understanding' – is much more typical of the tendency in later Heaney to use classical parallels as expressions of intellectual and psychic self-scrutiny. Now Hercules/Heracles, who was diametrically opposed to the earthbound giant Antaeus in earlier Heaney, has incorporated some Antaean qualities too: this Heracles is 'earthed' as well as 'heady'. The point might indeed be taken further: in Irish colloquial usage, the phrase 'stepping in and standing under' is traditionally used of helping to carry a coffin, reinforcing and darkening the associations of the word 'earthed'. This, I will suggest, is in keeping with the more negative presentation of pastoral in later Heaney: much more negative than the rather warm-hearted presentation of the child's coming to an understanding of the sadness of the world in the sentimental anti-pastoral of *Death of a Naturalist*.

Before comparing the pastoral in the early volumes, especially *Death of a Naturalist* (1966) and *Door into the Dark* (1969), with its function in *Electric Light*, I want to recap on what it was doing in those early volumes. Those early books, as all their admiring critics noted, were characterised by an exact evocativeness in the way they handled country themes; this was linked to Heaney's giftedness as a poet who evoked place, something he traced himself in his essay called 'Mossbawn' and elsewhere. That early precise, agricultural language was indeed extraordinarily evocative:

> Threshed corn lay piled like grit of ivory
> Or solid as cement in two-lugged sacks. (*DN* 17)

Anyone who has ever run dry corn through their fingers, or lugged a full sack of it, is powerfully reminded of those things by these lines; they have what Richard Kell (one of the most alert and perceptive of the early reviewers) saluted in his *Guardian* review as Heaney's 'gift of finding a new and consummate phrase to evoke physical qualities'. But it was also striking that this rural poetry was by no means an uncontaminated idyll; the poems tended to end more as anti-pastoral than pastoral. The first poem of *Death of a Naturalist* and in all the subsequent selected editions is 'Digging', which celebrates the skills with the spade of the poet's ancestors but concludes with the declaration that he, following the Horatian dictum, will dig with the pen: a pen though which, disturbingly, is 'snug as a gun'. There are other equally familiar, less complicated anti-pastoral moments: the rotting of the blackberries into 'a rat-grey fungus', and especially the title-poem, ending with the metamorphosis of the frogspawn which was collected with such delight into the terrifying vision of the mature toads whose

> ... slap and plop were obscene threats. Some sat
> Poised like mud grenades, their blunt heads farting.
> I sickened, turned, and ran. The great slime kings
> Were gathered there for vengeance and I knew
> That if I dipped my hand the spawn would clutch it. (*DN* 16)

But of course the pastoral itself was from its origins a contested form, as is shown for example in the opening chapter of Sydney Burris's fine book on Heaney. Burris notes that pastoral had a 'dual emphasis on lyricism and social responsibility',[7] so it offered itself as *the* form in which there was a conflict between realism and conventionalism: in Heaney's terms, between public responsibility and artistic licence. One of Heaney's first substantial critical pieces, indeed, was his 1975 *Times Literary Supplement* review of the *Penguin Book of English Pastoral Verse*, reprinted as the first essay in the final section of *Preoccupations*.[8] Heaney's main argument is that pastoral continues to be useful and expressive into the twentieth century, beyond the point at which the Barrell and Bull anthology stops. Clearly, he is seeing that pastoral still offers something for his particular purposes.

From the first Heaney's imagination, however 'pastoral' in the more genial sense (Heaney begins his review with this) his early poetry might seem, has had an inclination towards the vulnerable and the unstable. In these early volumes there is not much explicit classical reference (Narcissus occurs memorably once); but the *generic* influence of the classical farm-poems is very important. Poems like these find their definition in a pastoral tradition. Soon, however, the classics have a much more explicit role when Heaney's writing turns to Northern Irish events of political violence in *North*; but of course it is not now the pastoral classics. It is Greek tragedy with its emphasis on Nemesis, or the appeal to Tacitus to report the Northern Irish fairly: their taste for 'neighbourly murder', that terrible oxymoron, and how they 'slaughter / for the common good' (*N* 16, 45). The first of the two parts of *North* are framed by the conflict between Hercules, a figure of skill and cunning, and the giant Antaeus who could only be defeated by being lifted away from contact with the Earth. In the opening poem 'Antaeus' the sympathy is with the giant against the 'new hero'; but in the final poem 'Hercules and Antaeus', the triumph of Hercules is described in terms of contempt for the 'sleeping giant' who is dismissed in a much-quoted phrase as 'pap for the dispossessed' (*N* 53).[9]

From the following volume *Field Work* on there is a marked two-way pull in the use of the classics: between the terrors which culminate in 'Mycenae Lookout' in *The Spirit Level* in 1996, and the yearning towards the rural which shares *Field Work* with Heaney's great elegies, in poems like the 'Glanmore Sonnets' for Ann Saddlemyer who leased her house in Co. Wicklow to the Heaneys. This is the place where the uncontaminated *rus* seems maybe possible at last:

> Vowels ploughed into other: opened ground.
> The mildest February for twenty years (*FW* 33)

But for the most part, in much of the poetry of the next twenty years, between this volume and *The Spirit Level*, classical reference seems to be heavy-hearted, 'Greek with consequence' ('Lustral Sonnet', from 'Glanmore Revisited'; *ST* 35), not the Theocritan-Horatian-Virgilian bucolic. Heaney feels in his most serious writing that responsibility to public events still requires the classics of tragedy and epic; he has not yet resigned himself to the last Horatian obligation – 'il faut cultiver le jardin'.[10]

But when at last, in 2001, eclogues became the central form, quite explicitly, in *Electric Light*, in order to understand the meaning of this volume as a whole we need to scrutinise what exactly the employment of eclogue suggests, and what the relationship is of this version of pastoral to the country poems of those early volumes. In asking this question and examining the evidence, I will draw on the raising of such issues by Rui Cavalho Homem in an important and enlightening interview with Heaney. In that interview Heaney says artlessly of the origins of and inspiration for those poems: 'the fact of the matter is that I read a new translation of Virgil's *Eclogues* three or four years ago' which inspired in him 'a simple reader's delight'.[11] Other explanations were offered: his journey to Greece in which he saw the goatherd in a petrol station, described in one of the 'Sonnets from Hellas' (*EL* 38); writing an essay for a volume on the Irish playwright J. M. Synge on whose estate the Glanmore cottage was; the news that Heaney's niece was pregnant, so a significant child was imminent, as in Virgil's *Eclogue* iv; his interest in Alberto Caeiro, the shepherd-persona of the Portuguese poet Fernando Pessoa, and so on.

It is important to stress though that these things are only circumstantial; as Heaney puts it they 'establish a context', providing the material with which the poet works rather than the poems' purpose, or their overall meaning in the developing Heaney corpus.[12] They don't explain why eclogues are so prominent in *Electric Light* as a whole. With Heaney we always need to ask why he selects his influencing texts and chosen ancestors; early in his career he noted that his 'roots were crossed with his reading', for example when he read the English translation of P. V. Glob's book *The Bog People* in 1969 and found in it 'befitting emblems of adversity' for Northern Ireland (*P* 57).[13] Similarly he said of the medieval Irish Sweeney story of the Ulster poet defeated by a churchman and driven south 'there is something here for me': something that eventually produced *Sweeney Astray*. So the crucial question to ask of the eclogues is: what are the 'roots', broadly speaking, which are crossed with this reading – crossed with Virgil in particular?

To address this question, we must first review the evidence in some detail, the explicit eclogues in *Electric Light*: there are three of them, bearing very different relations to the Virgilian originals, the *Eclogues* or *Bucolics*. These were based on the *Idylls* written by the Greek poet Theocritus in the first half of the third century BC, two and a half centuries before Virgil. One of Heaney's poems is close enough to be called a version or, to use the term of Dryden and Lowell, an imitation; the poem is called, simply, 'Virgil: Eclogue IX' (*EL* 31–4). The original is one of the two eclogues (the other is *Eclogue* i) which have traditionally been interpreted as commenting on the land grievances in Virgil's time, in 41 BC. One might apply Heaney's term 'clearances' to them; the reader of English poetry is also reminded of the suggested impact on the poetry of John Clare of enclosures at the end of the eighteenth century. In the introduction to the Oxford World's Classics edition of the *Eclogues* and *Georgics* translated by C. Day Lewis, R. O. A. M. Lyne says: '*Eclogue ix* alludes to the land confiscations in much the same way as *Eclogue i* and partners that poem. But it is more pessimistic – and has a sharper edge'.[14] It is typical of Heaney's strengths to alight on the eclogue which has the sharpest, or the most political, edge. It is striking that this is the eclogue that he represents most faithfully: not the more celebrated *Eclogue* iv, or the first or last of the series. There is indeed 'health and worth' in any talk about land.

The situation in Virgil's poem is an encounter between the poet Lycidas and the small-landowner poet Moeris who complains that an outsider has taken over his farm, so it is this outsider's goats that Moeris, now only a tenant, is taking to market. Lycidas expresses surprise, believing that all the local land had been saved for its holders by the poetry of Menalcas (in *Eclogue* v Menalcas is closely identified with Virgil himself), whereupon Moeris declares that poetry has no power in a world where soldiers hold sway. Indeed Menalcas, in common with Moeris himself, might have been put to death if they hadn't both known when to maintain a discreet silence. Moeris and Lycidas then reflect on what a disaster to poetry the loss of Menalcas would have been, before Lycidas asks Moeris to recite a poem which he does – 'Huc ades, O Galatea; quis est nam ludis in undis?', beautifully translated by Day Lewis as, '*Come to me, Galatea. What sport have you in the ocean?*'[15] (We might note in passing that Day Lewis says that he 'used rhythms of English and Irish folk-song for translating the singing-matches in the *Eclogues*' (vi): another consideration likely to attract Heaney's attention.) Lycidas goes on to recall another of Moeris' songs in which the star of Caesar rises to make the crops fruitful. Moeris then laments that his voice 'is not what it was' (Day Lewis's felicitous phrase for 'vox quoque Moerim / iam fugit ipsa').[16] But the two poets conclude by agreeing to sing as they go, since 'singing shortens the road' in Heaney's idiomatically Irish words.

It is surely not being over-fanciful to see several recurrent Heaney themes in this poem, despite the apparently artless tone. It is not so much its broadly post-colonial themes of land confiscation, though of course they too have a resonance in the Irish context. The more weighty connection is with the relative strength of artistic and secular authority: whether poetry is effective in a world where military force holds sway. The suggestion is that the poets here have survived by keeping quiet. In the end they sing anyway, because singing entertains – 'shortens the road' – despite the fact that Moeris' voice is not what it was.[17]

There is an obvious congruence and mock-modesty about all of this, of the same order as Heaney's saying in the Homem interview that he was taken by Lycidas (the Heaney figure in the exhange) being 'not certain' of his talent despite the fact that 'people in the country call me bard':[18] as a student-poet Heaney had signed himself *incertus*, the 'not certain'. But the deeper question remains: why exactly is Heaney translating this poem? It has always been clear why Heaney chooses to translate what he does; indeed he often clarifies it for us himself, as in the case of the medieval Irish *Buile Suibhne* mentioned already, the story of the Ulster poet displaced by historical circumstances.[19] Likewise, the Golden Bough from *Aeneid* VI provides an obviously apt introduction to the negotiations with the afterlife and the underworld in *Seeing Things*. The critical challenge now is to decide what kind of book this is, to which these Virgilian poems of pastoral poetic contest and discussions of land confiscation are appropriate. We might also note here a charge to which the easy charm of parts of this book might seem to be open (and against which it is important to defend it, in order to understand what the temper of these poems is) of a kind of poet's complacency and mock-modesty. The poem which I will particularly address in this context is 'Known World': a poem which begins and ends with a cavalier assertion of the poet's freedom and lightheartedness in old Yugoslavia in 1979, but in which 'that old sense of a tragedy going on / Uncomprehended, at the very edge / Of the usual, it never left me once' (*EL* 21). This shadowing never wholly leaves *Electric Light* either, despite the apparent moments of insouciance.

Leaving those more important considerations in suspense for the moment, we should consider the other eclogues in the book. There are two of them, one of which like 'Virgil: Eclogue IX' acknowledges Virgil explicitly. 'Bann Valley Eclogue' (which occurs earlier in *Electric Light*) has as an epigraph the opening line of the most famous of Virgil's *Eclogues*, iv, 1: 'Sicelides Musae, paulo maiora canamus –', 'Sicilian Muses, now we sing of greater things for a while.' The age-old celebrity of this eclogue (concerning a new birth to be sent from high Heaven – 'a virgin too will return') was due to its interpretation as a prophecy in 40 BC of the coming of Christ. Heaney explained to Cavalho Homem that the connection with *Eclogue* iv was the pregnancy of his niece, particularly in the half-line '*casta fave Lucina*' – in Day Lewis's version: 'Look kindly, chaste Lucina, upon this infant's birth'.[20] Virgil in the Middle Ages was co-opted both as Christian prophet from this passage, and as magician (perhaps because of the powerful passage of Sibylline frenzy early in *Aeneid* VI, already given prominence by Heaney in 'The Golden Bough' at the beginning of *Seeing Things* in 1991). That Heaney is concerned with the eclogue passage interpreted as Christian prophecy (or at least as something beyond a niece's pregnancy – 'the child that's due', the 'Child on the way') is evident from the task set by Virgil for his interlocutor 'Poet' in Heaney's poem. He is to include a series of words in his poem, sounding like a kind of sestina exercise in a poetic workshop: '*Carmen, ordo, nascitur, saeculum, gens*' are all words which occur between lines 4 and 9 of *Eclogue* iv. In the event it turns out to be a kind of five-element semantic variant on the sestina, concentrating on the meaning rather than the form of these words. Later Heaney's poem further borrows the phrase '*pacatum orbem*', the first and last words of Virgil's line 17: 'a world made peaceful'.

This phrase from Virgil establishes clearly what is confirmed by several other poems in *Electric Light*: after the anger and self-justification of *The Spirit Level*,[21] this is a volume offering a cautious welcome to peace. In Northern Irish terms it is at first reading a peace-process book, and Heaney is trawling through the classics for the texts that lend themselves to that; clearly, a great epic of civil war like the *Aeneid*, even if is to result in the *pax Romana*, does not suit. However, in the end the function of eclogue here proves less univocally positive or peaceful than this first reading suggests. As in *Death of a Naturalist*, there is as much anti-pastoral as pastoral, and of a much more searing kind which cannot be got out of the poet's mind in *District and Circle* either.

The bearing of Virgil's *Eclogue* iv on Heaney's poem is general rather than particular. To the terminology of Virgil's prophetic and momentous commission he has already added two of the most resonant phrases from Christian narrative: '*And it came to pass*' which introduces amongst other things the biblical telling of Christ's nativity, and '*In the beginning*' from the start of John's Gospel. Later in *Electric Light*, in 'The Real Names', a poem which works into its development received idioms and terms from other sources, the phrase 'in the beginning' recurs to mean no more than in Heaney's childhood. Like Virgil's poem Heaney's 'Bann Valley Eclogue' centres on the birth of a child, associated with a new age of hope. But this poem is a much more anxious performance, trapped in the everyday, than Virgil's which is one of his strangest works, quite apart from its imputed Christian links – a kind of Golden Age poem in reverse, foreseeing a new blessed era in which the ground will not need to be broken by the plough, nor clothes need artificial means of colouring. It may be, of course, that this unrealised ideal age contrives to bring an uneasiness into Heaney's peace-process volume, his *pacatum orbem*. In any case Heaney's poem seems to lack the courage of its convictions, dominated by images of uncertainty, such as the millenarianism of the 2000 eclipse – 'Planet earth like a teething-ring suspended / hang[ing] by its world-chain' (*EL* 12) – with a suggestion of the world-threatening trials of Othinn recalling less sanguinely the astronaut's view of the Earth in 'Alphabets':

> The risen, aqueous, singular, lucent O
> Like a magnified and buoyant ovum ... (*HL* 3)

The most disturbing of those uncertain images, when seen within Heaney's whole development, is one which I suggest becomes dominant in his subsequent writing: the anticipatory 'sluicing the milk-house floor' (*EL* 12). This picture recalls two of the most devastating moments in Heaney's later poetry: the first, 'A clean spot / Where ... had been' the head of the murdered reservist witnessed by Heaney's brother, and recalled in the great poem of salutation 'Keeping Going' in *The Spirit Level* (*SL* 10–12); and the second, 'The Augean Stables', the fourth of the 'Sonnets from Hellas' in *Electric Light*, describing the murder of the Gaelic Athletic Association clubman Sean Brown, imagining

> Hose-water smashing hard back off the asphalt
> In the car-park where his athlete's blood ran cold. (*EL* 41)

The process of cleaning – of sluicing – tends in Heaney to have the classical association of the ignoring or expunging of horrors, above all in his most horrifying poem, the Cassandra section of 'Mycenae Lookout' in *The Spirit Level*: 'A wipe / of the sponge, / that's it' (*SL* 33), which Vendler examines in its Greek context.[22]

Turning to the last of *Electric Light*'s eclogues, 'Glanmore Eclogue', we encounter a poem which is formally close to Virgil's structures but much more fully adapted to Heaney's own purposes, having cut almost all ties with the originals in its circumstantial details. In fact the poem begins with an echo of *Eclogue* i, the other land-dispossession poem in which Meliboeus asks Tityrus why he came to Rome. Tityrus describes his inspiring encounter with the young prince, assumed to be Octavian/Caesar Augustus who consoled him for his dispossession, although homesickness for his native territory is the emotional centre at the poem's end.

Heaney's eclogue is *à clef* in a clear way, but this time it is remote from any Virgilian parallel; we might call it secondary or applied eclogue. The exchanging pastoral figures are 'Poet' – whose experiences are Heaney's own – and 'Myles' (spelt in the unusual manner of the Irish comic novelist and journalist, Myles na Goppaleen, *alias* Flann O'Brien, *alias* Brian O'Nolan, *his* 'real name'). The poem is set moreover not in the present but in the 1970s, when Heaney moved to Glanmore and was the tenant of the Canadian scholar Anne Saddlemyer.[23] It is a striking feature of *Electric Light* that many of its poems have to be read in the light of events from an earlier historical period: something which Heaney does increasingly through his career, as Vendler demonstrates. The benefactor who facilitates the poet's writing is called Augusta 'because we arrived in August'; perhaps, but Augusta is of course the name of Lady Gregory, Yeats's patron who provided *him* with 'house and ground', facilitating his writing. This woman (Saddlemyer), the poet says, 'changed my life' (*EL* 35). The house in Glanmore, Co. Wicklow, which she rented to the Heaneys at a low rent and which they subsequently bought, was on the estate of the family of J. M. Synge, the author of *The Playboy of the Western World* and other dramatic masterpieces of the Celtic revival at the start of the twentieth century. Myles reassures the poet that his patron, though an outsider, has 'every right, / maybe more right than most' to be there. She is an authority on the writings of Meliboeus, identifiable as Synge from these lines: 'All the tramps he met tramping the roads / And all he picked up, listening in a loft / To servant girls colloguing in the kitchen' (*EL* 35), referring to two of the best-known details of Synge's writing career: he signed himself as 'Tramp' or 'Tramper' in some of his early diaries; his observing of tramps is described in W. J. McCormack's admirable biography, *Fool of the Family*.[24] The clinching reference connecting Heaney's eclogues with Virgil's *Eclogues* i and ix then follows: the Synge word 'stranger' followed by an italicised quotation:

> A stranger on a wild night, *out in the rain falling …*
>
> (*EL* 36; italics in the original)

The poet reflects whimsically,

> Meliboeus would have called me 'Mr Honey.'

'Honey' is phonetically very close to 'Heaney', but of course it is the common term of address to Christy Mahon in Synge's *Playboy of the Western World*. Myles concludes (and here he is closest to Flann O'Brien/Myles na Goppaleen who studied and translated Old Irish poetry, several sections of which are included in his comic masterpiece *At Swim-Two-Birds* (1939), including poems paralleled by sections of *Sweeney Astray*) with a poetic request for an Old Irish song:

> Our old language that Meliboeus learnt
> Has lovely songs. What about putting words
> On one of them, words that the rest of us
> Can understand, and singing it here and now? (*EL* 36)

The Poet complies, in keeping with his role as the Heaney of *Sweeney Astray*, with a song of cuckoo and bog-cotton and wild deer, of warriors and fish and sea. Above all it has a reference to one of the most loved of all the poems in Old Irish, in a language that parodies the style of the early-twentieth-century translators such as Kuno Meyer:

> A little nippy chirpy fellow
> Hits the highest note there is (*EL* 37)

catches perfectly the diction of those early translations of the poem often titled 'The Blackbird of Belfast Lough'. We see later that one of the pastoral-darkening devices that Heaney employs echoes this poem in an ominous voice of rural wisdom in the closing poem of *District and Circle*, 'The Blackbird of Glanmore':

> I said nothing at the time
> But I never liked yon bird. (*DC* 75–6)

In the 'Glanmore Eclogue' then, Heaney is writing his own eclogue, with a strong element of the affectionate pastiche, reinforced from an Irish tradition. So what do we conclude about his using the eclogue form at all? At first glance, it is, as I said at the start, a return to country poetry after the harshness and jaggedness of *The Spirit Level*, a return seemingly confirmed by the prevailing concerns and title of *District and Circle* (2006). But it is a dramatic departure from the country poems of *Death of a Naturalist* which were praised for their evocation of pastoral as 'the thing itself': what it is really like for the imaginative child growing up on a farm. In this way the anti-pastoral was just as apt as the pastoral, and of course it is just as nostalgic-evocative. But now there is a dramatic shift: to put it strongly, it is a move from the least literary presentation of the rural to the most artificially literary, the Virgilian and Theocritan idyll.

Or so it seems. But the final question remains: is this formal-sounding shift characteristic of the spirit of *Electric Light* as a whole? One way in which it is not typical immediately suggests itself. Heaney has said that he had considered calling the volume, after one of its most substantial poems, 'The Real Names'. But nothing could describe the eclogue, including Heaney's, less well. In the eclogue everyone has an adopted name. (In a different context we might be tempted to pursue this briefly. What are the real names in the poem of that name? Was Owen Kelly, 'loping and gowling', really himself or really Caliban? The teacher instructs 'Frankie McMahon, you're Bassanio' (*EL*, 45, 48). In the same way, we might wonder whether Synge or Meliboeus was 'the real name' in 'Glanmore Eclogue', and whether Myles is Flann O'Brien.)

Our present question though is this: is it really the case that Heaney, who since *North* has tended to draw on the Classics for his darkest and most despairing subjects, could turn to their ostensibly more artificial and equable genre, the pastoral, to indicate a more cheerful turn in his own later writing? At first glance it might seem so: in 'Glanmore Eclogue' Myles tells 'Poet' (the Heaney who is settling in Wicklow in the early 1970s): 'You've landed on your feet', and it ends with a 'lovely song' of summer (*EL* 35). But that was the early 1970s, a hoped-for age of innocence as in 'The Glanmore Sonnets' of *Field Work*. In any case that volume has already contained 'After a Killing' and later finds room for the great elegies 'Casualty' and 'The Strand at Lough Beg'. 'Virgil Eclogue IX' strikes more explicitly dark notes about the following thirty years: 'The things we have lived to see' (*EL* 31). 'Bann Valley Eclogue' sets out upon a 'song worth singing' for 'the child that's due', but ends up 'sluicing' the milk-house floor (*EL* 11, 12). 'The Augean Stables' begins on an arty, comfortable note with 'My favourite bas-relief: Athene showing / Heracles where to broach the river bank' but ends with the hideous murder of Sean Brown and the grimly inartistic 'asphalt / In the car park where his athlete's blood ran cold' (*EL* 41). The wonderful title-poem starts 'In the first house where I saw electric light', a setting of excitement and progress, you might think, but ends desolately in the graveyard 'among beads and vertebrae in the Derry ground' (*EL* 81). This pattern of subverted pastoral – of the positive denied or questioned – is everywhere in *Electric Light*. The eclogue is set up to be shot down, a possibility which, as Heaney himself has repeatedly made clear, is native to the pastoral form. This is consistent too with Rand Brandes's demonstration in Chapter 2 of this volume that Heaney's tendency has been to change from more optimistic to pessimistic titles; the working titles often prove too sanguine or too 'literary'.

This defeat of the positive is true above all in what I think is the volume's most important poem, 'Known World' (though – deliberately harsh as it is – it is not the most attractive poem: that accolade is perhaps due to 'Out of the Bag'). '*Nema Problema!*', 'Known World' begins, proceeding through a self-regarding catalogue of drinking poets from the late 1970s, most of whom are far from household names in 2000. Looking back, Heaney wishes he had then known

> Hygo Simberg's allegory of Finland,
> The one where the wounded angel's being carried
> By two farm youngsters across an open field. (*EL* 21)

The 1970s Heaney surely was to encounter this haunting allegory on the cover of Paul Durcan's prize-winning and desolate volume *Daddy! Daddy!* in 1990; these very anti-pastoral children deepen the implicit anxiety that pervades Heaney's poem. Belgrade takes him back to Belmullet, and by a remote connection to a grim childhood association (Heaney's evocative powers incidentally have never been more exact) –

> The flypaper hung from our kitchen ceiling,
> Honey-strip and death-trap, a barley-sugar twist
> Of glut and loathing ... (*EL* 20)

The poem goes on, as I have already said, to note that the sense of tragedy at the edge of the usual 'never left [him] once' (*EL* 21); neighbourly murder is still in fashion, *nema problema* or not. And the 'Real Names' question is asked in its most crucial form, reverting to the famous question of tribal guilt raised in 'Casualty' (*FW* 23). The form now is: 'How does the real get into the made-up? / Ask me an easier one' (*EL* 21).

So, by the time the poet is flying out from 1970s Belgrade 'courtesy of Lufthansa', we are not reassured by the final line, written in 'May 1998' as the Balkans war is reaching its terrible dénouement in more 'neighbourly murder': '*Nema problema. Ja.* All systems go' (*EL* 23). As a small indicator, the '*Nema problema*' has lost its lightening exclamation mark. But we do not need such small indicators. *Electric Light* was a book of denied consolation: a peace process under permanent challenge; a light-heartedness that cannot be sustained against death or its Angel, or against *Beowulf*'s Hrethel, not even allowed to mourn his dead son fully. After all, it should not surprise us that the eclogue falls short of consolation in a volume that begins 'where the checkpoint used to be. / Where the rebel boy [Roddy McCorley] was hanged in '98' (*EL* 3) – now in another '98, we might note. Indeed this poem spells it out as clearly as the closing poem does at the end:

> Where negative ions in the open air
> Are poetry to me. (*EL* 3)

Heaney's cautious art is always on guard. And the open-air quality of the country poem, classical or otherwise, has never been proof against the negative. In the end the eclogue too remains 'Greek with consequence' (*ST* 35).

The wider implication for Heaney's employment of the classics in his work as a whole is that his view of the Greek and Roman writers, even when they are not laden with the tragic or mythic weight of *Antigone* or *Philoctetes*, is dark.[25] Their cultural and literary-historic centrality means that they are not to be taken lightly. Here we encounter a striking central paradox: much of Heaney's critical writing has argued that poetry can help – that it can offer 'redress', in one way or another. And yet the poetry itself seems less confident of this capacity, unsurprisingly given the era in which it is rooted, Northern Ireland in the last third of the twentieth century. Heaney's evocations of the everyday are always liable to be invaded by disaster, as indeed the everyday of that era was. And that sense of foreboding and threatened disaster 'never left [him] once' (*EL* 21). This tendency in the poetry, it is tempting to say, seems almost to be a psychological norm in Heaney: one perhaps of which he is aware, since his is 'an art that knows its mind' ('Squarings' xxxvii, *ST* 97). For example, the declared intention to be more positive and open in the move from *North* to *Field Work* must have been made knowing that the volume will contain 'After a Killing' and 'Casualty'. The options available to the writer of pastoral are clear: it can be conventional or founded in reality; it can be idyllic or threatened. Heaney has never allowed himself the luxury of settling for the conventional or the idyllic or the easy. And by making the problematic, negative choice in all cases, he has shown the form to be 'adequate to our predicament', and just as befitting an emblem of adversity as tragedy is.

NOTES

1. Marianne McDonald, 'The Irish and Greek Tragedy', in *Amid Our Troubles: Irish Versions of Greek Tragedy*, ed. Marianne McDonald and J. Michael Walton (London: Methuen, 2002), p. 37. McDonald is the dedicatee of Heaney's *Burial at Thebes* (2004).
2. I would like to thank Carle Bonafous-Murat and Maryvonne Boisseau of Sorbonne Nouvelle, the organisers of the conference there in June 2002 where part of this essay was originally given, as well as Clíona Ní Riordáin and Adolphe Haberer.
3. For Heaney's use of Greek tragedy before *The Burial at Thebes*, see the contributions by the poet himself ('*The Cure at Troy*: Production Notes in No Particular Order'), and by Helen Vendler ('Seamus Heaney and the *Oresteia*: "Mycenae Lookout" and the Usefulness of Tradition') in *Amid Our Troubles*, ed. McDonald and Walton, pp. 171–80, 181–97, respectively.
4. For a very brief itemising of these up to *Opened Ground* (1998), see Bernard O'Donoghue, 'Seamus Heaney and the Classics', in *Omnibus* 36 (Cambridge, September 1998), pp. 21–3. There are of course many more substantial explorations of particular classical usages in Heaney: for example, B. Arkins and P. F. Sheeran, 'Coloniser and Colonised: the Myth of Hercules and Antaeus in Seamus Heaney's *North*', *Classical and Modern Literature: A Quarterly* 10.2 (Winter 1990), pp. 127–34.
5. John Donne, *Complete Poems*, ed. C. A. Patrides (London: Everyman, 1994), p. 25.
6. The distinguished translation of *The Georgics* by Heaney's friend and occasionally editor Peter Fallon (*The Georgics of Virgil* [Oldcastle: Gallery Press, 2004]) may make preparing another contemporary Irish translation seem otiose to Heaney.

7. Sydney Burris, *The Poetry of Resistance: Seamus Heaney and the Pastoral Tradition* (Athens: Ohio University Press, 1991), p. x.
8. Seamus Heaney, 'In the Country of Convention', review of *The Penguin Book of English Pastoral Verse*, ed. J. Barrell and J. Bull (London: Allen Lane, 1975); reprinted in *P* 173–80.
9. It is significant that this triumph is underlined by the inclusion of the second poem but not the first in Heaney's *Opened Ground*, pp. 129–30. The phrase 'pap for the dispossessed' has become notorious as the title of David Lloyd's attack on Heaney, subtitled 'Seamus Heaney and the Poetics of Identity', first published in *Boundary* in 1985, and republished in Lloyd's important *Anomalous States: Irish Writing and the Post-Colonial Moment* (Dublin: Lilliput Press, 1993). This brilliant essay on Heaney's relation to the defects of the Irish Revival is curiously spoiled by suddenly turning at the end into an *ad hominem* rant against the poet.
10. Heaney has established that this is his conscious view of the eclogue in his talk delivered to the Royal Irish Academy on 6 June 2002, published as 'Eclogues *In Extremis*: On the Staying Power of Pastoral', *Proceedings of the Royal Irish Academy* 103C: 1 (2003), pp. 1–12.
11. Rui Cavalho Homem, 'On Elegies, Eclogues, Translations, Transfusions: An interview with Seamus Heaney', *European English Messenger* 10:2 (Autumn 2001), pp. 30, 25.
12. Ibid., p. 26.
13. In 'Belfast', originally in *the Guardian* in 1972; reprinted in *P* 37. For Glob's book, see p. 205 n. 5 here.
14. Virgil, *The Eclogues; The Georgics*, tr. C. Day Lewis, with an introduction and notes by R. O. A. M. Lyne, Oxford World's Classics (Oxford: Oxford University Press, 1983), p. xix. In fact Day Lewis's translation of the *Eclogues* was done in 1963, and of the *Georgics* in 1940. I am drawing on this version because, although Heaney tells us he was deriving his 'simple reader's delight' from a new translation in the 1990s, he was aware of Day Lewis as a notable predecessor-translator: an Anglo-Irish poet and English Poet Laureate. Fallon's *Georgics* (see note 6) are later than *Electric Light*.
15. Virgil, *Eclogues*, p. 40.
16. Ibid., pp. 53–4.
17. Heaney returns to this theme which has always absorbed him in '*Cure at Troy*', pp. 173ff.
18. Homem, 'On Elegies', p. 30.
19. 'Something here for me' was Heaney's memorable phrase for this encounter, in an interview with Dennis O'Driscoll (*Hibernia* 8:11 [October 1979]).
20. Virgil, *Ecologues*, p. 18 l. 8.
21. For an interesting historical rationale for this anger, particularly in 'Mycenae Lookout', see Vendler, 'Heaney and the *Oresteia*', pp. 181ff.
22. Vendler, 'Heaney and the *Oresteia*', p. 184. We might note that one of the finest poems in *District and Circle*, 'Quitting Time', serves to exorcise the violent association of sluicing, by showing it to be also a normal cleansing of the farmyard at the end of the working day (*DC* 69).
23. Heaney returns to this indebtedness by dedicating *District and Circle* to Saddlemyer in 2006, using some lines from this poem as the epigraph.

24. W. J. McCormack, *Fool of the Family: A Life of J. M. Synge* (London: Weidenfeld and Nicolson, 2000), pp. 91 and 218ff.
25. I have not dealt here with Heaney's translations of the Greek tragedies where the adequacy to the condition of the modern world, especially in Northern Ireland, does not need labouring. What I have argued is that Heaney has drawn even on the less fraught classics for warning parallels, in keeping with his view of the classics as inherently significant.

8

DAVID WHEATLEY

Professing Poetry: Heaney as Critic

Like Walt Whitman, the term 'critic-poet' contains multitudes. As currently used, it encompasses everything from a poet who writes occasional book reviews to lecturers publishing academic monographs to the Oxford Professor of Poetry. There are critic-poets such as Dr Johnson and T. S. Eliot whose prose dwarfs their poetry in volume and surrounds it like a protective cocoon. There are those in whom poetry and prose appear to coexist harmoniously, though for every multitasking Randall Jarrell or W. H. Auden there will be another whose competing muses jealously demand that a choice be made. For Matthew Arnold and William Empson, two writers who become ex-poets, the hyphen in 'critic-poet' could indicate a minus sign, while for Edward Thomas it represents a happy escape from journalism to the torrent of poems composed in the last two years of his life. There are those like Ezra Pound who are pedagogues in both their poetry and prose, enforcing their critical vision on two fronts, and others such as D. J. Enright or Patricia Beer with no manifestos to peddle, merely a well-stocked sensibility that overflows easily into large amounts of elegant essays and reviews. One size emphatically does not fit all.

His critical prose has always been important to Seamus Heaney. In his essay 'A Piece of Prose', Christian Wiman defends poets' prose as an ideally ad hoc, casual art: the work of a skilled craftsman, perhaps, but in one of his or her off-duty moments. A poet's prose, he writes, will always be 'considerably less than the real work, mere means, a very careful sort of public appearance, a bit of money, maybe, a bit of a headache, probably, a piece of prose'.[1] Reading this, a contemporary Sir Philip Sidney or Shelley might consider himself duly rebuked. Heaney's prose may lack the grandiloquence of *A Defence of Poetry*, but aside from a handful of book reviews, there are very few Heaney essays which do not hint at a larger animating poetics. *Finders Keepers*, his 2002 selection from thirty years of lectures, essays and reviews, runs to forty items and over four hundred pages of text. His range is generous and impressive: he has written on Irish poetry in both Irish and

English, with particular attention to Kavanagh and Yeats, and English poetry from *Beowulf* and Christopher Marlowe to Ted Hughes, Geoffrey Hill and Philip Larkin. He has explored American poetry in the form of great exemplars such as Robert Lowell and Elizabeth Bishop, and engaged profoundly with the poetry of Central and Eastern Europe (Herbert, Holub, Miłosz and Mandelstam). But if one note predominates in Heaney's prose that helps to place him in relation to the other critic-poets cited above, it is the autobiographical. More so than Eliot's, Auden's or Jarrell's prose works ever were, Heaney's are rooted in his own life and the narrative of his growth as a writer. *Preoccupations*, a volume of *Selected Prose 1968–1978*, begins with two mini-memoirs of Heaney's childhood in rural Co. Derry and of life in Belfast in the early years of the Troubles, and continues with their autobiographical style in its first extended critical essay, 'Feeling into Words'. Thirty-five may seem a little premature for a poet to conduct a retrospect (the essay was delivered as a lecture in 1974), but Heaney bases his argument on a series of memories from childhood and readings of his own work. The effect is a combination of the 'insouciance' and 'confidence' he finds in his early attempts at verse, as we move from remembered popular songs and doggerel to a sophisticated discussion of technique versus craft in poetry and the interaction of 'territorial piety' and 'imperial power' (*P* 41, 57).

Nor is this aspect of Heaney's style limited to his childhood. His second prose volume, *The Government of the Tongue*, appeared in 1988, the year between his seventh collection, *The Haw Lantern*, and the momentous political events of 1989. The connection is more than accidental, as in poems from *The Haw Lantern* such as 'From the Republic of Conscience' and 'The Mud Vision', Heaney displayed a change of direction heavily indebted to the parable style of the Eastern European poets he champions in *The Government of the Tongue*; and throughout that volume Heaney meditates on poetry as a form of witnessing, with all the comparisons that implies between the Irish poet and the poets of Czechoslovakia, Poland and Russia (comparisons that have not gone uncontested). His third prose volume, *The Redress of Poetry* (1995), draws the same insistent connection between critical prose and personal witnessing when, in 'Frontiers of Writing', Heaney describes attending a dinner at an Oxford college at the height of the hunger strikes of 1981. The previous week a Republican hunger striker from a neighbouring family of Heaney's in Co. Derry had starved himself to death, and in Oxford Heaney discovers that the bedroom he will be occupying is that of a serving Tory minister in the British government of the day. The poet is deeply exercised by this close-to-home reminder of his Irish beginnings in such close conjunction with a public sign of his acceptance into the heart of the British establishment. No matter what the occasion, it seems, the narrative of Heaney's life is always to hand as a point of reference, of self-examination and authentication. Or as he tells us in 'On Poetry and Professing', 'The great advantage a poet has is the fact that he or she is likely to possess a credible personal language' (*FK* 71). Professorial formality dignifies the personal anecdote and the personal anecdote in turn softens the professorial formality.

Such is the personal character of Heaney's prose, but as we read and respond to it, we face a choice: are these essays of interest primarily for what they tell us about Elizabeth Bishop, John Clare or Yeats, or for what they tell us about Heaney himself? Peter McDonald warns against too easy a slippage from the former to the latter: 'Our interest in poets' criticism ought to be a *critical* interest, and not an aspect of our veneration for the poets concerned.'[2] Ideally for Heaney, the one need not exclude the other: he chooses his subjects carefully for their usefulness to his own art, and frequently bases his readings on accounts of his own artistic development. This may account for another salient feature of Heaney's prose: its remarkable benevolence and good humour. Artists as varied as Clare, Gerard Manley Hopkins, Theodore Roethke, Hugh MacDiarmid and Stevie Smith are the subject of Heaney's excited and intelligent panegyric. For all that he has paid tribute to T. S. Eliot, there is no equivalent in Heaney to the radical reshaping of the canon in his own image performed by the young Eliot, with its assault on Milton and enthronement of the then-unfashionable metaphysicals. The obvious father figure for any Irish poet to overthrow in Oedipal fashion is Yeats, whom Heaney, were he so minded, could replace with the more amenable and down-to-earth Kavanagh. What he does, however, short-circuits any Bloomian anxiety of influence: he simply takes both. If Heaney's criticism is binary in nature, its preferred stance is less either/or than both/and.

In what follows, I propose to examine Heaney's criticism in relation to an abiding theme of his essays: poetic authority. Poetic authority is more than the magisterial pose of a writer like Yeats or Lowell; it is a form of truth-telling detectible in the smallest detail of voice and style. Here is Heaney's definition of poetic authority, from the essay 'Sounding Auden':

> By poetic authority I mean the rights and weight which accrue to a voice not only because of a sustained history of truth-telling but by virtue also of its tonality, the sway it gains over the deep ear and, through that, over other parts of our mind and nature. (*GT* 109)

Heaney's equation of authority with weightiness and voice is another abiding motif. In many of his poems, images of earthiness and weight are identified with the ungainsayable there-ness of nature and rural life, but also with the kind of unshakeable balance for which the Heaney of 'Whatever You Say, Say Nothing' has become proverbial. Where voice is concerned, Heaney is the most onomatopoeic of critic-poets, wedding signified and signifier in a seamless pre-Saussurean union: 'What was a mosscheeper,' he asks in 'Mossbawn', 'if not the soft, malicious sound the word itself made ...?' (*P* 18). As his readings of Clare, Mandelstam and Hopkins bear out, the union of sound and sign in nature is a model for the higher union again of writer and achieved poetic voice, such as he finds in Clare: 'an immense, creative volubility where human existence comes to life and has life more abundantly because it is now being expressed in its own self-gratifying and unhindered words' (*RP* 82). Heaney's image of self-confirmation – the voice issuing from and returning gratifyingly to the self – is another example of the groundedness and balance towards which his critical idiom so frequently gravitates.

For the most part Heaney presents this even-handedness as a virtue, as in the discussion of the scales that opens the title-essay of *The Redress of Poetry*, but there are times when the unruly material of poems disturbs the balance beyond the critic-poet's control. In the poem 'Weighing In', for example, Heaney's obsessive sense of fair play and impartiality gives way to exasperation. 'And this is all the good tidings amount to,' he complains, 'This principle of bearing, bearing up / And bearing out', against which he wishes for once 'To refuse the other cheek. To cast the stone' (*SL* 17). Even here though, the challenge to authority takes the form of a weight, not added to the scales but still solidly, stonily *there*. In his critical writings too, Heaney knows all about striking a balance and attempting to satisfy the competing claims of the imagination's freedoms and responsibilities. Yet here too, the forces opposing art sometimes weigh in so heavily that the 'redress' of art seems beyond the mere prose writer's powers. In 'Feeling into Words' Heaney indulges in gentle reminiscence of his beginnings as a writer before reaching the outbreak of the Troubles in 1969. Thereafter, 'the problems of poetry moved from being simply a matter of achieving the satisfactory verbal icon to being a search for images and symbols adequate to our predicament' (*P* 56). The writer is no longer his own creature, but stands arraigned before political tragedy, and bound to the collective fate of 'our predicament', as he describes and testifies to it again in other essays such as 'Belfast' and 'Through-Other Places, Through-Other Times: The Irish Poet and Britain'.

At moments of crisis like this, it is to Heaney the poet that Heaney the prose writer turns for a supporting witness. In the introductory essay of *The Government of the Tongue*, he recounts a crucial instance of this choice between freedom and responsibility. As Heaney and the musician David Hammond make their way to a recording studio in Belfast, a number of bombs go off. They continue on their way, but 'the very notion of beginning to sing at that moment when others were beginning to suffer seemed like an offence against their suffering' (*GT* xi), and the two men go home. In the already cited example from 'Frontiers of Writing', Heaney weighs up the competing claims of his lecture in Oxford and his personal dilemma as an Irish nationalist at the time of the hunger strikes, and reaches the opposite conclusion: this time there is no question of the furious noises-off disrupting the occasion, and, troubled though he is, Heaney stays put. What unites these examples is Heaney's need to do the right thing, and bear artistic witness accordingly; and, as the example of his essays on Plath, Mandelstam and Miłosz shows, Heaney's criticism is often at its most revealing when he pronounces on artists in the similar position of having to reconcile the claims of common human justice and the more unrelenting logic of art.

The first example I wish to discuss is Heaney's 1995 Nobel lecture, *Crediting Poetry*. This comes thirty years into his career, but in its 'down-to-earthness' (*CP* 12) returns the critic-poet to his beginnings, from which the vocation of poetry has led him outwards into the world, from the 'Stockholm' on the dial of his childhood radio to the Stockholm podium from which he now 'credits' his art, a journey he compares to 'walking on air' (*CP* 11). Heaney's title invites attention, coming so soon after the similarly ambiguous 'The Redress of Poetry' which he had used as a lecture title in 1989. Like his other book title, *The Government of the Tongue*, 'the Redress of Poetry' toys with the subjective/objective genitive ambiguity which so pleases Stephen Dedalus in the Nestor chapter of *Ulysses*. Is it we who govern the tongue and watch our words, or, in our innocence of the deeper workings of language, is it the tongue that governs us? Is it we who must offer redress to poetry, in our unliterary age, or we who receive it from that therapeutic art? Is it we who must credit poetry or poetry which inexhaustibly credits us? The answer in each case, ideally, is both, as Heaney pledges himself to a relationship of symbiotic reciprocity with his art:

> I credit poetry, in other words, both for being itself and for being a help, for making possible a fluid and restorative relationship between the mind's centre and its circumference ... I credit it because credit is due to it, in our time and in all time, for its truth to life, in every sense of that phrase. (*CP* 12)

With his imperative phrasing ('credit is due'), Heaney suggests a marketplace of value in which the normally private art of poetry has suddenly staked an unignorable claim. By being honoured as it has been, Heaney's lyric utterance is validated in the public sphere: these are words that carry weight. 'Money is a kind of poetry,' wrote Wallace Stevens, a poet who famously had lots of it; and, conversely, poetry is a currency of value invested in the poet even as it is *he* who credits *it*. If all the poet has to offer in a time of conflict is the 'meagre heat' of the sparks his art throws up (to borrow a phrase from his poem

'Exposure', which Heaney quotes in its entirety), his act of witness has still been underwritten to the point where Heaney can compare himself implicitly to Anna Akhmatova and Paul Celan, working out his private dilemmas in public in a way that remains 'true to the impact of external reality and ... sensitive to the inner laws of the poet's being' (*CP* 16). At the centre of the lecture is a gruesome example of violence from the Northern Irish Troubles, in which a group of workmen is stopped by gunmen and any Catholics instructed to step forward. The workmen mistakenly believe that the sole Catholic among them will be shot, and as he steps forward one of his workmates squeezes his hand in a signal of solidarity; mistaken solidarity, it turns out, since it is the Protestant workers who are then gunned down. 'It is difficult at times to repress the thought that history is about as instructive as an abattoir,' Heaney comments (*CP* 18), but in choosing to describe the scene the poet must believe his motives are more than voyeuristic. The crime is Dantean in its terror, in its stark confrontation of humanity and murderousness, but also in the way Heaney salvages from it the workman's small redeeming human gesture. 'Can you describe this?' as the woman in the prison queue asks Anna Akhmatova, 'And I said "I can."'[3]

Heaney then counterpoints this atrocity with the tale of St Kevin of Glendalough and the blackbird, the subject of a poem from *The Spirit Level*. Observing a bird building a nest on his outstretched hand, the saint stands immobile rather than disturb it. Sometimes, Heaney reminds us, wise passivity is the real challenge for the witnessing artist, when clumsy action would spoil everything. As the lecture moves towards a conclusion, Heaney turns to the tutelary example of Yeats, even taking the opportunity to rebuke his predecessor for a moment in 'The Municipal Gallery Revisited' when his art appears to be 'flourishing rather than proving itself', and conducting a leisurely 'lap of honour' (*CP* 24). He cites 'Nineteen Hundred and Nineteen' and 'Meditations in Time of Civil War' as examples of 'that completely adequate art' he has in mind instead, in which (once again) the full satisfactions of poetry are achieved without diluting the tragic dimension of right art in the midst of historical 'wrongness' (*CP* 27, 29). But as he acknowledges in his admission that he too is enjoying a 'lap of honour', this is not one of those moments in Heaney's prose when his natural instinct to strike a tidy balance is going to be disappointed, and in truth the lecture's closing cadences show us Heaney on autopilot ('Poetic form is both the ship and the anchor. It is at once a buoyancy and a holding'; *CP* 29), settling for the emolliently affirmative over anything more unpredictable or disconcerting.

For my second example, I would like to consider Heaney on a writer it would be not just reckless but calamitous to approach in a spirit of critical autopilot: Dante. Bernard O'Donoghue has noted Heaney's 'absolute concentration on lyric poetry' in his criticism,[4] to the exclusion of Shakespeare for example; but, while the epic scale of Dante's work has rendered him as fixed a figure as Yeats in Heaney's poetry, since at least the time of *Field Work*, it is odd that his one extended essay on Dante, 'Envies and Identifications: Dante and the Modern Poet', should have been omitted from *The Government of the Tongue* (an abridged version appears in *Finders Keepers*).[5] With a writer who looms large in Heaney's pantheon such as Patrick Kavanagh, there is always the suspicion that as a safely minor figure he can be moulded to Heaney's will. With Dante there is no such possibility, and instead what we find is Heaney the follower, just as in the *Commedia* Dante himself casts himself in the role of mere follower to Virgil as guide. Almost as though taking cover, Heaney approaches Dante first by way of Eliot's 'Little Gidding' and later Osip Mandelstam's 'Conversation about Dante'; so, while the subject of Heaney and Dante is deserving of a monograph to itself, I will be restricting my remarks here to Heaney's approaches to Dante through these other two exemplary figures. Mandelstam wrote of 'nostalgia for world culture', and as Heaney quotes Eliot's lordly pronouncements about Dante's 'universality' the thrill of connection to such an authoritative and bountiful culture is unmistakable. His comments on Eliot are a revealing mix of the poetic rapacity and submissiveness he finds in Eliot and by implication in himself too: 'He had always taken what he needed from [Dante] and at this stage what he needed was a way of confirming himself as a poet ready to submit his intelligence and sensibility to a framework of beliefs which were inherited and communal' (*FK* 173).[6] Where Heaney parts company with Eliot is over the issue of the vernacular. Contrasting Dante and Shakespeare, Eliot locates the Italian poet in a realm of 'classically ratified' purity, free of the rough edges and mongrel admixtures of Shakespeare's English, and of interest to him for his ability to 'turn values and judgements into poetry', as the Eliot of *Four Quartets* was also so concerned to do (*FK* 174).

'This Dante is essentially lyric', Heaney writes of the Dante that interests him most, and as early as the opening lines of the *Commedia* he finds examples of word music that makes a 'swarming, mobbish' sound in his mouth ('*smarrita*', '*selva selvaggia*'), 'as barbarous as Hopkins' in its way (*FK* 176, 173). But this is Mandelstam's Dante, not Eliot's. Just as Virgil can only accompany Dante some of the way on his journey, the crux between the poet of values and judgement and the poet of stridulent Tuscan consonants precipitates Heaney's transition from Eliot to Mandelstam. Mandelstam began to appear in Heaney's work just before Dante (in *North* rather than *Field Work*), and Heaney's discovery of the Russian poet must count as one of the great discoveries of his imaginative life. Many of my examples from Heaney's prose have highlighted his passion for tropes of symmetry and reciprocity, and just as Heaney plays his part in sponsoring Mandelstam's reception in English, Mandelstam now plays his part in making Dante available to Heaney. When he lays out a selection of quotations from Mandelstam's 'Conversation about Dante', Heaney is acting in accordance with Mandelstam's love of quotations: 'A quotation is a cicada', he writes, a small voice singing in the grass of its host text.[7] Among this menagerie of quotations, one in particular answers to Heaney's onomatopoeic aesthetic: as he learned Italian, Mandelstam notes, he felt the 'centre of gravity' of his speech move forward in his mouth to his lip. He quotes and relishes examples of Dante's 'peculiar labial music': 'It's as if a nurse had participated in the creation of phonetics' (*FK* 176).

Sharing Mandelstam's relish of the 'smacking, sucking and whistling sounds'[8] of Dante's Italian, Heaney manages to keep his distance from the drier deliberations of Eliot's essay. It is only fair to add, then, that among the brilliant and swaggering maxims Mandelstam pours forth, not a few go entirely against the grain of Heaney's poetics. As a veteran of Acmeism, an offshoot of Russian symbolism, Mandelstam had a strong belief in the autonomy of the word from what it signifies: 'poetry is not a part of nature ... let alone a reflection of it'.[9] His delight in Dante's *d* and *z* sounds notwithstanding, Mandelstam distances poetry from what he calls 'sounding' with a distinctly anti-phonocentric argument: 'we hear in it only the crossing of two lines, one of which, taken by itself, is completely mute, while the other, abstracted from its prosodic transmutation, is totally devoid of significance and interest'.[10] Mandelstam's position is complex, and any full discussion of it would involve an account of contemporary trends in Russian symbolism and futurism, his arguments with Andrei Bely, and his own poetic practice in works such as 'Octets'. Heaney bypasses all of this to lead the discussion back to questions of biography and the poet as witness: what Mandelstam's Dante reflects, for him, is the crisis in the Russian poet's life in the 1930s. 'Conversation about Dante' dates from 1933, the year before Mandelstam's ill-starred private reading of the 'Ode to Stalin' which led to his exile to Cherdyn and Voronezh. For Heaney, Mandelstam's efforts to reach an accommodation with socialist realism were bound to come to nothing, and while one consequence of this was the poet's exile, another was his liberation into a view of art as 'free, natural, biological process ... a focus for all the impulsive, instinctive, non-utilitarian elements in his creative life' (*FK* 178). The essay ends with an image of the poet breaking free from Soviet ideology, finding in Dante 'a guide who wears no official badge, enforces no party line' (*FK* 178–9).

The essay is a moving tribute from one artist to another, even if our misgivings about Heaney's use of Mandelstam do not quite go away.

Heaney does not pretend to be writing a literary-historical account of Russian poetry in the first half of the twentieth century, and is no doubt correct in guessing his readers will find the tragedy of Mandelstam's life more compelling than an account of the niceties of Acmeism versus socialist realism. If he is liberated here from one form of artistic constraint, the threat remains that he should become imprisoned in the story of his martyrdom, and its usefulness to Heaney's own situation, a threat that his treatment in *The Government of the Tongue* does nothing to assuage. Similarly, Heaney's talk of 'free, natural, biological process' should not obscure the real aesthetic disagreements that are being glossed over in 'Envies and Identifications'. When he argues onomatopoeically in *The Government of the Tongue*, but in the absence of any working knowledge of Russian, that a Mandelstam stanza 'has the resonant impact of late Yeats' (*GT* 79), according to an unnamed Russian poet, he is presuming a natural familiarity too far between himself and the Russian poet. A triangular relationship is established between Heaney, Yeats and Mandelstam, but on the level of wilful identification rather than critical demonstration. Paradoxically, this identification can have the effect of blurring the critical object before our eyes, inhibiting the more straightforward or technical description of Russian or Polish poetry Heaney might have given us instead, but which he has chosen not to. Heaney's elective affinity with Dante and Mandelstam achieves much – *Station Island* and *The Haw Lantern* could hardly have been written without them – but, to return to Peter McDonald's insistence that we take a '*critical*' interest in Heaney's prose, this does not exempt Heaney from serious questions about the use to which he has put them, as the probing readings these essays have received elsewhere more than demonstrates.[11]

One final test case for Heaney's criticism is the work of Philip Larkin, sometime librarian of Queen's University Belfast, but a writer whose name Heaney graduated without hearing once, according to his memoir of studying poetry as an undergraduate in that city (*FK* 39). Heaney's poem about Larkin at the beginning of *Seeing Things*, 'The Journey Back', is at best an ambivalent example of Dante's influence, drawing the English poet back from the shades for him to 'surprise' Heaney by quoting the Italian poet (*ST* 7). (Surprising indeed for a poet who never showed any inclination to do so during his lifetime.) In Heaney's prose, Larkin features in 'Englands of the Mind', where he holds up the Norman corner of the English poetic equation, in tandem with the Anglo-Saxon Ted Hughes and the Latin Geoffrey Hill. He features again in 'The Main of Light', an affectionate if slightly patronising tribute which aligns Larkin firmly with the 1950s Movement compromise (in Donald Davie's phrase) of 'a poetry of lowered sights and patently diminished expectations' even if he 'did not completely settle' for it (*GT* 22).

(Heaney's insistence that Larkin's collected work 'would fit happily under the title *Englanders*', forgetting his forays into Prestatyn, Dublin and Belfast, betrays an anxiety to restrict Larkin to a specifically national mode.) But it is in 'Joy or Night: Last Things in the Poetry of W. B. Yeats and Philip Larkin' that Heaney makes his major critical statement on the English poet. Given his habitually benevolent tenor, 'Joy or Night' is all the more notable for the hostile stand it takes against the defeatism Heaney detects in Larkin's 'Aubade'. As we will see, the implications of his stance go far beyond a local argument about the merits of a single poem written in 1977 by a depressed librarian in Hull.

Larkin's 'Aubade' is a famously comfortless poem. The poet wakes at dawn to the terrified realisation that he is going to die, and rejects all religious consolation but, equally, rejects the humanist consolation that '*No rational being / Can fear a thing it will not feel.*' What he feels instead is naked, sweaty terror. Contrasting this with the defiance he finds in Yeats's work, Heaney pronounces Larkin wanting. In Lawrence's phrase, it seems he 'does the dirt on life':

> 'Aubade' does not go over to the side of the adversary. But its argument does add weight to the negative side of the scale and tips the balance definitely in favour of chemical law and mortal decline. The poem does not hold the lyre up in the face of the gods of the underworld; it does not make the Orphic effort to haul life back up the slope against all the odds. For all its truth-breaking truths and beauties, 'Aubade' reneges on what Yeats called the 'spiritual intellect's great work'. (*RP* 158)

Heaney quotes Miłosz on Larkin: for the Polish poet there is a straightforward dereliction of the poet's duty to uphold 'faith in life everlasting', and the 'centuries-old mutual hostility between reason, science ... and poetry' (*RP* 158) (though Heaney's other Eastern European exemplar, Miroslav Holub, might have something to say about that). Heaney does not echo Miłosz exactly, sidestepping religion to embrace 'the condition of overlife' embodied by the achieved poem, which places itself 'on the side of life' against 'chemical law and mortal decline'. But even as he backtracks on Miłosz's Catholic dogmatism, Heaney runs into problems of his own. By now the sceptical reader is entitled to answers from Heaney to some difficult questions, such as: Has his negative reading of 'Aubade' disproved Larkin's beliefs about death, or merely found fault with it as a poem? Does the successful poem refute death or merely state the case against it? If the former, is art an accessory of, or substitute for, religion? How do we tell the difference between a belief and an imaginative statement of belief? Is all art 'on the side of life'? If so, how can this be a value judgement and not just a tautology? Is it an artistic or a moral shortcoming if a writer fails to come down 'on the side of life?' What might an art look like that is not 'on the side of life', and is it beyond Heaney's powers to describe (or produce)?

Unlike Miłosz, then, Heaney is not basing his objections to 'Aubade' on theological grounds. It is not because what Larkin says about death is wrong that Heaney finds it unpalatable: rather, it is a question of literary good behaviour and Larkin's unseemly flouting of it. Larkin does not pay sufficient obeisance to the Yeatsian 'phantasmagoria' of mythic resource in the face of bodily decrepitude and death, and this necessarily leads to immature and imperfect art. Heaney complicates his argument when he contrasts Larkin unfavourably with Samuel Beckett, 'a very clear example of a writer who is Larkin's equal in not flinching from the ultimate bleakness of things, but who then goes on to do something positive with the bleakness' (*RP* 159). The implication is that by indulging in black humour, as Beckett does, he has done 'something positive' with his despair, and somehow absolved us from having to take it seriously. But this is to praise Beckett only at the cost of neutering his work. How would Heaney answer an indignant Beckett who insisted that, no, he really did mean it? By now Heaney's nervous insistence on art that contributes 'something positive' is looking like too high a price to pay for our continued assent to such a reductive and blinkered reading of Larkin's poem.

Following the example of F. R. Leavis, much mid-twentieth-century British and Irish criticism took as its supreme value the epic yet blank category of 'life': life is what we find in great literature, and great literature is where we look to find out about life. It does not require a belief in the anti-humanism of literary theory to find this a dubious tautology, but in his appeals to 'life' Heaney argues from a position of unmistakably Leavisite vitalism. Writing is on the side of 'life' or, in the Heaneyesque coinage, 'overlife', and anything failing to muster the necessary good cheer in its defence stands self-condemned of treachery and desertion. Whatever his other merits, Larkin has placed himself beyond the pale; but the same could just easily be said of Paul Celan, Tadeusz Rózewicz or Michaux (not, whatever else they are, poets of 1950s Movement compromise). When Beckett asks of Axel Kaun, 'Is there something paralysingly holy in the vicious nature of the word that is not found in the element of the other arts?' and expresses a desire to 'leave nothing undone that might contribute to [language] falling into disrepute',[12] he is stating a position in every way at odds with the positivities of Heaney's argument. At this point, touching on one of the limits of Heaney's criticism, the simplest solution is to echo Tim Kendall's assessment of *The Redress of Poetry*: namely, that Heaney 'defines and celebrates one kind of poetry, not poetry in general'.[13] Heaney is a gifted reader of Kavanagh, Clare, Auden and

Lowell, but will never be the critic we turn to on Samuel Beckett, John Ashbery or J. H. Prynne.

Peter McDonald addresses a related issue in a probing essay on *Finders Keepers*. Examining Heaney's use of the word 'vocation', McDonald points to the ability of Heaney's affirmative instincts to carry his opinions before them in his prose, giving us only 'the good news' about poetry in a spirit of Arnoldian uplift but baulking at anything more uncomfortable:

> [T]his is the prose of a man whom the audience always applauds, and for whom the uncertainties, contradictions, difficulties, and ambiguities of language and memory are always going to be reassuringly resolved in the end ... However we admire the performance, it is less critical exertion and all-out struggle than it is a relaxed lap of honour.[14]

One answer to McDonald's strictures is that Heaney is simply not an authoritarian critic, and not concerned to police the canon or impose himself on his material; his few, muted references to literary theory suggest a horror of a kind of criticism which would presume to supplant its object. When we bring up names such as Ashbery or Prynne we are making a category error: they are simply not in Heaney's tradition, nor is he in theirs. But, granted all these objections, why should we have a problem with a critic-poet who would rather praise than damn, who would rather write about poets he knows than those who are alien to him, and who uses autobiography in ways that occasionally encroach on the strictly critical integrity of what he is up to? One last time, are we reading Heaney for what he has to say about others or what he reveals about himself?

I began this essay with a taxonomy of the different kinds of critic-poet, and before reaching a judgement on Heaney's standing among them, I would like to consider the verdict of Adam Kirsch on one of the best-loved critic-poets of all, Randall Jarrell. Kirsch argues that 'Intelligent admiration', such as he finds in Jarrell, 'is the best way to teach poetry, to incite in a novice the desire to read. But it is not criticism, which assumes an audience already interested and somewhat knowledgeable.'[15] This is the audience that Jarrell fails at those key moments when, instead of coolly explicating the greatness of his favourite poets, of Whitman, Robert Frost or William Carlos Williams, 'he explicitly abjures criticism, even speech, and just points dumbly'. For Kirsch this is a failure of critical will to power, the kind of will to power that drives critics to abandon all impartiality and gloriously (or ingloriously) impose themselves on their subjects. In the case of Eliot on Shelley or Arnold on Dryden and Pope, the resultant readings may be entirely wrong-headed yet still strike us as 'right', because '[the critics] are forcefully expressing their own sensibility'. For a reader of Kirsch's persuasion, Heaney would appear for the most part to fall into the category of an intelligent admirer and advocate rather than a true critic. And, it must be said, the list of what Heaney does *not* do in his criticism is indeed extensive and suggestive of serious limitations. Unlike T. S. Eliot or Marianne Moore, he has never yoked his critical authority to an editorial chair and created not just an individual body of work but a critical atmosphere that defines a generation; unlike Yeats, Robert Graves and Ted Hughes, he has not written an extended poetics on the lines of *A Vision, The White Goddess* or *Shakespeare and the Goddess of Supreme Being*; there exists a whole constellation of twentieth-century poets Heaney's thoughts on whom are unknown to us, including figures as diverse (to take only Americans) as Duncan, Niedecker, Oppen, Zukofsky, Olson, Creeley, O'Hara, Kees, Merrill, Spicer, Ammons and the L=A=N=G=U=A=G=E poets; unlike Pound he has not harnessed his criticism to the cause of radical experiment, made it his business to champion the cause of young unknowns, made the reputation of any emerging writers or, conversely, offered an entirely new and unprecedented reading of a canonical poet; and unlike Winters or Davie his criticism is entirely lacking in programmatic denunciation and ferocity, not that these things in themselves are any guarantee of critical strength.

The one instance of a strongly negative reading, I have argued, is also the essay in which Heaney's findings are at their most debatable. If we follow Kirsch's argument, the very tenacity of Heaney's wrongness on Larkin can be read as no more (or less) than an expression of the strong critic in action. But if Eliot on Shelley or Arnold on Pope are examples of strong critics, their wrongness only makes sense against the backdrop of so much besides that is right; and in Heaney's case too, the many more essays not discussed here – on Dylan Thomas, Marlowe, Brodsky, Bishop, MacDiarmid, Thomas Kinsella and Edwin Muir, among others – form solid evidence of the critical authority that mitigates for his lapse on Larkin. To adopt a Heaneyesque strategy of weighing up, it is only natural justice even as we find fault not to lose sight of all that makes this criticism so valuable. These essays are a record, with few contemporary equals, of a writer responding with critical magnanimity to his subjects and succeeding at the same time in taking what he needs from them to further his own art. If his use of Mandelstam and other Eastern European poets seems misjudged, his capacity to avoid the charges of egotism and appropriation in responding to so many other poets is entirely praiseworthy. He has written a critical prose that is in its own way creative, a prose that, in Neil Corcoran's phrase, 'seems to steady itself for the new poem that will flower from the encounter' with its subjects;[16] and if this dilutes the critical purity of the enterprise, or denies it the stature of the very best criticism, the poetic dividend that results from these encounters has been its own form of compensation. No critic should ever wish that a poet spent more time writing essays than writing poems, but neither could any critic see Heaney's prose as having interrupted or deflected its author's creativity. We value these essays not just for their insights into Heaney's poetry, but for their integral part in the creative process of his work as a whole; and that, in the magnificent understatement that closes the poem 'Tollund', must in every way be judged 'Not bad' (*SL* 69).

NOTES

1. Christian Wiman, 'A Piece of Prose', in *Twentieth-Century American Poetics: Poets on the Art of Poetry*, ed. Dana Gioia, David Mason and Meg Schoerke (Boston: McGraw-Hill, 2004), p. 488.
2. Peter McDonald, 'Appreciating Assets', review of *Finders Keepers*, *Poetry Review*, 92:2 (Summer 2002), p. 79.
3. Anna Akhmatova, *Selected Poems*, tr. Stanley Kunitz and Max Hayward (London: Collins Harvill, 1989), p. 99.
4. Bernard O'Donoghue, *Seamus Heaney and the Language of Poetry* (Hemel Hempstead: Harvester Wheatsheaf, 1994), p. 144.
5. The full text of 'Envies and Identifications' can be found in *Irish University Review* 15:1 (Spring 1985), pp. 5–19.
6. The tussle between personal freedom and submission to authority goes deeper than anxieties of poetic influence: Neil Corcoran notes the deep imprint 'the corrective confessionalism' of Catholic theology has left on Heaney's critical vocabulary (*The Poetry of Seamus Heaney: A Critical Study* [London: Faber and Faber, 1998], p. 210).
7. Osip Mandelstam, 'Conversations about Dante', *The Collected Critical Prose and Letters* tr. Jane Gary Harris and Constance Link, ed. Jane Gary Harris (London: Collins Harvill, 1991), p. 401.
8. Ibid., p. 430.
9. Ibid., p. 397. See Robert Tracy's introduction to his translation of Mandelstam's *Stone* (London: Collins Harvill, 1991), pp. 18ff., for a useful account of Acmeist theory.
10. Mandelstam, 'Conversation about Dante', p. 397.
11. I am indebted here to Justin Quinn's Chapter 6 in this volume, 'Heaney and Eastern Europe', which contains a further discussion on this topic.
12. Samuel Beckett, 'German Letter of 1937', in *Disjecta: Miscellaneous Writings and Dramatic Fragment* (London: John Calder, 1983), p. 172. The translation from German is by Martin Esslin.
13. Tim Kendall, 'An Enormous Yes?: The Redress of Poetry', in *The Art of Seamus Heaney*, ed. Tony Curtis (Dublin: Wolfhound Press, 2001), p. 238.
14. Peter McDonald, 'Appreciating Assets', p. 79.
15. Adam Kirsch, review of Randall Jarrell's *No Other Book* and Mary von Schrader Jarrell's *Remembering Randall, Times Literary Supplement* (6 August 1999), p. 24.
16. Corcoran, *Poetry of Seamus Heaney*, p. 233.

9

ANDREW MURPHY

Heaney and the Irish Poetic Tradition

In discussing the position of the aspirant Irish writer of the 1920s and 1930s, Terence Brown observes that, for such an author, 'the anxiety of influence pressed with a peculiarly intimate insistence. He was perhaps a rueful late guest at a literary feast celebrated as the Irish Literary Revival.'[1] The Revival – that flowering of Irish cultural endeavour from the 1880s to the 1920s, which drew heavily on a romanticised version of a mythical Irish past – cast a long shadow which extended, of course, well beyond the early decades of the twentieth century. Neil Corcoran, in his contribution to this present volume, discusses the ways in which Heaney struggled to come to terms with, in particular, the Yeatsian inheritance. In general terms, however, Heaney has clearly valued the work of the Revivalists, seeing them as offering a kind of cultural sustenance to their literary successors. A certain 'nourishment', he observes 'became available more abundantly to us as a result of the achievements of the Irish Literary Revival, and much of its imaginative protein was extracted from the sense of place' they provided (*P* 136).

The 'sense of place' evoked by Revivalist writers was a complex construct, being tied to specific locations (Coole Park, the Aran Islands, Thoor Ballylee, etc.), but also being heavily overlaid with mythologies of various kinds (Celticist, Ascendancy, Classical, etc.). At times the Revivalist writers also appeared to operate at one remove from their subject matter. Thus J. M. Synge famously observed in the Preface to *The Playboy of the Western World* that, when he was writing an earlier play (*The Shadow of the Glen*), he 'got more aid than any learning could have given me from a chink in the floor of the old Wicklow house where I was staying, that let me hear what was being said by servant girls in the kitchen'.[2] Synge appears in this image as a middle-class metropolitan straining to catch the accents and attitudes of ordinary rural life from a closeted distance. His writing has thus sometimes been criticised as presenting overdrawn caricatures, his characters speaking a language that fails to equate to any natural Irish speech.

While the later Heaney could certainly, as we have already noted, see beyond these criticisms, to understand the value of what the Revivalists achieved, it is likely that his younger self might have wished for a literature that was a little more immediately connected to the world of his own direct experience. In his early twenties, Heaney – a farmer's son with a degree in English from a Queen's University where he 'had not ever been taught by an Irish or an Ulster voice' (*GT* 7) – still experienced the rarefied world of the literary and the academic as something of a foreign country. He characterises himself as belonging, at this age, to a Northern Irish literary generation who 'stood or hung or sleep-walked between notions of writing ... gleaned from English courses and the living reality of writers from our own place whom we did not know, in person or in print' (*P* 28). An important turning point for Heaney at this early stage in his writing career was the discovery of the work of the Monaghan poet, Patrick Kavanagh. Kavanagh was himself also the son of farming stock (and he worked as a farmer for much of his early life), and he was a writer whose 'sense of place' differed markedly from that of the Revivalists, being drawn from rooted and immediate living experience. What Kavanagh offered Heaney was a sense of locatedness with which he could identify in a direct and immediate manner. He also presented the young poet with a mode of writing in which language, as Heaney himself puts it, 'is not used as a picturesque idiom but as the writer's own natural speech'. Again, Heaney notes, 'this points to Kavanagh's essential difference from the Revival writers' (*P* 138).

Early in the 1960s, Heaney encountered Kavanagh's work in the *Oxford Book of Irish Verse* (1958). Reading 'Spraying the Potatoes' (1947) he was, he tells us, 'excited to find details of a life which I knew intimately – but which I had always considered to be below or beyond books – being presented in a book' (*GT* 7). Heaney's observation here resonates with Kavanagh's own sense of his aesthetic project, which was precisely (in the earlier stretch of his career, at least) to claim a poetic value for the everyday and the commonplace. Thus, in 'Spraying the Potatoes', the trivial, conventional chatter of a pair of farmers is afforded the same status as regal discourse:

> He eyed the potato-drills.
> He said: 'You are bound to have good ones there.'
>
> We talked and our talk was a theme of kings,
> A theme for strings.[3]

In a much-repeated set of observations, Kavanagh drew a distinction between the 'provincial' and the 'parochial'. 'Parochialism and provincialism are direct opposites,' he observes: 'The provincial has no mind of his own; he does not trust what his eyes see until he has heard what the metropolis – towards which his eyes are turned – has to say on any subject.' By contrast, the 'parochial mentality ... is never in any doubt about the social and artistic validity of his parish'.[4] This doctrine closely matches Heaney's own sense, from early in his career, of the importance of home ground and native community.[5]

For Heaney, Kavanagh's work was profoundly enabling; reading Kavanagh, he tells us, helped to 'throw the switch that sends writing energy sizzling into a hitherto unwriting system' (*GT* 8). The filiations between Heaney's early work and Kavanagh's poetic vision are abundantly clear – so clear, in fact, that when Heaney was asked why he had never dedicated a poem to the older man, he replied simply 'I had no need to ... I wrote *Death of a Naturalist*.'[6] Kavanagh's influence is indeed obvious on every page of that first full-length collection (and on many later works as well). Heaney celebrates there the quotidian and the local, drawing his subject matter from the rural world of his childhood. The titles of the poems themselves bear this out: 'The Barn', 'Blackberry-Picking', 'Cow in Calf', 'In Small Townlands', to select just a few representative samples. In the later period of his career, Heaney finds further enabling value in another version of Kavanagh: a late Kavanagh, less tied to the immediate present, for whom 'the world is more pervious to his vision than he is pervious to the world. When he writes about places now, they are luminous spaces within his mind. They have been evacuated of their status as background, as documentary geography, and exist instead as transfigured images, sites where the mind projects its own force' (*GT* 5). For the Heaney of a collection such as *Seeing Things*, this formulation is of particular importance, as it facilitates his complex poetic negotiations between the material and the transcendent.

If Kavanagh offered a different 'sense of place' and of language from the Revivalists, he also afforded other kinds of resistance to their larger project, observing that, while it 'purported to be frightfully Irish and racy of the Celtic soil', in actuality it 'was a thoroughgoing English-bred lie'.[7] The bitterness of Kavanagh's condemnation here points to a certain sense of disjunction in Irish literary culture which set in during the early decades of the twentieth century. The fault line of this fracture can be traced back in part to the work of Daniel Corkery. Corkery's *Hidden Ireland* was first published in 1924, just two years after the greater part of the island of Ireland had attained independence from Britain as a 'Free State'. In his book, Corkery, in keeping with the general temper of the times, sought to push past Revivalism to trace an extended native Irish literary tradition. This programme had a certain ethnic, political and religious edge to it. The

Revivalists had, for the most part, come from Protestant backgrounds and had aligned themselves with a liberal strain in the Ascendancy tradition. In seeking a literary heritage Yeats, on the one hand, looked back to the nineteenth-century nationalist 'Young Irelander' poets ('Nor may I less be counted one / With Davis, Mangan, Ferguson ... ')[8] and, as Heaney himself has noted, 'honoured their patriotic fervour and wanted his own work to be coloured by the same sentiments – chthonic, national, Celtic'.[9] On the other hand, Yeats also constructed for himself an Ascendancy Protestant pantheon that included 'Goldsmith and Burke, Swift and the Bishop of Cloyne [George Berkeley]'.[10] Corkery, in the wake of independence, wanted, in essence, to establish an Irish literary line that he considered to be wholly native: undiluted by what was imagined to be 'foreign' influence. Part of this ambition involved an act of recovery – bringing back to attention an Irish-language literature which had largely dropped from sight during the long period of British rule. Corkery wished to convey to his readers the value of the work of such writers as Aogán Ó Rathaille (*c.* 1675–1729), Eoghan Rua Ó Súilleabháin (1748–84), Eibhlín Dhubh Ní Chonaill (*fl.* 1770), Bryan Merriman (1749–1805) and Antoine Raifteirí (1784–1835). In addition to this act of recovery, he also had a more polemical agenda, as he argued that the distinguishing marks of this literature were 'Nationality, Religion, Rebellion'.[11] Corkery's work thus spawned a sense of true Irish cultural identity as being exclusively native, Catholic, ideally Irish-speaking and – by implication at least – anti-British.

Corkery's book was written in a period of some optimism, as the fledgling Irish state struggled to achieve a sense of identity. In the year following the first appearance of *The Hidden Ireland*, J.L. O'Sullivan translated *Macbeth* into Irish and observed in his foreword that 'In a little while, it is our hope, we shall be Irish-speaking, Irish-reading. We have at the moment, in the desks of our National Schools, the boys and girls who will be the future writers of a new and vigorous school of modern Irish literature.'[12] O'Sullivan's confidence was misplaced; the Irish-language project conspicuously failed. Likewise, the Catholicism that Corkery had found to be so sustaining an element of native identity came increasingly to be felt as an oppressive and deadening force – not least because of the strict censorship laws that it prompted. By the end of the 1930s, the poet Austin Clarke was damning the new cultural regime with pithy economical force:

Penal Law

Burn Ovid with the rest. Lovers will find
A hedge-school for themselves and learn by heart
All that the clergy banish from the mind,
When hands are joined and head bows in the dark.[13]

At the same time, however, Clarke found the Irish-language poetic heritage – which Corkery had been instrumental in bringing to the foreground – to be fruitfully sustaining. He attempted a kind of cross-breeding of Irish and English prosody, producing, as Neil Corcoran has noted, 'a poetry heavily dependent on systems of assonance, alliteration, and internal rhyme rather than end-rhyme'.[14] Clarke was not the only poet who attempted a productive engagement with the extended tradition that Corkery had made more generally available. In the next generation Thomas Kinsella (who edited Clarke's *Selected Poems*) worked as both a poet and a translator, bringing the eighth-century Ulster cycle of heroic poems, the *Táin Bó Cuailnge* to a wider audience and also publishing, in 1981, an important anthology of Irish poetry in *An Duanaire: Poems of the Dispossessed, 1600–1900* – a collection which shared a certain amount of common ground with Corkery's original project. Kinsella has argued that 'the Irish tradition is a matter of two linguistic entities in dynamic interaction, of two major bodies of poetry asking to be understood together as functions of a shared and painful history'.[15] In the same generation as Kinsella, John Montague has also written poems which attempt to establish a sense of continuity between contemporary Irish life, landscape and culture and its deep native past.

Heaney has been influenced by all of these developments in a variety of different ways. He has honoured Eibhlín Dhubh Ní Chonaill's *Caoineadh Airt Ui Laoghaire* – a passionate lament for her dead husband, killed by English soldiers in 1774 – as 'an outburst both heartbroken and formal, a howl of sorrow and a triumph of rhetoric', which 'proclaimed for almost the last time the integrity of the Gaelic order and the ordained place of poetry within that order'. He has also applauded the 'hammer-and-tongs vernacular' and 'buoyant couplets' of Bryan Merriman's eighteenth-century *Cúirt an Mheán-Oíche*, proposing filiations between Merriman's work and that of the contemporary Irish-language poet Nuala Ní Dhomhnaill (*RP* 39, 40, 54). Heaney has offered his own translation of sections of Merriman's poem in *The Midnight Verdict*, reading it 'within the acoustic of the classical myth' of Orpheus.[16] A more ambitious project has been his translation of *Buile Suibhne* – the medieval story of a petty king, Sweeney, transformed into a bird by a saint's curse and doomed to wander the island of Ireland without finding rest, singing of his plight during the course of his journey. Part of the attraction of the narrative for Heaney is that it offers an insight into a culture that 'was clearly in the grip of a tension between the newly dominant Christian ethos and the older, recalcitrant Celtic temperament,' thus affording a point of entry into two conflicting native traditions (*SA* vii). Heaney began his work on *Sweeney Astray* by freely adapting from the original, drawing as much on the standard existing translation by J. G. O'Keeffe as on the Irish text itself. In time, however, he started 'to reshape stanzas from scratch, rhyming them and keeping my eyes as much to the left, on the Irish, as to the right, on O'Keeffe's unnerving trot' (*FK* 64). Sweeney has often been seen in the Irish tradition as a kind of figure for the poet (as expressive, rootless outsider), and Heaney has registered his own particular affiliation with this notion, especially given the rhyming resonance between his own surname and the name of the displaced king.

In addition to taking an interest in the texts of the Irish-language tradition, Heaney also connects with the nativist poetics pursued by John Montague, whose collection *The Rough Field* was published in the same year as Heaney's *Wintering Out*. Heaney himself astutely distinguishes between the poetic projects of Montague and of Patrick Kavanagh. He argues that, while both poets celebrate the local, their final objectives differ significantly:

> Montague's exploration follows Corkery's tracks in a way that Kavanagh's does not. There is an element of cultural and political resistance and retrieval in Montague's work that is absent from Kavanagh's. What is hidden at the bottom of Montague's region is first of all a pagan civilization centred on the dolmen; then a Gaelic civilization centred on the O'Neill inauguration stone at Tullyhogue. The ancient feminine religion of Northern Europe is the lens through which he looks and the landscape becomes a memory, a piety, a loved mother (*P* 141).

Heaney nicely suggests that when Montague walks the land of his native region 'he can think of himself as a survivor, a repository, a bearer and keeper of what had almost been lost'. By contrast, 'when Kavanagh walks through others' farms, he will think of himself as a trespasser rather than a survivor' (*P* 141, 142).

The poems included in the 'Severed Head' sequence of Montague's *The Rough Field* nicely illustrate the poetic disposition that Heaney identifies as characteristic of this fellow Ulster poet. The sequence begins in the present with 'The Road's End', detailing a walk across a familiar landscape, redolent of the speaker's own youth. In the final stanza, he contemplates a set of ruined cabins, 'deserted / In my lifetime', and recalls their old inhabitants. This sets the scene for the second poem, 'A Lost Tradition', in which the pastward movement intensifies, spiralling down through the centuries until we arrive at early modern Ireland and the era when the O'Neill clan dominated this region of Ireland. We reach this historical moment in part through Montague's glossing of the name of his own home county, Tyrone: '*Tír Eoghain*: Land of Owen, / Province of the O'Niall'. From here we move to a series of poems on the last of the O'Neill chieftains: Con Bachach, Seán an Diomas and Hugh. We then learn of Hugh O'Neill's final defeat by the English at the battle of

Kinsale and his eventual flight into exile together with the rest of the native northern Irish aristocracy in 1607 ('After Kinsale, 1604' and 'The Flight of the Earls'). The loss of the O'Neill dynasty decisively signalled the breaking of Irish power in the region and ultimately provided the occasion for the 'planting' of Scottish settlers in Ulster, the ancestors of the present-day Protestant community. The defeat of the native population is emblematised in the penultimate poem of the sequence in the suppression of the Irish language, with Montague's attenuated lines mirroring an asphyxiated expressiveness: 'Dumb, / bloodied, the severed / head now chokes to / speak another tongue.' The final poem, however, posits the emergence of a hybrid form of English, in which both Scottish planter and native Irish traditions are simultaneously inscribed: 'Names twining braid Scots and Irish, / Like Fall Brae, springing native / As a whitethorn bush.'[17]

The set of gestures and manoeuvres presented in this sequence of poems will be familiar to readers of Heaney. Indeed, the very verse forms would also be familiar, as so many of the poems in *The Rough Field* appear as thin columns on the page – a format characteristic of Heaney's work during the phase of what Bernard O'Donoghue has styled his 'artesian stanza'.[18] For Heaney, the narrowly constrained line allows him, precisely, to use the poem as a way of drilling down from the present into the past. Oftentimes, in Heaney as in Montague, the point of arrival of the poem is the early modern period, and Hugh O'Neill makes an appearance in Heaney's 'Terminus' – 'the last earl on horseback in midstream / Still parleying, in earshot of his peers' (*HL* 5) – just as he does in the 'Severed Head' sequence. Montague and Heaney have other figures from this period in common as well, such as Edmund Spenser, whose *View of the Present State of Ireland* (1595) is quoted by Montague in the 'Patriotic Suite' section of *The Rough Field* and by Heaney in 'Bog Oak'. Both poets also push through from the early modern to something more distant: through 'shards of a lost tradition'[19] to the dolmen world of pagan Ireland in Montague's case; through 'loam, flints, musket-balls, / fragmented ware, / torcs and fish-bones' (*WO* 16) to a northern European sacrificial fertility cult in Heaney's. Montague's etymologised geography (Tyrone = *Tír Eoghain* = land of Eoin; Garvaghey = *garbh acaidh* = the rough field) is matched by Heaney in poems such as 'Broagh' and 'Anahorish'. Anahorish is the anglicised version of *anach fhíor uisce*, translated by Heaney as the 'place of clear water', with the very name itself providing a glimpse through to the 'mound-dwellers' who were the aboriginal inhabitants of the place (*WO* 6). Both Montague and Heaney draw in this regard on the Irish poetic tradition of *dinnseanchas*, in which the placename provides a kind of linguistic and cultural map of the locale to which it is applied. Montague's desire to see Ulster Scots and Irish 'braided' together also finds its equivalent in Heaney's positing, in 'Broagh', a common language of place, intelligible to planter and native alike, but unavailable to outsiders, 'Broagh' itself being a kind of signifier shared only by the locals, because of 'that last / *gh* the strangers found / difficult to manage' (*WO* 17).

'Broagh' offers us a vision of union between planter and native, but it also reminds us that the fracturing of Irish literary culture that we find in the division between Corkery and the Revivalists is itself effectively a version of a greater historical schism. Corkery imagined a holistic Irish tradition that was native, Irish-speaking and Catholic. The Free State constitution of 1937 laid claim to an Ireland that consisted of the entire island, and it proclaimed the special importance of the Catholic Church in that Ireland. Corkery was dismissive of the cultural tradition of the Protestant Ascendancy – a tradition deeply cherished by Yeats. The Irish government seemed to feel that the presence of a British-identified Protestant community in the six-county statelet of Northern Ireland could simply be made to vanish by constitutional fiat.

Whatever the ideologues of the Free State (and, subsequently, the Republic of Ireland) might have imagined, the reality on the ground in Northern Ireland was quite different. Heaney grew up in a doubled country that was fractured by dual identities. As the 1960s turned to the 1970s, those fractures grew increasingly fatal. It was a period in which, to borrow from Paul Muldoon, 'Irish writers again and again' found themselves 'challenged by the violent juxtaposition of the concepts of "Ireland" and "I"'.[20] Heaney himself has observed that:

> Among poets of my own generation in the 1960s there was a general feeling of being socially called upon which grew as the polarization grew and the pressure mounted upon the writers not only to render images of the Ulster predicament, but also perhaps to show solidarity with one or other side in the quarrel. (*RP* 193)

Though Heaney has been accused in some quarters precisely of showing solidarity with one side only, he has certainly attempted to remain open to a sense of duality in the North's poetic traditions. An important figure for Heaney in this regard is John Hewitt, the left-leaning Belfast poet of Protestant stock, who aimed in much of his work to map out a planter position which could express sympathy for and also find an accommodation with a native sense of identity. The best known statement of Hewitt's vision is his poem 'The Colony' which finds an allegory for the Northern planter experience in the figure of a Roman colonist, settled in a remote outpost of the empire. The speaker in the poem wants to imagine that it would be possible to 'make amends / by fraternising, by small friendly gestures',

> hoping by patient words I may convince
> my people and this people we are changed

> from the raw levies which usurped the land,
> if not to kin, to co-inhabitants.

The poem closes in a defiant statement of belonging and a refusal to be displaced: 'we would be strangers in the Capitol; / this is our country also, no-where else; / and we shall not be outcast in the world'.[21]

In 'The Glens', Hewitt offers a similar image of simultaneous outsiderness and belonging. The speaker feels only a stiff sense of connectedness with his Catholic neighbours:

> I cannot spare more than a common phrase
> of crops and weather when I pace these lanes
> and pause at hedge gap spying on their skill
> so many fences stretch between our minds.

At the same time, however, he feels connected to this particular region in an elemental and ineluctable fashion: 'no other corner in this land / offers in shape and colour all I need / for sight to torch the mind with living light'.[22] Heaney's 'The Other Side' serves as something of a companion poem to 'The Glens', in that it imagines the same situation, but from the reverse perspective. In Heaney's poem, the Protestant neighbour is envisioned standing out in the yard, reverently waiting for the Catholic family he is calling on to finish saying their prayers. He 'taps a little tune with the blackthorn / shyly, as if he were party to / lovemaking or a stranger's weeping'. In the closing lines, the speaker imagines attempting to make a connection with the waiting neighbour, and considers essaying it precisely through the kind of phatic dialogue that Hewitt had registered in 'The Glens': 'Should I slip away,' he wonders, 'and talk about the weather // or the price of grass-seed?' (*WO* 26).

The value that Heaney finds in Hewitt is similar to what he finds in Kavanagh (and, indeed, in Montague): an ability to have faith in the local and in 'getting down in words what it was we grew up with' (*RP* 193–4). The key point of focus for Hewitt is the region rather than the state. As Heaney notes, he

> settled upon the region of Ulster itself as the first unit of his world, in the hope that a place that was both a *provincia* of the British imperium and an area of the ancient Irish province of Uladh or Ulster could command the allegiance of both Unionists *and* Nationalists. (*RP* 195)

While regarding this strategy as 'original and epoch-making, a significant extension of the imaging faculty into the domain of politics', Heaney nevertheless concludes that the imbalance of power in the North – and the Catholic community's lived experience of discrimination – necessarily meant that it was a programme that could never wholly succeed. Ultimately, Heaney argues, 'Hewitt's regionalism suited the feeling of possession and independence of the empowered Protestants with their own Parliament and fail-safe majority at Stormont more than it could ever suit the sense of dispossession and political marginalization of the Catholics' (*RP* 195–6).

An alternative poet proposed by Heaney as a standard-bearer for the integrative northern Protestant voice is Louis MacNeice. Biographically, MacNeice appears as a more complex figure. He was born in Belfast, the son of a Church of Ireland clergyman. His father was originally from the island of Omey, in Co. Sligo, in the south of Ireland. Through his father, MacNeice felt a strong sense of kinship with Connemara. Even the phrase 'The West of Ireland,' he noted in a memoir of his childhood, 'still stirs me, if not like a trumpet, like a fiddle half heard through a cattle fair ... The very name Connemara,' he writes,

> seemed too rich for any ordinary place. It appeared to be a country of wind-swept open spaces and mountains blazing with whins and seas that were never quiet, with drowned palaces beneath them, and seals and eagles and turf smoke and cottagers who were always laughing and who gave you milk when you asked for a glass of water.[23]

But MacNeice was also educated in the English public-school system, going on to attend Oxford University and to spend most of his life in England, working for the BBC. Though moulded by his upper-middle-class English experience, he retained a strong but deeply conflicted sense of his Irish identity. In *Autumn Journal*, written on the eve of the Second World War, he measures out precise doses of disgust for both traditions in Ireland – self-proclaimed nationalist martyrs and Lambeg drum-banging loyalists alike:

> The land of scholars and saints:
> Scholars and saints my eye, the land of ambush,
> Purblind manifestoes, never-ending complaints,
> The born martyr and the gallant ninny;
> The grocer drunk with the drum,
> The land-owner shot in his bed, the angry voices
> Piercing the broken fanlight in the slum,
> The shawled woman weeping at the garish altar.

At the same time, however, he imagines – if with a deep-running scepticism – a kind of value in the small-scale, isolated world of the island: 'Ireland is small enough / To be still thought of with a family feeling' and 'the waves are rough / That split her from a more commercial culture'.[24] In 'Carrick Revisited', written immediately after the war, MacNeice registers a knot of identity, rooted in his childhood years spent in Carrickfergus, Co. Antrim, which his later life cannot unpick. Despite being 'Schooled from the age of ten to a foreign voice', early experience remains crucially formative for MacNeice, 'Like a belated rock in the red Antrim clay / That cannot at this era change its pitch or name'.[25]

MacNeice's *Collected Poems* was one of the very first books Heaney bought on graduating from Queen's in 1961 (*GT* 8), and his complex and conflicted national fidelities have long held a deep appeal for Heaney. Unlike Hewitt, Heaney argues, MacNeice 'did not allow the border to enter into his ... imaginings: his sense of cultural diversity and historical consequence within the country never congealed into a red and green map' (*RP* 198–9). In 'Frontiers of Writing', Heaney draws on MacNeice to resolve his figure of the 'quincunx' – a geometric conceit which attempts to synthesise Irish literary culture into a unified whole. The quincunx consists of a centrally-placed round tower of 'prior Irelandness', which can be taken as indicating in part the nativist Irish-language tradition; in the west is Yeats's Thoor Ballylee, standing for the Revival; in the east, Joyce's Martello tower, symbolic of 'his attempt to marginalize the imperium which had marginalized him by replacing the Anglocentric Protestant tradition with a newly forged apparatus of Homeric correspondences, Dantesque scholasticism and a more or less Mediterranean, European, classically endorsed world-view' (*RP* 199); and, in the south, Edmund Spenser's Kilcolman Castle represents the cultural concomitant of the English imperial project. The final element in this scheme is Carrickfergus Castle, in the north, a geographical correlative for MacNeice. The Belfast poet here serves to draw together all the other figures into a single point of unity: 'by his English domicile and his civil learning', he is an aspect of Spenser, 'by his ancestral and affectionate links with Connemara an aspect of Yeats and by his mythic and European consciousness an aspect of Joyce'. Heaney argues that MacNeice 'can be regarded as an Irish Protestant writer with Anglocentric attitudes who managed to be faithful to his Ulster inheritance, his Irish affections and his English predilections' (*RP* 200).

In Heaney's scheme, MacNeice operates as a kind of two-way valve for the greater literary system, providing 'a way in and a way out not only for the northern Unionist imagination in relation to some sort of integral Ireland but also for the southern Irish imagination in relation to the partitioned north' (*RP* 200). In terms of the rough, unyielding reality of politics and culture on the ground in Ireland, it is hard not to feel that this is a rather pious hope – of a piece with Heaney's rather extraordinary expectation that his translation of *Buile Suibhne* might have stimulated 'some sympathy in the Unionists for the Nationalist minority who located their lost title to sovereignty' in the 'Gaelic dream-space' of the poem (*FK* 61). (Small hope of that in the ultra-loyalist enclaves of east Belfast, we might feel.) And quite whether MacNeice can bear the full weight of importance that Heaney invests in him is perhaps another issue to be considered here. Neil Corcoran has noted that 'MacNeice has become the name for desirable kinds of hybridity and plurality in a culture of positions often fixed into calcification', but he has also noted an important contrast between MacNeice and Hewitt, in that MacNeice died in 1963, while Hewitt lived on to 1987, thus offering 'the spectacle of a poet actually attempting to cope with the increasing depredations of [Northern Ireland] after 1968'.[26] MacNeice's career thus rather conveniently predates the period of conflict in Northern Ireland which served so strongly to shape the literary culture of Heaney's own generation.

The quincunx, we might say, offers an easy balanced rendering of the complexities of Irish literary history: too easy, in some respects. Edna Longley astutely comments, in *The Living Stream*, that as far as 'seeing *Irish literature* steadily and seeing it whole' is concerned, 'such an enterprise faces institutional, constitutional and theoretical obstacles'.[27] The complexity of that history is, in a sense, reflected in the rather fractured structure of this chapter on Heaney and the Irish poetic tradition. The tradition itself is fragmented, and attempting to map Heaney's career against it necessarily involves a kind of historical shuttling: from the Revival forward to Kavanagh, then back to the poets of the Irish-language tradition, forward to Montague, back to Hewitt, thence to MacNeice. We have noted that the formative experience for Heaney as a poet – the moment at which he felt the surge of a 'writing energy sizzling into a hitherto unwriting system' – was his encountering Kavanagh's poems in the *Oxford Book of Irish Verse*. In his introduction to that volume, Donagh MacDonagh asks, 'What constitutes an Irish poet?'[28] It is far from easy to provide an adequate answer to this question.[29] For the Revivalists, the Irish-language poets were largely unknown. For Corkery, the Revivalists for the most part represented an alien element – a rippling obstruction in the stream of the native tradition. Cultural questions, in an Irish context, always intersect with politics and history, and with issues of nationality, language and religion – precisely those nets that Joyce's Stephen Dedalus was desperately attempting to 'fly by'.[30] In 'Belfast', Heaney suggests that Hewitt, MacNeice and W. R. Rodgers, as northern Protestants, each attempted to address the problematics of Irish identity in British Northern Ireland: 'They did not hold apart and claim kin with a different litter' (*P* 33). All three, Heaney suggests, attempted fruitfully to engage with the question posed by Shakespeare's stage-Irishman Macmorris in *Henry V*: 'What ish my nation?' It is a question that still resonates in the literary culture of the island of Ireland, prompting worthwhile responses, if no final answers.[31]

NOTES

1. Terence Brown, *Ireland's Literature: Selected Essays* (Mullingar: Lilliput, 1988), p. 91.
2. J. M. Synge, *The Playboy of the Western World* (London: Methuen, 1961), p. 39.
3. Patrick Kavanagh, *Collected Poems* (London: Martin Brian & O'Keeffe, 1972), p. 78.
4. Patrick Kavanagh, *Kavanagh's Weekly* no. 7 (24 May 1952), p. 2.
5. Heaney credits the nurturance he received in Philip Hobsbaum's Belfast Group with helping him to make the transition from provincial to parochial: 'now, of course, we're genuine parochials. Then [in the mid-1960s] we were craven provincials. Hobsbaum contributed much to that crucial transformation' (*P* 29).
6. Heaney quoted in Michael Parker, *Seamus Heaney: The Making of the Poet* (London: Macmillan, 1993), p. 32. The influence of the English writer Ted Hughes on *Death of a Naturalist* should not, however, be overlooked. See, in particular, Neil Corcoran's comments on Hughes's influence on Heaney in *The Poetry of Seamus Heaney: A Critical Study* (London: Faber and Faber, 1998).
7. Patrick Kavanagh, *Collected Prose* (London: MacGibbon & Kee, 1967), p. 13.
8. W. B. Yeats, 'To Ireland in the Coming Times', *Yeats's Poems*, ed. and annotated by A. N. Jeffares (London: Macmillan, 1989), pp. 85–6.
9. *W. B. Yeats: Poems Selected by Seamus Heaney* (London: Faber and Faber, 2004), p. xiv.
10. Ibid., 'The Seven Sages', pp. 355–7.
11. Daniel Corkery, *The Hidden Ireland: A Study of Gaelic Munster in the Eighteenth Century* (1924; Dublin: Gill and Macmillan, 1967), p. 8.
12. J. L. O'Sullivan (S. Labhrás uá Súilleabháin), *An Brón-Chluiche Macbeit* (Dublin: Cahill & Co., 1925), n.p.
13. Austin Clarke, 'Penal Law', *Selected Poems* (Portlaoise: Dolmen, 1976), p. 22.
14. Neil Corcoran, *After Yeats and Joyce: Reading Modern Irish Literature* (Oxford: Oxford University Press, 1997), p. 15.
15. Thomas Kinsella (ed.), *The New Oxford Book of Irish Verse* (Oxford: Oxford University Press, 1986), p. xxvii.
16. Seamus Heaney, *The Midnight Verdict* (Oldcastle: Gallery Press, 1993), p. 11.
17. John Montague, *Collected Poems* (Oldcastle: Gallery Press, 1995), pp. 33, 37, 38.
18. Bernard O'Donoghue, *Seamus Heaney and the Language of Poetry* (Hemel Hempstead: Harvester Wheatsheaf, 1994), p. 6.
19. Montague, *Collected Poems*, p. 33.
20. Paul Muldoon, *To Ireland, I* (Oxford: Oxford University Press, 2000), p. 35.
21. John Hewitt, *Collected Poems, 1932–1967* (London: MacGibbon & Kee, 1968), p. 79.
22. Ibid., p. 23.
23. Louis MacNeice, *The Strings are False: An Unfinished Autobiography* (London: Faber and Faber, 1982), pp. 216, 217.
24. MacNeice, *Collected Poems* (London: Faber and Faber, 1966), pp. 132, 133.
25. Ibid., p. 225.
26. Corcoran, *After Yeats*, pp. 133, 134.
27. Edna Longley, *The Living Stream: Literature and Revisionism in Ireland* (Newcastle: Bloodaxe Books, 1994), p. 9.

28. Donagh MacDonagh and Lennox Robinson (eds.), *The Oxford Book of Irish Verse: XVIIth Century–XXth Century* (Oxford: Clarendon, 1958), p. xvii.
29. MacDonagh's own answer was that 'a poet may be Irish in three ways: by birth, by descent, by adoption' (ibid.). This accounts for some of his more quixotic inclusions – most notably Nahum Tate and Emily Brontë.
30. James Joyce, *A Portrait of the Artist as a Young Man*, ed. Jeri Johnson (Oxford: Oxford University Press, 2000), p. 171.
31. My thanks to Jonathan Allison and Neil Corcoran for their valuable feedback on this chapter.

10

DILLON JOHNSTON

Irish Influence and Confluence in Heaney's Poetry

Excepting perhaps primitive or infantile wordplay, protective or playful, such as that with which Baby Tuckoo opens Joyce's *A Portrait of the Artist As a Young Man*, we might say no one has written a solitary poem. Poems arrive in the context of other poems read or written by the poet, and by other poets of his or her region, sect, nation or globe. These contexts may even be arranged hierarchically, as the slightly older Baby Tuckoo does on the flyleaf of his geography book when he identifies himself as the young 'Stephen Dedalus / Class of Elements / Clongowes Wood College / Sallins / County Kildare / Ireland / Europe / The World / The Universe', although he might add a temporal scale to situate himself in other periods in the poet's life or relate him to other epochs or centuries. For various reasons critics of the poet Seamus Heaney have often limited the context for his poems, interrupting these concentric poetic circles in which we might read him after 'Seamus Heaney / Belfast / Ulster', perhaps because, as with young Stephen, 'It made [them] very tired to think that way.'[1]

For example, Neil Corcoran, one of Seamus Heaney's most perceptive critics, has published a study entitled *Poets of Modern Ireland* (1999), in which, in his six chapters on living poets, he has only included Heaney and other poets who emerged in the sixties from what is called 'the Belfast Group', with no living poets from the Republic of Ireland. We can understand readers' fascination with a group of talented poets – including in this case Derek Mahon, Michael Longley, James Simmons, Seamus Deane and, a little later, Tom Paulin, Ciaran Carson, Medbh McGuckian, Paul Muldoon and Frank Ormsby – emerging at one time and in one place, and such a fascination is compounded when this talent, like that of poets of the First World War or of the English Civil War, appears during a political crisis and violent upheaval which seems to enlarge these poets' role and impose a common tragic topic. Nevertheless, because reading Heaney in relation to the Group preoccupies mostly English critics, such criticism can be seen as having exclusionary and even Unionist intentions. Heaney, himself, in an essay on 'Vision and Irony in

Recent Irish Poetry', has included only contemporary Ulster poets.[2] In other essays, Heaney has identified himself as an Irish poet, but he has also tried in his own translations, critical prose and dedicated poems to widen his poetic associations not only to Britain but also to classical Greece, Dante's Christendom, the United States and Eastern Europe, thereby escaping the exclusive context either of the Belfast Movement or of Catholic Ireland.

What is neglected or under-represented when Heaney criticism narrowly focuses on Ulster poetry is not only the colonial but also the pre-colonial context of the entire island, the ways in which Heaney and other Northern poets share with living poets from the Republic certain shaping influences. To counter this neglect we might read Heaney in relation to poets from all over the island: from older Ulster poets who preceded the group, to contemporary poets from the Republic, such as Thomas Kinsella and Eiléan Ní Chuilleanáin, from whom he is usually partitioned. To the extent that this essay is a study of influence, it focuses on the confluence of similar ideas between and among poems rather than on one poet's anxious revision of a poetic forerunner, according to Harold Bloom's theories of 'misprision' and 'anxiety of influence'.[3]

This distinction sharpens if we consider early influences from the North on the poetry of Heaney, especially from the poetry of John Hewitt and John Montague before the resurgence of the Troubles. While lacking the brilliance of his contemporary compatriot Louis MacNeice, Hewitt, nevertheless, laid down several challenges for Ulster poets emerging in the 1960s: to find common ground with the other tribe while being honest to one's own sectarian differences; to write out of one's own regional, rather than global, concerns; to begin with the texture and gravity of one's own topography and language. Although we cannot specify the extent to which this last challenge shaped the thoroughly tactile quality of Heaney's early poetry,[4] as late as 2001 he referred to the ending of Hewitt's 'The Colony' (1950): 'I still love a line like Hewitt's "heavy, clay-sucked stride." That's the kind of music I was after in the beginning and I wouldn't ever want to sign away my right to it.'[5] Hewitt sought a pre-industrial space which he found in the West of Ireland ('The Swathe Uncut') or more often in the Glens of Antrim from which he had collected the verse of 'rhyming weavers' who epitomised his notion of 'Regionalism'.

Aspects of social politics and political economy flow between Protestant and Catholic neighbours in 'The Hill-Farm', published in Hewitt's 1969 volume, and 'The Other Side' which was published in Heaney's *Wintering Out* (1972). In Hewitt's poem, on a dark night a Protestant farmer's errand brings him to the door of his Catholic neighbours where, as the mother leads the family in evening prayers, 'curtained light / thrust muffled challenge to the night'. Alone in the dark, the Protestant speaker remains 'far from that faith-based certitude, / here in the vast enclosing night, / outside its little ring of light'.[6] The religious imagery of circles of light and darkness dimly suggests the Protestants' representation of themselves as occupiers of a garrison state, surrounding the Catholic minority in the North but in turn besieged by the island's encircling Catholic majority. Heaney's poem also places the Protestant neighbour in the outside dark, awaiting the end of the rosary. However, the Catholic speaker imagines himself stepping out of the darkness of the yard to 'go up and touch his shoulder / and talk about the weather / or the price of grass-seed' (*WO* 36). The apparently clichéd and trivial topics – weather and market prices – actually concern survival and real values, and therefore bind neighbours together, as in that original sense of *religion* Heaney often cites. To Hewitt's sceptical Protestant in his existential darkness, Heaney's speaker offers agrarian community, as his poem *redresses* Hewitt's, in one of Heaney's later senses of that word: 'poetry as an answer', 'poetry ... adjusting and correcting imbalances in the world, poetry as an intended intervention into the goings-on of society' (*RP* 191–2).

Another older Ulster contemporary who influenced Heaney, John Montague, could seem the Catholic complement to Hewitt, as Hewitt and Montague did when they travelled together in 1969 as 'The Planter and the Gael', offering readings sponsored by the Arts Council of Northern Ireland. Heaney's most biographical critic Michael Parker has written, 'In the poetry of John Montague, in particular, Heaney identified a duality of rootedness and exile which corresponded to his own, a maturity of feeling and expression to emulate.'[7] The duality, often manifested as ambivalence, which Montague came to call 'global regionalism', was evident in the early poem 'The Water Carrier' which Heaney admitted was a model for his own early *ars poetica* 'Personal Helicon'.[8] For both poets the childhood memory of waterholes, wells and springs remains a source of inspiration. Whereas Heaney recalls the wells as a site of unregulated and obsessive play ('they could not keep me from wells'), Montague fulfils humanity's ancient chore of hauling water. Montague is fastidious, stepping 'carefully across slime-topped stones'[9] whereas Heaney would 'finger slime' or 'drag ... long roots from the soft mulch' (*DN* 57).

Aside from the title (which substitutes the Muses' mountain for their spring) and a self-mocking reference to Narcissus (the classical image of self-absorption), Heaney's poem remains local and egocentric. On the other hand, Montague makes an effort to universalise his local memory: 'Recovering the scene, I had hoped to stylize it, / Like the portrait of an Egyptian water carrier', but he is 'entranced', arrested at the threshold of 'memoried life'. Montague's close is remarkably like Hewitt's last lines in

'Substance and Shadow': 'My lamp lights up the kettle on the stove / and throws its shadow on the whitewashed wall, / like some Assyrian profile with, above, / a snake, or bird-prowed helmet crested tall.' For Hewitt, such iconic images from another place and time dissolve into 'the screes of doubt' whereas local images remain 'sharp, spare, simple, native to / this small republic I have charted out / as the sure acre where my sense is true',[10] as if unmediated by memory. Montague, however, turns from the iconic to the mystery of memory, not a 'sure acre' but an entrance to 'some living source, half-imagined and half-real', much closer to Heaney's later interest in that border he calls 'the Frontier of Writing'.

The circulation of influences between Montague and Heaney has been traced by several critics, and most thoroughly by Rand Brandes who says of Heaney's 'Fosterling',

> As a prologue to part two of *Seeing Things* (1991) ... 'Fosterling' attests both to Montague's initial influence on Heaney, helping him to read 'the immanent hydraulics' of the land and language, and to Montague's liberating poetics: 'Me waiting until I was nearly fifty / To credit marvels.'[11]

Beyond these comments, 'Fosterling' can be read as a farewell to the poetic water-sources Heaney shared with Montague and to 'my lowlands of the mind / ... the doldrums of what happens' which were a restriction of the full Fenian birdsong of 'the music of what happens' (*ST* 50) to which Heaney had aspired earlier in his career. At this point he arises from his Antaeus-like adherence to the earth – a mere halving or even quartering of the material world of air, earth, fire and water – towards the full, lightening cosmos which his new poetry will inhabit.

The ascent of Heaney's poetry in *Seeing Things* from earth to sky was labelled irreverently as 'surf und turf' by Paul Muldoon.[12] Such bold parodic jabs by the younger Faber poet and former student of Heaney have been tabulated and thoroughly examined by critics, notably by Edna Longley and Neil Corcoran. Corcoran has argued that the apparently 'impudent, presumptuous, disconcertingly brilliant pupil wilfully running rings around his earliest mentor' actually contributes to a healthy exchange, where 'the most painfully difficult matters of cultural authority ... are negotiated at the level of brave articulation and explicitation, rather than suppression or sublimation'.[13]

Because Corcoran traces the trajectory of Muldoon's missiles against Heaney after the Corcoran article written in 1997, he sees no need to extend his account of each impact. However, we might look at one more of Muldoon's responses to Heaney because it makes clear the difference between the deliberate, polemical or personal exchanges among Northern poets and the more contextual influences poets from the North share with those from the Republic. In *The Spirit Level* (1996) Heaney extends an idea he entertained in the earlier volume *Station Island* that the stages of human creation and construction are preserved in the completed structure: 'the constant sound of hidden river water / the new estate rose up through – / with one chop of the trowel he sent it all / into the brick for ever' ('The Sandpit'; *SI* 55). The later poem 'The Gravel Walks' from *The Spirit Level* also presents the continuum of civilisation from pastoral origins – 'River gravel. In the beginning, that.' – to the completed concrete metropolis, from nature's raw material to human empire (with echoes of Conrad's *Heart of Darkness*) and dominion over nature:

> And cement mixers began to come to life
> And men in dungarees, like captive shades,
> Mixed concrete, loaded, wheeled, turned, wheeled, as if
> The Pharaoh's brickyards burned inside their heads. (*SL* 39)

Just as he reveres pristine, riverbed gravel – 'The kingdom of gravel was inside you too' – so he recognises the 'honest worth' and constructive discipline of the building material: 'But the actual washed stuff kept you slow and steady / As you went stooping with your barrow full.' In its closure, the poem, which supports ambivalence and the maintenance of two states of mind, advocates a middle position, 'somewhere in between / Those solid batches mixed with grey cement / And a tune called "The Gravel Walks" that conjures green' (*SL* 40). The last line surprisingly substitutes for personal origins and pastoral youth a traditional musical reel, an artefact of a pre-industrial culture (celebrated in the flute-playing of Matt Molloy) which evokes the greenness of nature and of a more innocent society.

In the title-poem of Muldoon's volume *Moy Sand and Gravel* (2002) where two six-line stanzas rhyme *abacad*, the fourth and sixth lines rhyme between stanzas. The fourth lines locate romantic sites – 'movie stars' heads' and 'the Blackwater's bed' – and the final two lines of each stanza link two illusions, those of Hollywood endings and of bucolic beginnings that convey the illusion that nature can be sanitised and tamed for our use, 'as if washing might make it clean'.[14] Muldoon's corrective here seems directed against Heaney's sense that we can recover origins and gravitate between pastoral gravel and gravel in its usable state, in other words, between pastoral origins and civilisation. More a nudge at, than a jab against, Heaney, Muldoon's poem offers a corrective, and a 'redress', to Heaney's pastoralism.

Whether redressing or simply mocking, Muldoon maintains throughout his poetry what Edna Longley calls a 'running demurral with Heaney'.[15] Deliberateness and explicitness of exchange – whether Michael Longley's letters and dedications to other Northern poets, or Mahon's regular, and Simmons's occasional, dedications – arise more rarely between Ulster poets and poets from the Republic, but, to quote Edna Longley again, 'there is ultimately no iron border between poetry written by Northerners and Southerners. Not least of the overlaps is the poets' fruitful awareness of one another, the cross-border influences now at work.'[16] In tracing this exchange, one can borrow Longley's authority without repeating her discussion because the poets she selects to represent the Republic, Brendan Kennelly and Paul Durcan, neither fancy the well-wrought lyric nor care to follow Yeats's or the Northern poets' standards of craft or trade.

The 'cross-border influences' that are most ignored and most 'now at work' may be not so much the 'poets' fruitful awareness of one another', of which Longley speaks, but shared settings – cultural, geographical, topographical, religious, colonial and post-colonial – within the broader context of the entire island. These aspects are often shared unconsciously and may even arise both from the streams of the unconscious and from ancient currents and eddies. Although Heaney undoubtedly shares with other poets in the Republic influences from what he calls 'hidden springs', those he shares with Thomas Kinsella and Eiléan Ní Chuilleanáin concern the matter foremost in the following discussion: personal and cultural identity as they are acquired through relations the poems establish with the dead. Both Heaney and Kinsella feature legendary, even prehistoric figures, hibernating or comatose, who are enclosed in natural crypts or caves awaiting rebirth. Heaney, Kinsella and Ní Chuilleanáin represent the father and mother as mediators, an intermediary between the poets and the dead generations of an earlier culture, but also as the psychopomp, guiding the resurrected body back from entombment and restoring it to the mourning poets.

Kinsella's 'Survivor' begins, 'High near the heart of the mountain there is a cavern.' The poem continues dramatically, in the mysterious cavern-dweller's own words:

> Curled in self hate. Delicious
>   Head heavy. Arm too heavy.
> What is it, to suffer:
>   The dismal rock nourishes.[17]

In response to 'neighbourly murder', Heaney's speaker in the volume *North*'s 'Funeral Rites' declaratively rather than dramatically imagines megalithic burials: 'I would restore / the great chambers of Boyne, / prepare a sepulchre / under the cupmarked stones.' Those murdered in the Troubles, Heaney imagines within terms of Nordic myth, would be 'disposed like Gunnar / who lay beautiful / inside his burial mound, / though dead by violence // ... chanting / verses about honour' (*N* 17–18). In 'Sacrifice' Kinsella's holding-chamber or sepulchre takes on characteristics of Austin Clarke's psychiatric ward in *Mnemosyne Lay in Dust* (1966) or a cell in some gulag: 'I have been in places ... The floors crept, / an electric terror waited everywhere' (*KCP* 116), but this torment eases:

> I was lying in a vaulted place.
> The cold air crept over long-abandoned floors,
> Carrying a taint of remote iron and dead ash.

In '38 Phoenix Street' Kinsella narrates the near-fatal entombment of his neighbour in the First World War:

> Sealed in his sad cave. His horror erecting
> Slowly out of its rock nests, nosing the air.
> He was buried for three days under a hill of dead ... (*KCP* 168)

In Heaney's 'North' the burial chamber from Icelandic myth becomes the *file*'s composing room: 'Lie down / in the word-hoard, burrow / the coil and gleam / of your furrowed brain' (*N* 20). In a mid-sixties poem, which Heaney brings forward to preface cave-burial poems in *North* (1975), the mythic giant Antaeus says, 'Down here in my cave // Girdered with root and rock / I am cradled in the dark that wombed me' (*N* 12). In the sequel 'Hercules and Antaeus', he refers to 'the hatching grounds / of cave and souterrain' (*N* 52–3).

As in the concepts fundamental both to Ireland's ancient burials and to Irish modernism, based by Yeats on cyclic history and the return of heroes, resurrection – the tomb becoming womb – is at least implicit in both Heaney's and Kinsella's cave burials. Heaney attributes this expectant posture to Kinsella in the third Ellmann Lecture at Emory University (1988), acknowledging the centrality of this cave-penned warrior to Kinsella's poetry:

> Kinsella is, in fact, the representative Irish poet in that his career manifests the oath-bound, unrewarded plight of the *comitatus* in Yeats's black tower. In his work, we can watch the ancient correspondence between the nation's possibilities and the imagination of its poet – represented originally by the Milesian bard Amergin – discover itself again in a modern drama of self-knowledge and self-testing.[18]

Heaney's enlistment of Kinsella in Yeats's posse – 'Stand we on guard oath-bound! // *There in the tomb the dark grows blacker*' – implicitly ascribes to Kinsella Yeats's nationalist expectation of the new cycle, the return of light and the restoration of their heroic order, although Yeats distinguishes his warriors from later politicised nationalists who 'come to bribe or threaten'.[19]

However, in these various cases of entombment, neither Kinsella nor Heaney emphasises revival or resurrection of heroic Ireland. In Kinsella's *New Poems* (1973) and after, he evokes the twelfth-century *Book of Invasions* and Ireland's earliest legendary immigrant poets Fintan, Tuan and Amergin, each of whom endures an interim of decline and renewal between one of six successive invasions. Presented dramatically and cryptically or as background to more contemporary poetic settings, Kinsella's narrative of possession, loss and repossession becomes an analogue for humanity's processes of growth and decay, whether collective (history, myth, art) or individual (love, domesticity, reproduction, maturation and ageing). Just as important as this idea basic to *The Book of Invasions* – that rather than trekking an expansive frontier we must delve into ourselves and our relations to win again what we possess – Kinsella borrows from diverse sources the various levels of narration: the narrator of these invasions, the monkish scribe who set them down with marginal glosses, the third-person contemporary and the autobiographical narrator who recounts his own retakings, returns and renewals, in layers of the narrative.

For an example of the frequent reprises of the six invasions, 'Morning Coffee' first alludes to other earlier poems by Kinsella: 'We thought at first it was a body / Rolling up with a blank belly onto the beach / The year our first-born babies died. // A big white earthenware vessel / Settled staring up / Open mouthed at us' (*KCP* 307). What appears initially as the foetal flotsam from 'Ballydavid Pier' connects in the third line with the first of the six invasions by the people of Partholon all of whom except the chronicler-poet Tuan perish from a plague. The body, re-identified as 'a big white earthenware vessel', evokes from earlier Kinsella poems the 'ordeal cup', a crucible of birth and bitter life. The passage concerns origins, as in the fresh beginning of Eve, not born of woman and therefore with 'blank belly'.[20] The need to account for origins, 'in the beginnings', Kinsella suggests, becomes the motive behind literature: in Tuan's words, 'Soon we were making up stories / about the First People / and telling them to our second born' (*KCP* 307).

Kinsella revises poems frequently and thoroughly, as another expression of his self-excavation. Less often, Heaney revisits and revises earlier poems, as he does in the pairing of 'Antaeus', dated 1966, and 'Hercules and Antaeus', a new poem in *North*, where he contradicts the earlier view, expressed by his persona Antaeus, that he is stronger unweaned from his mother earth and rooted in 'the hatching grounds / of cave and souterrain' (*N* 52–3). Helen Vendler interprets succinctly: '"Pap for the dispossessed," comments Heaney bitterly, thinking of the way the oppressed batten on myths of ultimate victory ... living in "a dream of loss and origins".'[21]

Whereas the sectarian violence that further polarises Catholics and Protestants in the North introduces an ambivalence into Heaney's poetry, he like Kinsella sees the poetic quest for origins as illusory but consoling. In Heaney's 'Funeral Rites', the need for vengeance is allayed by 'ceremony, customary rhythms' to which 'the whole country tunes', as 'we' imagine Gunnar disposed in the tomb and 'chanting / verses about honour' (*N* 18–19). Although Kinsella and Heaney draw on quite different myths in quite different ways, they both share the topics of entombments, possible resurrections and the role of poetry in representing 'a dream of loss and origins' in 'making up stories / about the First People' (*KCP* 307).

For both Kinsella and Heaney, fathers are not the origins or among 'the first people', but rather transitional figures going between an artisan-class generation and their own scholarly and intellectual lives. With no evidence of exchange or influence between the poets, remarkably they both represent their fathers as Hermes, the type for intermediaries, messengers and, even, psychopomps. In addition to scattered individual poems about the father, both poets devote entire sequences – Kinsella's *The Messenger* and Heaney's 'Crossings' – to the father as Hermes, who goes between the Other World and this, but also, uncannily, between his own corpse and his grieving son.

Two years after his father's death, Kinsella published *The Messenger* (1978), which attempted to compensate for, if not redeem, the father's last embittered years, enabling the son to come to terms with the sickening image of his corpse. In dreams the poet has found 'something to discourage goodness': 'A dead egg glimmers – a pearl in muck / glimpsed only as the muck settles' (*KCP* 209). Recalling the insensitive comment of a well-wisher at his father's funeral – 'His father before him ... Ah, the barge captain ... / A valued connection. He will be well remembered ... / He lived in his two sons' (*KCP* 210) – Kinsella must convert the imagined maggot to 'the eggseed goodness', validating his father beyond the charge of being a mere hyphen between generations. To achieve this, he reverses the stages of his father's life. The narration regresses from the besotted and disempowered pensioner back through his maturity as a union founder at Guinness, to his courtship in Wicklow, his youthful assistance of his own father as part-time cobbler, and then to his first day of employment as a uniformed messenger boy mounting his bicycle, before the sequence returns to the affirmative memory of grandchildren, diverse and vital, following the wheeled coffin, and, as in *The Book of Invasions*, converting death and defeat to fresh beginnings and retakings of life.

Among the various referents for the Peppercanister volume's title, *The Messenger*, we have to number the figure of Mercury on the cover of the chapbook, a parody of the monthly devotional journal which features Christ baring his Sacred Heart; the sperm-dragonfly that hovers over his parents in the moment of his conception; and, climactically, the father setting out on his first job with the Post Office: 'A new messenger boy / stands there in uniform, with shining belt! // He is all excitement: arms akimbo, / a thumb crooked by the telegram pouch, / shoes polished, and a way to make in the world' (*KCP* 218). In enthusiasm and innocence, the father's fresh beginning redeems images of his death and transfers the emphasis of his funeral from corpse-rot to generational rebirth, from putrescence to eager potential that recurs generationally: 'all shapes and sizes, / grandchildren, colourful and silent' (*KCP* 219).

For reasons similar to Kinsella's, Heaney also identifies his father with Hermes. Despite the poet's deep filial love, his attenuation from his father, which finds expression in celebrated poems published before the Troubles such as 'Digging', 'Follower' and 'Ancestral Photographs', results from the son's break both from the farming community, from the agrarian succession from father to son and from the father's own displacement from his role as cattle-dealer when changes in country customs replace fairs with more regularised cattle-marts: 'No room for dealers if the farmers shopped / Like housewives at an auction ring. Your stick / Was parked behind the door and stands there still' (*DN* 27).

A quarter of a century later, in the 'Crossings' section of *Seeing Things*, the poet apotheosises his father from 'solid man ... with an ashplant' to Hermes, 'god of fair days, stone posts, roads and crossroads, / Guardian of travellers and psychopomp', who becomes a guide through doors, a tunnel of trees, St Brigid's 'girdle of straw rope', and across water's flow on a kesh or causey and stepping stones (*ST* 85, 89, 88, 90). The enigmatic opening poem concludes with a reference to Iris, suggesting the transference through vision between mind and material world but also the earlier form of Hermes, Iris as rainbow and messenger. Although 'Crossings' occupies only one quarter of 'Squarings', the second half of *Seeing Things*, it becomes elevated by translations from Virgil and Dante which serve as Prologue to the entire volume – in which the son assumes the role as psychopomp who ferries his father from a burning Troy and acquires not an ashplant but a golden bough to guide him 'beyond the limit' – and Epilogue – in which Charon replaces Hermes and restrains Virgil and Dante from crossing into Hades. Between these 'carryings across' from Virgil and Dante, some of the most powerful poems in the book, such as the first part of 'Seeing Things', concern risky transporting, almost all spatialisings of temporal crossings between the past and present.

The second part of 'Man and Boy' resonates backward from 'Crossings' and forward from Heaney's poetic sequence about the death of his mother, 'Clearances'. The most cited lines of 'Clearances' convert the usual grieving over loss in time, such as Lear's 'Never ...', to vacated space: 'The space we stood around had been emptied / Into us to keep ... a space / Utterly empty, utterly a source" (*HL* 31, 32). In 'Man and Boy', Heaney inserts both a visual and audible emblem for this gravid vacancy, a source for melancholy: 'In earshot of the pool where the salmon jumped / Back through its own unheard concentric soundwaves / A mower leans forever on his scythe' (*ST* 14). The startling word 'forever' vaults us out of mere recollection past Marvell's mower to the grim reaper garnering souls, as it anticipates the emptying of the grandfather's and, implicitly, the father's space. The second stanza returns us to an ostensibly autobiographical level: 'He has mown himself to the centre of the field / And stands in a final perfect ring / Of sunlit stubble' (*ST* 14). Heaney's father as a boy then becomes the go-between relaying news from this ominous mower to Heaney's grandfather: '"Go and tell your father," the mower says / (He said it to my father who told me) / "I have it mowed as clean as a new sixpence"' (*ST* 14). Whether as those obols for the eyes or final wages, this sixpence reinforces the news of the task's completion. The father then fulfils his task and his type as Hermes: 'My father is a barefoot boy with news, / Running at eye-level with weeds and stooks / On the afternoon of his father's death. // The open, black half of the half-door waits. / I feel much heat and hurry in the air. / I feel his legs and quick heels far away' (*ST* 15).

The earnestness and urgency of the go-between, the contrast of the quick and the dead, may remind us of Kinsella's father in *The Messenger* when he 'unprops the great Post Office bicycle ... It faces uphill. The urchin mounts. I see / a flash of pedals. And a clean pair of heels!' (*KCP* 218). Heaney's setting also reflects Kinsella's henyard in a celebrated early poem, 'Hen woman' – 'The noon heat in the yard / smelled of stillness and coming thunder.' – where the two cottage doors suggest enclosures for death and for the unconscious:[22] 'The cottage door opened, / a black hole / in a whitewashed wall so bright / the eyes narrowed' (*KCP* 97). The ending of 'Man and Boy' recognises the reversal in roles that results from ageing. Shifting into a future or habitual tense, he recalls that 'when he will piggyback me,' he becomes, in a reference to his opening translation from Virgil, 'light-headed and thin-boned, / Like a witless elder rescued from the fire' (*ST* 15). In a similar reversal, the messenger who sets out alone, wheeling 'the great Post Office bicycle' in Kinsella's poem is, in turn, wheeled in his coffin accompanied by his grandchildren.

The appearance of similar motifs, images and representations surely owes less to any direct borrowings than to a complex of historical, economic and social causes that cross borders and pervade the island. A common religion, for example, may not bind together Protestant or Catholic co-religionists from across the border, but as each community faces changes and problems that bridge the Boundary, responses within each church inevitably transcend borders. In common with some other poets from the Republic and the North, Seamus Heaney often assumes what might be called a counter-reformational stance, highly qualified but, nevertheless, distinct from British positivism and a too restrictive sense of reason. Indeed Yeats had named the adversary of the poetic as the 'mechanical theory',[23] although few contemporary poets would see themselves siding with Yeats in such a cause.

In an interview with John Brown, Heaney said, 'What I've found myself doing more and more, especially in interviews like this, is emphasizing the purely religious, transcendental importance of Catholicism' and declaring 'the beauty and salvific effect of growing up with the idea of God in his eternal present around and about and above you everywhere, growing up with ideas of continuous creation, of guardian angels, of sanctifying grace, a universe shimmering with light'.[24] Heaney's religious language here echoes his declaration to turn from the earth-bound music he once subscribed to – 'poetry / Sluggish in the doldrums of what happens' – to poetry that will 'credit marvels ... So long for air to brighten, / Time to be dazzled and the heart to lighten' (*ST* 50), lines which effectively serve as prologue to the second half of *Seeing Things*, to 'Shifting brilliancies' which owe something to Derek Mahon's imagery in 'Light Music' (1977) and his *Courtyards in Delft* (1981).

Perhaps the most celebrated poem in 'Squarings' recounts the appearance above a monastery of an air-borne ship which tangles its anchor in the altar-rails so that a crewman has to try unsuccessfully to free it:

> 'This man can't bear our life here and will drown,'
>
> The abbot said, 'unless we help him.' So
> They did, the freed ship sailed, and the man climbed back
> Out of the marvellous as he had known it. (*ST* 62)

Although Heaney's poem conveys poetic truths – such as that art gives us the perspective to lever marvels from our quotidian life and that we live in bilateral universes, experiential and imaginative – it does not fully credit marvels. Rather than conveying authority, the attribution 'The annals say' heavily qualifies the story by placing it within the seventeen-century quasi-folk compendium *The Annals of the Four Masters*.

We might look at a poem with some similarities by Eiléan Ní Chuilleanáin, a seriously underrated poet who rarely, if at all, has been linked with Heaney. Ní Chuilleanáin bases her poem 'Fireman's Lift' on a visit in 1963 to Correggio's great baroque ceiling mural in the Duomo of Parma. Although her mother is never named, we are to understand that the dates – 'Parma 1963 – Dublin 1994' – refer to the mother and daughter's visit to Parma and to the mother's death three decades later. The collective effort portrayed in Correggio's mural *The Assumption of the Virgin*, to hoist the bodily Mary to heaven, is implicitly extended to the poet's mother. In an interview in the mid-1990s, Ní Chuilleanáin said, 'When I found myself compelled to write about Correggio's *Assumption of the Virgin*, ... I could only concentrate on one aspect, the way it shows bodily effort and the body's weight.' The baroque architecture and painting are the machinery for the Virgin's airlift: 'The back making itself a roof / The legs a bridge, the hands / A crane and a cradle'.[25] In this ekphrastic poem, however, only words and poetic form transmit this baroque collusion of paint, plaster, arch and architrave. Ní Chuilleanáin's enjambed lines, alliterative pauses and assonantal chiming project the sound incrementally as they imitate this collective boost of Mary's incarnate self in what the poet calls playfully a 'fireman's lift'. In the poem's closing lines, the significance of 'purchase' and 'weight', the adhesive /u/ syllables – *usc, ung, urch, und, oud* – and the drawn-out closing hectasyllabic, all emphasise that body goes with soul in this final heave toward the terminal bourn: 'As the muscles clung and shifted / For a final purchase together / Under her weight as she came to the edge of the cloud'. Rather than more ethereal ascensions, both Ní Chuilleanáin's and Heaney's poems recount assumptions, in which the successful liberation of the Virgin and of the tropospheric ship requires overcoming bodily weight and gravity. As does Ní Chuilleanáin, Heaney emphasises the participants' physicality: 'the big hull rocked to a standstill', 'A crewman shinned and grappled... / And struggled' (*ST* 62).

Yet, at least three factors weigh against this essentialising of the Irish poet as Catholic. By having their portrayal and narrative mediated through legend and art, both poets overcome pious gravity. While the baroque painting enlarges the human figure to a not-quite-credible gigantism, the opening attribution in Heaney's poem, 'The annals say', may induce images of slightly cartoonish humans with profile noses flattened on full-frontal faces such as those, say, in Giraldus Cambrensis's twelfth-century *Topography of Ireland* (which Heaney has drawn on elsewhere). Secondly, the presentation or even priority of the body seems widespread throughout Irish poetry, whether Catholic or Protestant. In a letter shortly before his death, Yeats wrote 'Man can only embody truth but he cannot know it.'[26] In 'The Linen Workers', the Protestant poet Michael Longley records an assumption with indelible bodily details:

> Christ's teeth ascended with him into heaven:
> Through a cavity in one of his molars
> The wind whistles: he is fastened for ever
> By his exposed canines to a wintry sky.[27]

Derek Mahon consistently recounts spirit as inescapably bound to body, 'When we start breaking up in the wet darkness',[28] and after. It is also arguable that in the 1990s both poets are reacting against the growing secularism that accompanied increasing Irish prosperity, redressing upward mobility with transcendent loftiness. Finally, we must recall that the polarity and alternation of earth and heaven – 'going down and down' and 'climb[ing] back out' (*ST* 62) – remain one of Heaney's lifelong ambivalent alternations.

Of the concentric contexts within which we may read Heaney, an understanding of his regional roots in Ulster and his literary associations with the English language and British culture are unquestionably important. However, if we consider as well the living poets of the Republic and the shared experience of geography, religion, social customs and traditions, history, the arts, much of which precedes 1923 or even 1800, we may perceive the deeper sources of Heaney's poetry, not as conscious borrowings but something deeper and more pervasive, almost a shared unconscious, 'As if we moved in the first stealth of flood / For remember ... the swim and flow / From hidden springs ...' ('A Retrospect', *ST* 42).

NOTES

1. James Joyce, *A Portrait of the Artist As A Young Man*, ed. Seamus Deane (New York and London: Penguin Books, 1992), pp. 12–13.
2. Seamus Heaney, 'The Pre-Natal Mountain: Vision and Irony in Recent Irish Poetry', in *The of Place of Writing* (Atlanta, CA: Scholars Press, 1989).
3. Harold Bloom, *The Anxiety of Influence: A Theory of Poetry* (Oxford: Oxford University Press, 1973).
4. *The American Heritage Dictionary* (2000) illustrates the meaning of *tactile*, 'conveying an illusion of tangibility', with a quotation from Helen Vendler: 'Heaney must thus continue to be a poet rich in tactile language.'
5. John Brown, *In the Chair: Interviews with Poets from the North of Ireland* (Co. Clare: Salmon, 2002), p. 81.
6. John Hewitt, 'The Hill-Farm', *The Collected Poems of John Hewitt*, ed. Frank Ormsby (Belfast: Blackstaff Press, 1991), p. 125.
7. Michael Parker, *Seamus Heaney: The Making of the Poet* (Iowa City: University of Iowa Press, 1993), p. 36.
8. Ibid., p. 231 n. 52.
9. John Montague, 'The Water Carrier', *Collected Poems* (Winston-Salem, NC: Wake Forest University Press/Loughcrew, Oldcastle: Gallery Press, 1995), p. 189.
10. Hewitt, 'Substance and Shadow', *Collected Poems*, p. 191.
11. Rand Brandes, '*Well Dreams: Essays on John Montague*, ed. Thomas Dillon Redshaw (Omaha, NE: Creighton University Press, 2004), p. 312.
12. Paul Muldoon, *The Prince of the Quotidien* (Winston-Salem: Wake Forest University Press/Loughcrew, Oldcastle: Gallery Press, 1994), p. 14.
13. Neil Corcoran, *Poets of Modern Ireland: Text, Context, Intertext* (Cardiff: University of Wales Press, 1999), pp. 123, 135.

14. Paul Muldoon, 'Moy Sand and Gravel', *Moy Sand and Gravel* (London: Faber and Faber/New York: Farrar, Straus and Giroux, 2002), p. 8.
15. Edna Longley, *The Living Stream: Literature and Revisionism in Ireland* (Newcastle: Bloodaxe Books, 1994), p. 169.
16. Ibid., p. 220.
17. Thomas Kinsella, *Collected Poems: 1956–2001* (Manchester: Carcanet, 2001), pp. 110–11. Hereafter referenced in the text as '*KCP*'.
18. Seamus Heaney, *The Place of Writing* (Atlanta, GA: Scholars Press, 1989), p. 63.
19. W. B. Yeats, 'The Black Tower', *Yeats's Poems*, ed. and annotated by A. N. Jeffares (London: Macmillan, 1989), p. 455.
20. The controversy raised by the anti-evolutionist Philip Gosse in *Omphalos* (1857) and entertained by Madam Blavatsky and probably Yeats, is revisited by Stephen Dedalus in *Ulysses* when he imagines 'naked Eve. She had no navel. Gaze. Belly without blemish' (James Joyce, *Ulysses* [New York: Random House, 1986], p. 32).
21. Helen Vendler, *Seamus Heaney* (Cambridge: Harvard University Press, 1998), pp. 89–90.
22. In 'Bog Oak' (*WO* 1972), Heaney has: 'I might tarry / with the moustached / dead ... // ... as a blow-down of smoke / struggles over the half-door' (*WO* 14).
23. W. B. Yeats, 'A General Introduction for My Work', *Essays & Introductions* (New York: Macmillan, 1961), p. 518.
24. Brown, *In the Chair*, pp. 83–4.
25. Eiléan Ní Chuilleanáin, *The Brazen Serpent* (Winston-Salem: Wake Forest University Press/Loughcrew, Oldcastle: Gallery Press, 1994), p. 10.
26. W. B. Yeats, *The Letters of W. B. Yeats*, ed. Allan Wade (New York: Macmillan, 1955), p. 922.
27. Michael Longley, 'The Linen Workers', *Collected Poems* (London: Cape, 2006), p. 119.
28. Derek Mahon, 'Consolation of Philosophy', *Collected Poems* (Oldcastle: Gallery, 1999), p. 50.

11

NEIL CORCORAN

Heaney and Yeats

I

Terence Brown ends his critical biography of Yeats with a chapter on his 'afterlife', an account of the various ways in which his work survives in subsequent writing. He says there that Seamus Heaney 'has engaged as critic with the poetic achievement of Yeats more fully than any other Irish poet since MacNeice'[1] – who published the first critical book on Yeats in 1941. In fact, Heaney's writings on Yeats to date would almost make a book too – relatively slim, but intellectually substantial. These are also usually instances of Heaney at his best as a critic, provoked into some of his most alert and challenged acts of attention.

A collection of Heaney on Yeats would begin with two essays of 1978. One, 'The Makings of a Music: Reflections on Wordsworth and Yeats', sustains a contrast between a poetry of 'surrender' and a poetry of 'discipline'. The other, 'Yeats as an Example?', adds a question mark to the title of an essay by W. H. Auden to suggest how deeply problematic a figure Yeats is for Heaney. 'Yeats as an Example?' is central to my sense of this relationship, and I shall return to it shortly.[2] Other essays would include the uncollected 'A Tale of Two Islands: Reflections on the Irish Literary Revival', published in 1980, in which the Protestant Anglo-Irish Yeats is compared with the nineteenth-century Catholic apostate novelist William Carleton.[3] Then there is an essay of 1988, 'The Place of Writing: W. B. Yeats and Thoor Ballylee', in which Heaney meditates on the various meanings of the Norman tower in the West of Ireland in which Yeats lived for a few years, and which he figured extensively in his poetry. The essay is one of three – the others are frequently allusive to Yeats too – which made a short book, also called *The Place of Writing*, published in the United States in 1988,[4] excerpts from which were reprinted in the prose collection *Finders Keepers* in 2002.

This putative collection of Heaney on Yeats would continue with an essay of 1990 called 'Joy or Night', which compares attitudes to death in Yeats and

Larkin, decisively favouring Yeats as 'more vital and undaunted' (*RP* 160, 147). It would include the lengthy essay written for *The Field Day Anthology of Irish Writing* in 1991, a revised version of which forms the introduction to the Faber selection of Yeats which Heaney published in 2000.[5] And it would end with the Nobel Prize acceptance speech delivered in Stockholm in 1995 entitled 'Crediting Poetry', which he subsequently reprinted at the end of his not-quite-collected volume, *Opened Ground: Poems 1966–1996*, in 1998.[6] An account of his own career as a poet in relation to the circumstances of Northern Ireland since 1969, this lecture is also much taken up with Yeats, that earlier Irish winner of this same prize. Peter McDonald has said that 'this feels like the last word on a topic Heaney knows must now be dropped',[7] but it is hard to agree that this must necessarily be so, given that Yeats remains as the supreme model for poetic persistence into old age.

Yeats has been, then, a constant presence in Heaney's criticism since the late 1970s, and a central figure in his consideration of poetic influence. Auden, in his elegy for Yeats on his death in 1939, famously said that 'The poet became his admirers.'[8] One of the admirers Yeats has most crucially become is Seamus Heaney.

The strenuousness of Heaney's ongoing engagement with Yeats is of keen interest not least because it sets him in the midst of one of the most fraught and contentious debates in recent Irish literary and cultural criticism, in which the voice of Seamus Deane has been particularly penetrating, with its articulation of Yeats's later career as an exercise in 'the pathology of literary Unionism', and with its inveighing against a criticism complaisantly tolerant of certain presumptively Yeatsian procedures in contemporary Northern Irish poetry which appear to propose that 'The literature – autonomous, ordered – stands over against the political system in its savage disorder.'[9] But it is of keen interest also because Heaney's place in Irish national life is of a kind that no Irish poet since Yeats has enjoyed, or endured. One consequence of this has been that, as early as the mid-1970s, Yeats was adduced in critical discussions of Heaney with the clear implication that he was to inherit the mantle. This must have been at least as daunting as it was encouraging; and it put Heaney in the way of the scepticism of his younger contemporary Paul Muldoon, who, in a prominently placed review of *Station Island* (1984), said that 'a truly uninvited shade' to the title-poem's purgatorial setting would advise this poet 'that he should resist more firmly the idea that he must be the best Irish poet since Yeats, which arose from rather casual remarks by the power-crazed Robert Lowell and the craze-powered Clive James, who seem to have forgotten both MacNeice and Kavanagh'.[10] That advice may not have been entirely innocent of this reviewer's jostling for his own place in the firmament; and I have written elsewhere of the complexities of the Heaney–Muldoon entanglements.[11] But the review certainly makes it plain that the relationship between Heaney and Yeats which I am discussing here is an affair of peculiar delicacy, in which the bold but wary subtleties of Heaney's negotiations over the years may have been almost matched by the subtleties of suspicious scrutiny to which they have been subjected.

I am interested here, however, in the way Yeats figures in Heaney's poems as well as in his critical prose. Any full treatment of this would prominently consider the sequence 'Singing School' in *North* (1975), whose title derives from Yeats's poem 'Sailing to Byzantium', and whose epigraphs set a quotation from Yeats's *Autobiographies* against another from Wordsworth's *Prelude* in a way that makes, of itself, an ironic political point; and it would examine many other poems in that volume too. It would think about the poem 'The Master' in the sequence 'Sweeney Redivivus' in *Station Island*, where the anonymous figure of authority is dressed in very Yeatsian imagery; and it might think about that poem all the more because Heaney in fact identifies the master in an interview as Czesław Miłosz.[12] It would consider 'A Peacock's Feather', published in *The Haw Lantern* (1987), but punctiliously dated 1972 – an extremely significant date in recent Irish history, about which I shall have more to say in a moment. This is an apparently occasional poem written for the christening of a niece, but its ironically Marvellian octosyllabics offer a consideration of Anglo-Irish and class resentments in which prominent reference is made to Yeats's poems of Coole Park, the Irish house owned by his patron, Lady Gregory. A full treatment of the topic would also examine the references to Yeats in the sequence 'Squarings' in *Seeing Things* (1991), in some of which we would discover, I think, a poet learning from Yeats's astonishing poem 'The Cold Heaven' one way of registering a religious sensibility without using the terms of religious orthodoxy. More generally, Heaney is a poet of antitheses – of time and eternity, world and other-world, earth and air – in the way Yeats is. Clearly, given this catalogue of instances, a full treatment of this relationship would need a book; but in this essay I want to isolate what seems to me one exceptionally significant moment of it, by bringing four texts into relationship: Heaney's essay 'Yeats as an Example?', written in 1978 and published in *Preoccupations* in 1980; Yeats's poem 'The Fisherman', published in *The Wild Swans at Coole* in 1919; Yeats's most famous political poem, 'Easter, 1916'; and Heaney's poem 'Casualty', published in *Field Work* (1979).

'Yeats as an Example?' is one of the most spirited of Heaney's earlier essays, in which we witness his approach to another writer with the clear awareness that this is going to be a significant phase of self-development. The essay notices, as much criticism has, something cold, violent and implacable in Yeats's art, and asks if this can be regarded as in any way exemplary.

Heaney does admire what he calls Yeats's 'intransigence', and admires too the way 'his vision did not confine itself to rhetorics, but issued in actions' (*P* 100). He respects, that is to say, the inextricability of the life and the work in this poet who maintained a theory of their separation. He then offers a quite unpredictable reading of a couple of moments from the life. One is from the 1890s, in the first flush of Yeats's enthusiasm for spiritualism, and the other from 1913, when he spoke in outrage against Irish middle-class philistinism. He did so on this occasion because Dublin Corporation had refused to fund a gallery for a collection of Impressionist paintings offered to the city by Lady Gregory's nephew, Hugh Lane. Where others have found only Yeats's silliness or snobbery in these episodes, and have ridiculed him, Heaney reads them as moments in which Yeats admirably 'took on the world on his own terms, defined the areas where he would negotiate and where he would not'. Heaney assumes that 'this peremptoriness, this apparent arrogance, is exemplary in an artist, that it is proper and even necessary for him to insist on his own language, his own vision, his own terms of reference'. Such admiration is in fact tempered in the essay as a whole by a concerted attempt to find in Yeats's work moments which are not peremptory or arrogant at all, but rather instinct with a kind of saving humanitarianism. The end of the essay, for instance, finds Yeats's poem 'Under Ben Bulben' unfortunate, even ethically obnoxious, in itself and particularly so as the intended final poem of his *Collected Poems*. Heaney would, he says, 'put a kinder poem last' – and finds such a thing in 'Cuchulain Comforted' (*P* 100).

But, to understand why, nevertheless, Heaney might approve of Yeatsian 'arrogance', I want to quote the second of his two instances from the life. His comment on it then leads into a quotation from 'The Fisherman'. The passage is a piece of raillery taken from the Anglo-Irish novelist George Moore's autobiography, *Hail and Farewell* (1925). Moore gives an account of the Lane controversy and of a lecture of his own on the Impressionists, which Yeats attended, and then Yeats appears, the victim of Moore's mocking and arrestingly engaging prose:

> As soon as the applause died away, Yeats who had lately returned to us from the States with a paunch, a huge stride, and an immense fur overcoat, rose to speak. We were surprised at the change in his appearance, and could hardly believe our ears when, instead of talking to us as he used to do about the old stories come down from generation to generation he began to thunder against the middle classes, stamping his feet, working himself into a temper, and all because the middle classes did not dip their hands into their pockets and give Lane the money he wanted for his exhibition. When he spoke the words, the middle classes, one would have thought that he was speaking against a personal foe, and we looked round asking each other with our eyes where on earth our

> Willie Yeats had picked up the strange belief that none but titled and carriage folk could appreciate pictures ...
>
> We have sacrificed our lives for art; but you, what have you done? What sacrifices have you made? he asked, and everybody began to search his memory for the sacrifices Yeats had made, asking himself in what prison Yeats had languished, what rags he had worn, what broken victuals he had eaten. As far as anybody could remember, he had always lived very comfortably, sitting down invariably to regular meals, and the old green cloak that was in keeping with his profession of romantic poet he had exchanged for the magnificent fur coat which distracted our attention from what he was saying, so opulently did it cover the back of the chair out of which he had risen ...[13]

This passage has the confidence, and perhaps the condescension, of Moore's own certain knowledge that he is himself, as the scion of a (Catholic) Big House far grander than Lady Gregory's, socially several cuts above 'our Willie Yeats'. Nevertheless, the critique of Yeats's aristocratic pretensions hits its target. Animated by animosity, Moore deflates Yeats in a rhetoric of bathos. And one might expect Seamus Heaney to have some sympathy with this, since he seems congenitally incapable of any such behaviour himself. He does of course note the 'theatricality' of Yeats's performance, but he regards it as deliberate. Yeats is busy creating out of himself, he says, 'a character who was almost as much a work of imagination' as James Joyce's Stephen Dedalus. And, Heaney thinks, for the same reason: the exercise of intransigence is a protection, he says, of 'the imaginative springs, so that the gift would survive' (*P* 108) – by which he means, of course, the gift of poetry.

Most poets must dread the departure of the gift. There are, after all, many precedents in literary history for that, including Wordsworth, who is probably the most deeply informing presence in Heaney; and a lot is made in this essay of the fact that Yeats is particularly exemplary for a poet 'approaching middle age', as Heaney may well have considered himself in 1978, when he was nearing forty. Yeats is of course, paradigmatically, the post-Romantic poet who managed to go on writing and, indeed, produced some of his greatest work in, and about, old age. It is in this context of writerly survival that Heaney then quotes the ending of 'The Fisherman' and comments:

> The solitude, the will towards excellence, the courage, the self-conscious turning away from that in which he no longer believes, which is Dublin life, and turning towards that which he trusts, which is an image or dream – all the drama and integrity of 'The Fisherman' depend to a large extent upon that other drama which George Moore so delightedly observed and reported. (*P* 108–9)

The apparent silliness or snobbery of the behaviour, that is to say, is a way of making possible new developments in the art. The drama of the life and the drama of the art, which must superficially seem discontinuous, are in fact continuous at the deepest creative level.

'The Fisherman' is written in trimeters: three-stress lines, occasionally varied to two-stress ones by Yeats. The form is stately but also taut, even nervous. It seems to permit the possibility of a heightened tone while at the same time preventing any such thing from being too easily achieved; and this tonal hesitation is underlined by the irresolution of the poem's pararhymes. In its first verse paragraph Yeats has disdained the urban middle classes – 'The craven man in his seat, / The insolent unreproved' – and then he turns to the West of Ireland fisherman of the poem's title. Such a person must seem, on the face of it, an unlikely recipient of the work of William Butler Yeats but he is celebrated here as the work's ideal, and ideally demanding, audience:

> Maybe a twelvemonth since
> Suddenly I began,
> In scorn of this audience,
> Imagining a man,
> And his sun-freckled face,
> And grey Connemara cloth,
> Climbing up to a place
> Where stone is dark under froth,
> And the down-turn of his wrist
> When the flies drop in the stream;
> A man who does not exist,
> A man who is but a dream;
> And cried, 'Before I am old
> I shall have written him one
> Poem maybe as cold
> And passionate as the dawn.'[14]

What exercises Heaney throughout 'Yeats as an Example?' and what 'The Fisherman' explicitly considers too is the relationship between poet and audience. The questions raised by this encounter between one Irish poet and another concern the way a relationship with an audience may become a worrying element in the attempt to survive properly as a poet; the desirability of remaking yourself, at a point in your life when you have become a public person as well as a private poet, in order to resist certain expectations; the necessity of refusing certain kinds of invitation or co-option. These were all also issues which Yeats faced, in their most exacerbated form, in 'Easter, 1916', also written in trimeters, and in many ways an exemplar for the political poem in the modern period, and a poem which shadows, for instance, W. H. Auden's trimeter poem 'September 1, 1939'. Heaney's poem 'Casualty', published in *Field Work* in 1979, just a year after 'Yeats as an Example?' was written, makes it clear why such issues should be the focus of his attention when writing about Yeats in the 1970s; and the poem is in some significant ways the acknowledgement of debts.

'Casualty', one of several elegies in this volume, is Heaney's sole poem 'about' Bloody Sunday, one of the crucially defining moments in Northern Ireland's recent history, and a poem more emphatically about a public event than anything else he has written. Heaney's attitude to the killings, and to the judgement of the Widgery tribunal which followed them, has never, I think, been much in doubt. My assumption is that he shares the view of Catholic nationalists, and others, that the finding represented a fundamental injustice, and his Nobel Prize speech is explicit about how 'the "mere Irish" in oneself was appalled by the ruthlessness of the British Army on occasions like Bloody Sunday in Derry in 1972' (*OG* 454–5). He also published in *The Sunday Times* on 2 February 1997, to commemorate the twenty-fifth anniversary of the event, some of the lyrics of a broadside called 'The Road to Derry', written in 1972.[15] These read, in part, 'And in the dirt lay justice like an acorn in the winter / Till its oak would sprout in Derry where the thirteen men lay dead' – where the metaphor, drawing on the etymology of the word 'Derry' (from 'doire', the oakwood), carries implications of resentment and the necessity for reparation. It is also not irrelevant that it was later in 1972 that Heaney moved from Belfast to the Republic. What bearing, if any, the events of Bloody Sunday and their aftermath had on this move I am in no position to say, but it was the material of media speculation at the time, and the figure of the poet as 'inner emigré' in 'Exposure' in *North* (*N* 73) may be thought to reflect the move from North to South, just as one significance of the poem's title is undoubtedly the media 'exposure' which accompanied it.

Whatever the reactions of Heaney as a man and as the composer of a song lyric, however, his reactions as a poet are much more complex, and their complexity resides in, precisely, his sense of audience. 'Casualty' is, among other things, the register of that complexity. It involves a fundamental refusal to express perhaps anticipated nationalist sentiment, since it is an elegy not for the dead of Bloody Sunday, but for one man, a fisherman, killed by the Irish Republican Army in the reprisal bombing of a pub shortly afterwards: the word 'Casualty' of the title is the anonymising of this person in the usual neutrally exculpating way of the military, or paramilitary, strategist who also, of course, conventionally 'regrets' such casualties. That this is Heaney's only explicit consideration of Bloody Sunday, and that he waited seven years before he published it is in itself very revealing, particularly when we remember that Thomas Kinsella published an outraged satire called 'Butcher's Dozen' within a week of the publication of the Widgery report. In concentrating on the individual death, Heaney is honouring, first of all, a personal rather than a political obligation: the poem seems initiated by the commemorative and preservative desire to give a character back to this man who would otherwise be only an anonymous statistic. This is, that is to say, a real, as opposed to Yeats's ideal, fisherman: he is 'dole-kept' indeed, even though 'a natural for work' (*FW* 21), because Northern Ireland in the 1970s had one of the highest unemployment rates in Europe; and furthermore – and this is the one point in the poem at which nationalist resentment breaks cover – the vast majority of the unemployed were Catholic.[16]

There is no doubt that Heaney intends an allusion to Yeats's poem, since not only do both involve fishermen, but they share a metre and the subtle and tactical deployment of pararhyme, although Heaney varies the rhyme scheme itself. The connection between the poems was pointed out, in fact, by Blake Morrison in the first critical book on Heaney, in which Yeats, along with Joyce, is read as a 'governing spirit',[17] although not much more than this is made of the relationship. Heaney's revision of Yeats's ideal into a real man in a socially particularised Northern Ireland – rather than, as in Yeats, an idealised Connemara – is managed deftly: but it carries a large cultural freight. Some of this is explicated in a critical essay I referred to earlier, 'A Tale of Two Islands'. There, Yeats's vision of the West and its noble peasantry and hard-riding country gentlemen is read as 'not ennobling but disabling'.[18] Yeats's image of the fisherman, that is to say, shares with other such images and symbols in his work a mystificatory quality, offering the Irish a self-image which, if accepted, could only prove sentimentalising, nostalgic or fey, an image deriving from the cultural condescensions of a post-Arnoldian Celticity and a more recent Celtic Twilightery. That essay, and this element of the poem 'Casualty', are in complete harmony with the revisionist criticism of Yeats which has dominated the study of his work since the early 1970s.

But there is also in the poem a vivid evocation of the amiably masculine relationship between fisherman and poet, which nevertheless includes a strong sense of constraint. Where Yeats's fisherman – coldly isolated from all the appurtenances of modernity in an idealised, oneiric West of Ireland – is unambiguously the poet's ideal first audience, Heaney's, the poet tells us, finds his 'other life' – the life of poetry, that is – 'Incomprehensible' (*FW* 21). Yet it is the fisherman who raises the subject, seeking understanding, and the poet who refuses to pursue it, even if, understandably, 'shy of condescension' (*FW* 21) because to speak at all would be to speak about all they do not share. Arguably, however, this refusal is in fact the greater condescension, the committing by silence or elision of precisely the offence which the poet claims to wish to avoid; and a readerly unease at this point matches the deep social unease which attends the encounter. The poet of 'Casualty' falters where the poet of 'Digging', the first poem in Heaney's first full-length book, bridges a comparable gap with the metaphor of the pen as spade, and does so with apparent confidence ('I'll dig with it'; *DN* 14), but perhaps with a certain stridency which is itself a register of vulnerability. And when the word 'educated' does finally figure in 'Casualty', it does so almost as rebuke or taunt from fisherman to poet: 'Now you're supposed to be / An educated man. / Puzzle me the right answer / To that one' (*FW* 23). In some subsequent poems of Heaney's, as if in reparation for such actual condescension, poetry and fishing are soldered metaphorically together, and with a casualness which implicitly constructs a bridge: 'poetry, say, or fishing', in 'The Daylight Art' from *The Haw Lantern* (*HL* 9), for instance.

In 'Casualty' the question to which the fisherman asks the poet to 'puzzle the answer' is 'How culpable was he / That last night when he broke / Our tribe's complicity?' and it occurs after the poem's description of the funerals of the thirteen dead in its second section, where the fisherman's refusal of 'complicity' is opposed by that peculiarly ambivalent imagery used of the mourners, the 'swaddling band, / Lapping, tightening / Till we were braced and bound / Like brothers in a ring'. There is steadying resolve in this but there is also a hint of constriction. The complexity of this poem's sense of complicity is that it is the fisherman's refusal of it – specifically, his refusal to honour the IRA's curfew, those 'threats [that] were phoned' – which is paradoxically, but causally, both his freedom and his death: the fisherman become the fish, 'Swimming towards the lure / Of warm, lit-up places' (*FW* 23) and, doing so, lured to his death. And so the final part of the poem sets him as the object of this poet's agonised self-enquiry. In this respect, however – and this is a kind of allusive irony in 'Casualty' – this fisherman turns back into something much more like Yeats's ideal. In his ghosthood, Heaney's fisherman too is a man who does not exist, a man who is but a dream. And actually this staging of the encounter as a dialogue within the poem – which does not happen in Yeats – may represent a crossing of Yeats with Wordsworth, the poets also joined in 'The Makings of a Music'. The moment resembles the one in 'Resolution and Independence', where the poet says of the leech-gatherer that

> ... the whole body of the man did seem
> Like one whom I had met with in a dream;
> Or like a man from some far region sent,
> To give me human strength, by apt admonishment.[19]

No longer the socially realised character of his first appearance, but the symbolically challenging and questioning 'revenant', this fisherman cannot supply any actual answers, but only those the poet chooses to ventriloquise on his behalf and to draw from his example or admonishment: 'How culpable was he / That last night when he broke / Our tribe's complicity?' (*FW* 23) – where the word 'tribe', inflected with the demotic, also has the harshness of judgement.

I have just said that the fisherman 'turns back' into something more like Yeats's fisherman; and in doing so, I am using the language of the poem itself, where the image of the turned back is prominent, and so too is an imagery of the specular. 'Casualty' is preoccupied with watching, observing, seeing and being seen, and with how, in these processes of scrutiny, you might choose to turn, to turn your back, to turn back. It is a poem, that is to say, about how a poet, or a poem, might discover his, or its, own appropriate or 'proper' audience – this dead fisherman – and might do so by resisting another audience's – the 'tribe's' – expectations or assumptions. 'Casualty' is a refusal of instrumentality, an insistence on the virtue of reflection. Far from being what he has sometimes been accused of being – a poet who, whatever he says, says nothing – Heaney is here, schooled by the Yeatsian example in self-protective intransigence, insisting on the poet's right to do otherwise.

Questions of a rhetorical kind function crucially in 'Easter, 1916' too – 'O when may it suffice?'; 'What if excess of love / Bewildered them till they died?'; 'What is it but nightfall?'; 'Was it needless death after all?'[20] – and one may think that Heaney, in approaching a public political event, is at once accommodating himself to a Yeatsian tradition of the public poem and muting its tonalities in the more intimate register of address of 'The Fisherman'. If it is Yeats who looks at Heaney in 'Casualty', and the ghosts of Yeats's metres and rhetorical inflections which haunt Heaney's, the ethic of 'Casualty' is the emulation not of Yeatsian intransigence, such as Heaney found in the performing self of George Moore's anecdote, but rather of the urge to decision, singularity, authoritative independence. The mood of this in Yeats's 'The Fisherman' is passionately indicative and promissory, voicing itself in a cry; in Heaney it is still mutedly interrogative, although the poem's final use of the verb 'Question' is itself voiced in the imperative. The result is that 'Casualty' could never be accused, as Kinsella's 'Butcher's Dozen' – however justified its anger – perhaps could, of being itself complicit with military or paramilitary action or reaction. The poem's ellipsis and its self-questionings are a deeply meditated stepping to one side of the ethic of revenge. Even so, the questions about poetic responsibility in relation to public atrocity which are raised here, in the context of Bloody Sunday, with a painful, even piercing intensity, remain unanswered in the poem, only to be raised again and again in the work of this much-haunted and endlessly self-questioning poet.

II

'Casualty' powerfully suggests, I think, that the relationship between successor poets need not be, or need not be only, a matter of contestation and misreading, as it is in the influential work of Harold Bloom. It may also be a difficult education in the exemplary, and one found where you might least expect it: in Yeats, a haughty Anglo-Irish Protestant kowtowing to the aristocracy and sometimes venting anti-Catholic spleen, for instance, when you are Heaney, a Northern Irish Catholic from a farming background who was subjected in youth to some of the political results of the venting of anti-Catholic spleen. Form, which involves interrelationship as well as self-limitation, is a kind of society; and, if you are an exceptional poet, it is where you encounter the only true society of your peers, your only true first audience. As in all well-regulated societies, contractual relationships of obligation, indebtedness and responsibility obtain. But so too do relationships of challenge, enquiry, scrutiny and self-advancement. Relationships between poets may be corroborative as well as competitive, but only when they are bravely entered into; and this is a conclusion also reached by Fiona Stafford in her book *Starting Lines*, as part of an argument against the singularity or monodrama of Bloom's view of poetic influence where, in her reading of one of the 'Squarings' poems in *Seeing Things*, she derives the word 'corroborative' from Heaney himself.[21] Formal indebtedness of the kind I have considered here is something substantively, and ethically, distinct from intertextuality. In Julia Kristeva, the theorist who first, in her readings of Bakhtin, gave the term currency, intertextuality has nothing whatever to do with human agency, with intersubjectivity, but with the 'transposition of one (or several) sign-system(s) into another': the use of the term 'intertextuality' to denote the 'study of sources' is, she says, 'banal'.[22] It is far too late now in literary history and criticism to avoid that banality, and in any case I hope that what I have offered here has been something more complex in its poetics, ethics and politics than the *de-haut-en-bas* Kristevan phrase 'study of sources', which seems intended as a slur, might suggest. In my view, to attempt an engagement with form, to show how and why particular forms both derive from, and meet, specific contingencies, necessarily involves criticism in the processes of agency, and not only the agency of the individual poet, but the agency also of historical and political circumstance.

In any such consideration, questions of value also matter. Heaney is braced but not bound by the Yeatsian heritage, difficult as that is to approach and assimilate, and in this he differs from many lesser poets. 'Casualty' is not so much a Bloomian 'map of misreading' as the graph of a brave engagement with the best that is itself one of the signatures of the newly excellent. This engagement is figured explicitly in one of the 'Squarings' poems, xxii of the sub-sequence 'Settings'. It ends with a reference to Yeats as, this time, himself the revenant, now become the object of the poet's questions. These have their gnomic element, but they are to do with the cohabitation between what the poem calls 'spirit', which is, of course, a substantial word in Yeats, and what it calls 'perfected form' (*ST* 78). 'Spirit' I take to be what it is traditionally, the animating principle, cognate with the more explicitly religious term 'soul', which is a word the poem also risks. And 'perfected form' is, I think, the initially daunting architecture of the Yeatsian poem, or poetic sequence (that very Yeatsian form). The imagery of this 'Squarings' poem, with its birds, its dawn cold, its stone tower, its Big House statuary and horticulture, is all Yeatsian. The questions with which it concludes are those of a Seamus Heaney who, even if now undaunted, turns aside, in the parenthesis of the final line, with what seems a wry, even embarrassed, but saving, *moue* at this act of his own presumption: the poet suddenly become examiner of the schoolboy Yeats, asking impossibly large questions which, if they may be answered at all, may be answered only by the next, and then, again, the next poem:

> How habitable is perfected form?
> And how inhabited the windy light?
>
> What's the use of a held note or held line
> That cannot be assailed for reassurance?
> (Set questions for the ghost of W. B.)

NOTES

1. Terence Brown, *The Life of W. B. Yeats* (Oxford: Blackwell, 1999), p. 381.
2. Both are collected in *P*.
3. Seamus Heaney, 'A Tale of Two Islands', in *Irish Studies*, 1, ed. P. J. Drudy (Cambridge: Cambridge University Press, 1980), pp. 1–20.
4. Seamus Heaney, *The Place of Writing* (Atlanta, GA: Scholars Press, 1988).
5. Seamus Heaney, 'William Butler Yeats (1865–1939)', in *The Field Day Anthology of Irish Writing*, ed. Seamus Deane (Derry: Field Day Publications, 1991), vol. II, pp. 783–90 and Introduction to *W. B. Yeats: Poems Selected by Seamus Heaney* (London: Faber and Faber, 2000).
6. *OG* 445–67.
7. Peter McDonald, 'Faiths and Fidelities: Heaney and Longley in Mid-Career', in *Last Before America: Irish and American Writing: Essays in honour of Michael Allen*, ed. Fran Brearton and Eamonn Hughes (Belfast: Blackstaff Press, 2001), p. 15.
8. W. H. Auden, 'In Memory of W. B. Yeats', *Collected Poems* (London: Faber and Faber, 1991), pp. 247–9.
9. Seamus Deane, *Heroic Style: The Tradition of an Idea* (Derry: Field Day Publications, 1984), reprinted in *Ireland's Field Day* (London: Hutchinson, 1985), p. 50, and General Introduction, *Field Day Anthology*, vol. I, p. xxvi. Other important discussions of Heaney and Yeats are Jon Stallworthy, 'The Poet as Archaeologist: W. B. Yeats and Seamus Heaney', *Review of English Studies* ns 33: 130 (May 1982), pp. 158–74; and Jonathan Allison, 'Seamus Heaney's Yeats', *Yeats: An Annual of Critical and Textual Studies* 14 (1996), pp. 19–47.

10. Paul Muldoon, 'Sweeney Peregrine', *London Review of Books* (1–14 November 1984), p. 20.
11. Neil Corcoran, 'A Languorous Cutting Edge: Muldoon versus Heaney?', in *Poets of Modern Ireland: Text, Context, Intertext* (Cardiff: University of Wales Press, 1999), pp. 121–36.
12. Rui Carvalho Homem, 'On Elegies, Eclogues, Translations, Transfusions: An interview with Seamus Heaney', *European English Messenger* 10:2 (Autumn 2001), p. 30. ('But "The Master" is specifically about meeting with my hero, Czesław Miłosz. Many people think it's about Yeats because it's set in a tower and so on.')
13. George Moore, *Hail and Farewell* (1925), ed. Richard Cave (Gerrards Cross: Colin Smythe, 1985), p. 540.
14. W. B. Yeats, 'The Fisherman', *Yeats's Poems*, ed. and annotated by A. N. Jeffares (London: Macmillan, 1989), p. 252.
15. 'Nobel poet discloses his despair at Bloody Sunday', *The Sunday Times* (2 February 1997), p. 3.
16. I am grateful to Patrick Crotty for discussion of this point.
17. Blake Morrison, *Seamus Heaney* (London and New York: Methuen, 1982), p. 79.
18. Heaney, 'A Tale of Two Islands', p. 11.
19. William Wordsworth, 'Resolution and Independence', *Poems in Two Volumes and Other Poems 1800–1807*, ed. J. Curtis (Ithaca, NY: Cornell University Press, 1983), p. 123.
20. W. B. Yeats, 'Easter, 1916', *Yeats's Poems*, ed. Jeffares, p. 288.
21. Fiona Stafford, *Starting Lines in Scottish, Irish, and English Poetry: From Burns to Heaney* (Oxford: Oxford University Press, 2000), p. 294, where she quotes from Heaney's 'Foreword' to *Lifelines: An Anthology of Poems Chosen by Famous People*, ed. Niall Macmonagle (London: Penguin Books, 1993).
22. Julia Kristeva, 'Revolution in Poetic Language' (1974), reprinted in *The Kristeva Reader* ed. Toril Moi (Oxford: Basil Blackwell, 1986), p. 111.

12

GUINN BATTEN

Heaney's Wordsworth and the Poetics of Displacement

In an admired poem in the sonnet series 'Clearances' in memory of his recently dead mother, Seamus Heaney recalls her death in this way:

> ... we all knew one thing by being there.
> The space we stood around had been emptied
> Into us to keep, it penetrated
> Clearances that suddenly stood open.
> High cries were felled and a pure change happened.
>
> ('Clearances', vii; *HL* 31)

It may not be surprising that 'The Thorn' is the poem by Wordsworth which Heaney, after an opening discussion of the bog-like spots of time in *The Prelude*, chose for his point of focus in his crucial essay 'Feeling into Words'. At the centre of that Romantic poem is a cloaked, threatening, but also compelling female figure. She embodies what Wordsworth in *The Prelude* and elsewhere describes as Nature's vexed, redundant energies, its reflexive and recursive return of acts of human aggression towards her secret places. In the concluding pages of his essay Heaney puts that figure into a more specifically Irish context. Referring to the 'religious intensity of the violence' in Northern Ireland as 'a struggle between the cults and devotees of a god and a goddess', he calls that goddess an 'indigenous territorial numen, a tutelary of the whole island', citing the names given to her in Ireland: 'Mother Ireland, Kathleen Ni Houlihan, the poor old woman, the Shan Van Vocht, whatever'. Known earlier in Irish legend as 'Sovereignty', that female figure's very name 'has been temporarily usurped by a new male cult whose founding fathers were Cromwell, William of Orange and Edward Carson ... What we have is the tail-end of a struggle in a province between territorial piety and imperial power' (*P* 57).

Patricia Coughlan in 'Bog Queens' criticises Heaney for representing 'place' as female. 'Mother Ireland', represented in such statements as the one just quoted as oppressed by a foreign patriarchy that has usurped the native male's sexual possession of her, is in turn oppressed by the poet who represents her as vacating her place so that he, as the representative speaker for the plight of 'Ireland', may usurp it. Yet here, in that second or 'emptying' stage of disempowerment, a paradox emerges: in assuming the place of Mother Ireland, in displacing into his own voice her latent power, the Irish male poet, Coughlan contends, who elsewhere is '(phallically) digging and ploughing like his ancestors', ironically thereby 'becomes the culturally female voice of the subjugated Irish, about to inundate the "masculine" hardness of the planters' boundaries with "feminine" vowel-floods'.[1]

We must take seriously Coughlan's charge that there is an internal and logical inconsistency in Heaney's effort to be both maternal place and, as poetic son, the oedipal usurper (or reclaimant of place) – both source and subject – if we are to understand how Heaney's poetry in fact offers a fresh and appealing understanding of the way that masculine forms of embodiment may, contrary to expectation, identify with the maternal body. Notably in his use of such rhetorical paradoxes as the self-inwoven simile or the self-doubling term or image – for which the archetype might be Freud's own exploration of the etymology as well as the phenomenon of the 'uncanny' – Heaney challenges rather than underwrites the very convention that he seems to advocate in that citation from 'Feeling into Words'. This convention refers to place in order to ground an alleged distinction between source and subject, muse and poet, and in turn confirms a maternal relationship in which the son may desire, but not imitate, the mother.

We may note, for example, one of the most powerful – and most Wordsworthian – moments in Heaney's poetry of place and displacement: the moment quoted at the beginning of this essay, in which a maternal absence *penetrates* (transgresses) the poet who now must speak in, and even from *within*, that interior place cleared by her active absence. This extraordinary moment should remind Heaney's readers of those other places celebrated but also feared in his poetry, ruled by female figures who are by turns old and young, fierce and seductive, nurturing and destructive, powerful but absent. In such places, which include the bog and the water pump, Heaney in fact echoes the two sources of mysterious power in 'The Thorn' – the muddy ground and the upright tree, both of which are associated with maternal power. Indeed, he may even collapse them into a single image in the figure of the pump, a trope that notably undergoes transformation from 'Rite of Spring' to 'Mossbawn' to 'Changes'. In that last poem the nest, emptied of the mother bird who nevertheless in some way broods beside its 'single egg, pebbly white', becomes displaced into a site of emptiness within the self. Yet it is not the path to that actual place but rather the path to its displacement in memory – in this case a memory notably to be shared by a father and his daughter – that the father urges his own nestling to 'retrace … when you have grown away and stand at last / at the very centre of the empty city' (*SI* 37).

That image of the emptied place, figured by Heaney in 'Clearances' as the absence of a felled chestnut, is made coterminous with his mother's place in his life; that palpable absence particularly haunts Heaney in the essay that led him to retrace his own path as a Nature poet in the year just after his mother's death. In 'The Placeless Heaven' the chestnut transplanted from that favoured Heaney image, the 'jam jar' (itself, of course, an image of transformed purpose), is identified not (as in 'Clearances') with the mother but with himself as a poet. Here, the growing tree serves as an objective correlative of the poet's own growing sense of himself as an individual subject, as a subject who, while he may remain rooted in (maternal) place, also imaginatively supersedes it. The subject, as he writes, thereby acquires an 'indigenous afterlife' (*GT* 4). Yet the mother does not absent herself altogether from the afterlife. Also in that essay, Heaney reads Patrick Kavanagh's later poetry as a reconciliation, through a poem for his own mother, with the matriarchal authority of place in Ireland, freeing the poet tethered to a negative image of Mother Ireland in 'The Great Hunger' to write instead love poems to Mother Earth, fulfilling his own claim that 'naming these things is the love-act and its pledge'.[2]

Through his own mother Heaney learns to 'listen' for, as well as to 'loosen' the ties that bind him to maternal place, to recognise that the feminine power whose echoes he may seem to have 'co-opted and obliterated' through poetic representation persists as a model 'behind the linear black' of bereavement:

She taught me what her uncle once taught her:
How easily the biggest coal block split
If you got the grain and hammer angled right.

The sound of that relaxed alluring blow,
Its co-opted and obliterated echo,
Taught me to hit, taught me to loosen,

('Clearances', *HL* 24)

Heaney, keenly reading an English and Romantic patrimony in which the poet imaginatively *sounds* in order to *express* a maternal absence linked to place, has developed a politics and poetics of embodiment inseparable from his politics and poetics of displacement. Further, he situates the experience of embodiment *as* displacement within Ireland's particular history of dispossession, which includes famine (the land's failure to fulfil, maternally, the human need to 'incorporate' its bounty) and eviction, the clearance or 'emptying' of the land. These histories intersect and climax in 'Station Island', where the dead hunger striker, Francis Hughes, is represented through the poetic speaker's own discomfiting displacement (*SI* ix).

For Wordsworth as for Heaney, the poetic relationship to place involves displacement, in two senses. First, place (or Nature) is, through the active engagement of the senses, displaced into the self that will both preserve and imitate her power. Indeed, the self is already imitative of Nature or 'place' precisely in being a *place* that swallows (in bog-like fashion) and that which, in turn, is pursued or even swallowed by the entity that has been imaginatively incorporated: see, for example, Wordsworth's 'Boy of Winander' and Heaney's 'Toome'. Through such an act of displacement the poet comes to understand that his own exilic *experience* of displacement is part of what he shares not only with place but also, by extension, with 'place' as it is defined as maternal.[3] Heaney in *North*, like Wordsworth in 'Michael', locates violence less in the historical invasion or enclosure of place than in the occupation of the body *by* that place that has been invaded or enclosed. Through that place's *own* experience, the native (whether poet or agricultural worker) who lives there cannot help but become, in some sense, connected to the intrusive or enclosing power, whether it is the English law that reaches into Michael's hearth or the Viking invader whom Heaney locates in the bog that is his own imagination. Moreover, for both poets an external source of power figured as place or 'Nature' comes to the fore in times when political crisis is experienced as personal crisis. As that power is recognised by the self, it seems not only to become one's own but to be what is most *essentially* one's being or selfhood, whether it is Wordsworth experiencing a crisis of alienation on home turf in 1792 or Heaney recoiling from the recursive forms of terror and counter-terror in the 1970s. This interpenetrative figuring of place, power and the body suggests that Heaney's understanding of 'imperial' violence, 'territorial piety' and the maternal entity he calls 'the goddess' is in fact more nuanced than these contentious phrases in the 1974 essay 'Feeling into Words' might suggest (*P* 57).

We witness such swallowing of the source by that which it has generated in those examples in Heaney of the rhetorical paradox that Christopher Ricks terms the *self-inwoven* or *reflexive simile*, a device that 'describes something both as itself and as something external to it which it could not possibly be'.[4] 'The Grauballe Man' offers perhaps the clearest example of such a paradox: 'As if he had been poured / in tar, he lies / on a pillow of turf / and seems to weep // the black river of himself' (*N* 35). It is a characteristic trope, Ricks writes, of the 'gifted group of Ulster poets' who 'write out of an imagination of civil war'.[5]

In Heaney's poetry, arguably the most extended and purposeful of those examples are found in *North*, where the subject-poet's relationship to objects that have been buried in the Irish landscape or, more particularly, the bog, is either interiorised or doubled (made redundant) by the presence of those objects in the self. This is sometimes expressed in images that strikingly involve, in relation to place or source, *both* its internalisation and its redundancy. In 'Viking Dublin: Trial Pieces' the speaker describes the writing on a piece of Viking bone as the generation of an interior space: 'a small outline // was incised, a cage / or trellis to conjure in' (*N* 21). We might note that this line, in diction and intention, echoes Keats's poem about an interiorisation that is also a doubling of place, 'Ode to Psyche': 'the wreath'd trellis of a working brain'.[6] Turning one's own writing into the *source* of one's writing, the following description also makes the tongue double the work of the hand, engendering thereby a self-inwoven simile at its centre: 'Like a child's tongue, / following the toils // of his calligraphy, / like an eel swallowed / in a basket of eels, / the line amazes itself // eluding the hand / that fed it' (*N* 21). Later the speaker figuratively uses his own hand to reach into 'mother-wet caches' in the museum display for a 'trial piece' of Nordic art 'incised' by a child, beginning a process whereby that object, 'a longship, a buoyant / migrant line', becomes a source that 'enters my longhand, / turns cursive, unscarfing / a zoomorphic wake, / a worm of thought // I follow into the mud' (*N* 23). He follows the source, in other words, back to a maternal source that is now personal and bodily. Like the poet in crisis whom Wordsworth describes in Book X of the 1805 *Prelude*, this speaker – describing himself as Hamlet, the melancholy Dane, 'skull-handler, parablist, / smeller of rot // in the state' – is himself 'infused' with the state's (his source's) 'poisons' (*N* 23). The muddy bog into which this speaker follows his own thought is a 'zoomorphic wake' – the residual and bodily trace of the longship but also the memorial, funereal sign of its absence. That bog's relationship to the bodies buried there, like the self-inwoven simile, is exemplary of the place that swallows and preserves its subjects only, in turn, to be swallowed and preserved by *them*, each digesting and hoarding the other. Confusing those processes with thought itself – as Heaney himself does deliberately in finding for poetic and cultural memory in 'Feeling into Words' the objective correlative of 'Bogland' – the 'seeps' of Nature that digest the body in 'Bog Queen' become in turn the 'illiterate roots' that die and are internalised in the stomach's 'cavings' and 'hoards' (*N* 32).

Wordsworth's 'The Thorn' features not one but two such muddy, boggy sites, both of which are associated with an infant murdered by its mother. Now, in death, the 'moss' it has become threatens to drag her into the burial bog. In 'Feeling into Words', Heaney cites in full the most interesting of the poem's stanzas representing these strange spots. In the first citation, 'to the left' of the thorn, 'three yards beyond, / You see a little muddy pond / Of water never dry' (*P* 49). The other objective correlative of the infant grave, 'the beauteous hill of moss', appears in the second Heaney citation, where that arresting spot suddenly and forcefully comes alive in response to a show of public and institutional authority that would bring to justice the mysterious, nocturnal 'Woman in a scarlet cloak' (a figure both seductive and deadly who bears, as mentioned earlier, comparison with the Irish Kathleen Ni Houlihan). That woman haunts both the tree and the bog, in a stanza Heaney cites in full, concluding with the observation that '"The Thorn" is a nicely documented example of feeling getting into words, in ways that paralleled much in my own experience' (*P* 51), an assertion he follows with a reflexive statement not unlike the self-inwoven simile – or like the bog poem in its reference to the 'posthumous': 'although I must say that it is hard to discriminate between feeling getting into words and words turning into feeling, and it is only on posthumous occasions like this that the distinction arises' (*P* 52). Heaney even suggests that perhaps it is best to leave the graves of the self unopened, their secrets intact, lest the 'inquest' of naming them 'have the effect of confining them to what is named' (*P* 52).

Just as threatening as the opened bog-grave or the quaking sod – the unstable place or permeable boundary to which the subject engendered by it cannot return without at once swallowing and being swallowed *by* it – may well be the uncanny experience of the double who is often encountered in such haunted sites. In 'The Thorn' that redundancy manifests itself in the gnarled tree that is arguably an allegory for the withering of liberty. In a passage from Book Ten of the 1805 *Prelude* to which Heaney calls particular attention in 'Place and Displacement' (an essay written, significantly, just after the death of Heaney's mother), Wordsworth refers to 'the ravage of this most unnatural strife', whereby England, in declaring an 'unnatural' war against the ideal of liberty in France, displaced that war into what Wordsworth calls 'my own heart': 'I, who with the breeze / Had played, a green leaf on the blessed tree / Of my beloved country – nor had wished / For happier fortune than to wither there – / Now from my pleasant station was cut off' (*FK* 113–14). The thorn also serves, of course, as an objective correlative for the poem's version of the cruel mother, Martha Ray. For an Irish reader such as Heaney that thorn's decrepitude – 'It looks so old and grey' – might find associative links with the maternal figure for Ireland, mentioned by Heaney in 'Feeling into Words', who in her destructive aspect leads her sons to martyrdom.

This condition of being doubled by place, in which either half of this doubling – the self or its setting – is to a certain extent a situation of *dis*placement, seems particularly applicable to Northern Ireland. In 'Place and Displacement', Heaney writes that it is a place which, for the cultural nationalist, is at once governed from London and, imaginatively, inclusive of part of the Ireland that is not. As Heaney well knows, that sense of being torn between places was not unfamiliar to Wordsworth. He sought (in flight, it has been argued, from the surveillance of England's Home Office) to find in Goslar a new home with Dorothy, even as both siblings returned imaginatively from that place of foreign speech to Grasmere, where they together imagined yet another future home. Yet Wordsworth, who already had a home – an illegitimate daughter and her mother whom he had abandoned in France – surely reproached himself for that hope that 'home' might ever be a single, rather than a double, phenomenon. Likewise Heaney sought in Glanmore a second home from which he might write Wordsworthian poems that would nevertheless express his own Irish perspective on the politically troubled home-place – Northern Ireland – he had, in effect, abandoned. Darcy O'Brien in 'Seamus Heaney and Wordsworth: A Correspondent Breeze' writes of Heaney's 'sombre and self-critical mood' in December 1973, a period when he also told O'Brien, 'I've been getting a lot out of Wordsworth lately.'[7] In the final poem of the Glanmore sequence the speaker dreams disturbingly of himself and his wife (who jokingly resists serving in the role of 'Dorothy') as effigies in a cold pastoral. In the dream, while the couple resemble the legendary Irish lovers Diarmuid and Grainne, they also fulfil the death wish Wordsworth expressed, recorded by Dorothy in her journal and cited in full by Heaney in 'The Makings of a Music'. According to Dorothy, as the brother and sister once were lying together but 'apart' in a 'trench' surrounded by waterfalls, 'the sound of waters in the air – the voice of the air', led Wordsworth to suggest, 'it would be as sweet thus to lie in the grave' (*P* 68).

But Heaney is never more clearly modelling his own prose and poetry on that of Wordsworthian displacement than when, like his forebear, he writes the anniversary poem or essay that returns to a previous place of writing. Themes in the 1974 essay 'Feeling into Words' recur in 'The Makings of a Music' in 1977; 'Place and Displacement: Recent Poetry from Northern Ireland' was delivered (shortly after the death of Heaney's mother) as a lecture at the Wordsworth Summer School in 1984. That essay is in turn revisited nine years later in the Oxford lecture that became the concluding chapter in *The Redress of Poetry* 'Frontiers of Writing' (a title which itself echoes the Heaney poem that appeared, with 'Clearances', in *Haw Lantern*: 'From the Frontier of Writing'). Like the author of 'Tintern Abbey', the Wordsworth who repeatedly revisits the spots of time to dislocate and relocate them in the 1799, 1805 and 1850 versions of *Prelude*, Heaney knows that such spots – memories that collapse space and time into a condensed, obdurate place in consciousness – are, as Wordsworth writes, 'hiding places' of a 'power' that is simultaneously one's own and elusive of full possession or (to use Wordsworth's term) of 'restoration'.[8]

In a passage that first appeared in the 1799 *Prelude*, the second part of which, significantly, largely concerns itself with 'nourishment that came unsought',[9] Wordsworth figures the empty place or 'vacancy' that emerges in memory through the distance between a prior and the present self. This passage may have been a source for Heaney's own figurings of emptiness and memory in 'Changes' and 'Clearances': 'so wide appears / The vacancy between me and those days, / Which yet have such self-presence in my heart / That sometimes when I think of them I seem / Two consciousnesses – conscious of myself, / And of some other being' (27–31). What follows is an image of 'splitting' in relation to a crone figure – 'assiduous for the length of sixty years' – whose place has been usurped by a public structure, the Hawkshead Town Hall (32–45):[10] 'I found that it was split and gone to build / A smart assembly-room that perked and flared / With wash and rough-cast' (14–15).

The naming of the stone after the old dame suggests a local and English correspondent to the *dinnseanchas* tradition in Ireland, the naming of place that Heaney in 'The Sense of Place' calls a 'feeling, assenting, equable marriage between the geographical country and the country of the mind', a 'marriage that constitutes the sense of place in its richest possible manifestation' (*P* 132). To John Montague, an Irish poet who is also an avid and perceptive reader of Wordsworth, Heaney attributes a 'feminine image' of place in which, as for Wordsworth, 'the landscape becomes a memory, a piety, a loved mother'. This Wordsworthian aspect of Montague is represented by the term Heaney uses – 'sounding' – to describe Montague's displaced relationship to the Irish landscape, his 'sounding lines, rods to plumb the depths of a shared and diminished culture' (*P* 141).

In Wordsworth's poetry those sounding lines appear, as Heaney surely recollected,[11] at a memorable moment in Wordsworth's life: having just lost his mother, he is removed to Hawkshead Grammar School where (on a peninsula shaped, significantly, like ears) he observes a search party 'sounding' and probing with their 'long poles' to recover a dead body from the lake's depths. They restore, one might surmise, in ghastly and masculine form, the maternal body that is now palpably absent for the young boy. As if by association, that image restores to Wordsworth, in this first location of the spots of time in the 1799 *Prelude*, First Part, the first of two such spots displaced into memory. A woman wandering across the landscape bears a pitcher that suggestively evokes uterine life or urn burial, appearing to the five-year-old Wordsworth beneath an upright, thorn-like emblem on the hill's summit (a stone signal-beacon that might recall the old dame doubled by the native rock) beside what is twice called a 'naked pool'. She appears just after the boy encounters an image that seems similarly displaced from 'The Thorn':

'a long green ridge of turf' whose 'shape was like a grave' (311–20). While this passage opens with the hope that such memories 'retain / A fructifying virtue, whence, depressed ... our minds – / Especially the imaginative power – / Are nourished and repaired' (288–97), it is difficult not to find that hope dispelled by what Wordsworth calls (in line 322) 'the visionary dreariness' of this female figure of, and in, this place already associated by legend with the hanging of a man who murdered his wife by poisoning her.

While this fact, too, may suggest an English version of the *dinnseanchas* in which Irish places, according to Nina Witoszek and Pat Sheeran, are more typically named after and affiliated with those who died than with those who lived there,[12] the critic accustomed to the terms of a trite psychoanalysis would need no such grounds to argue that for Wordsworth, as for Heaney, the repossession of the land involves a symbolic marriage between a son who is also a bridegroom and the goddess of place. Such a critic might point to the ostensibly 'universal' condition of mothers and sons to understand the presence of such marriage tropes in the landscape poems of the Romantic, as of the Irish, poet. That critic would begin with the implications of two terms already associated by Wordsworth with the female herself who is associated with place – a 'split' stone that is itself a double of the female, and an overcoming of a 'depressive' condition associated with her (and the stone's) absence. That leaves the critic with a notion of the post-oedipal poet-son who, having split or severed his tie to the mother, persists in it, beyond loss itself through displacement of the incestuous wish into either 'normal' (heterosexual) marriage or the sublimation of art. In that act of sublimation, such displacement would involve a process called by Paul de Man, in his study of Wordsworth and allegory, 'the Romantic dialectic': 'the experience of the object takes on the form of a perception or a sensation', a strategy of internalisation whereby the self can 'borrow ... the temporal stability that it lacks from nature, and ... devise strategies by means of which nature is brought down to a human level while still escaping from "the unimaginable touch of time"'.[13] Here de Man cites M. H. Abrams: 'The best Romantic meditations on a landscape ... all manifest a transaction between subject and object in which the thought incorporates and makes explicit what was already implicit in the outer scene.'[14] That statement illustrates, de Man continues, the dilemma of the Romantic poet (and the Romantic scholar) who insists simultaneously on the priority of Nature and the priority of the self – a dilemma, we might note, that is well captured in the self-inwoven simile.

Mary Jacobus in 'Splitting the Race of Man in Twain: Prostitution, Personification, and *The Prelude*' claims that in the Romantic dialectic, notably in examples she cites from Abrams, 'the role of woman ... is to put man ... in possession of his desire' insofar as the possession is figured as the repossession of place (and, more particularly, of home) through, in Wordsworth's case, Dorothy.[15] In so doing, Wordsworth, in such sublime moments as his encounter with vacancy on Snowdon, avoids facing the very origins, or source, of the self in a primary and melancholic *effacement* of place, its constitution, as Jacobus continues (citing Julia Kristeva), in 'self-alienation, the earliest form of which is separation from the mother, that allows the most rudimentary form of signifying subject to come into being. [Kristeva's] account ... might be called not simply the natural Sublime, but (doubly naturalized) the maternal Sublime.'[16]

Yet there is another way of reading Wordsworth's experience of 'the homeless voice of waters' on Snowdon, available in part through Heaney's own canny reading of the Romantic dialectic as it is expressed in that related passage on the voice of waters, cited earlier, from Dorothy's journal. Wordsworth's relationship to Nature, Heaney insists, is not a sublation of (female) body into (masculine) mind; it is, instead, a penetration of Nature into, and onto, the incorporative but also imitative body of the male poet, much as Heaney figures that penetration in the penultimate poem of 'Clearances'. To use a term from Locke favoured by Heaney no less than Wordsworth, Nature 'impresses'.

Just what does Heaney learn from the Wordsworth whom he reads here, and, more particularly, how does he employ these gleanings from Wordsworth's use of sound/mother/place? As I have hinted, Heaney comes to portray the poetic body as itself a receiving station: the poet's feet do not only imitate those of the female wanderers (and his poetic practice – like the garrulous narrator's of 'The Thorn' – does not only imitate Martha Ray's repeated return to the same spot). In the terms of 'The Makings of a Music', they also circle round in bodily form, representing the diurnal round, or they plough (*P* 68, 65), making of feet of flesh the implements of voicing and writing as well as of agriculture. It is therefore hardly surprising that when Heaney moves from the archaeological excavation of bodies from the bog to the agricultural or 'field work' of the next volume, the violence in the North from which the speaker self-consciously fled to Glanmore and *Field Work* (see, for example, the troubled harvests of 'Triptych', *FW* 12–14) redounds, violently, not only in the images, close to home, of predatory rats or slain horses but more intimately in the necessary human acts of ingesting food or, more terrifyingly, even in *becoming* food, in 'Ugolino' (*FW* 61–4).

In Heaney's own diurnal and nocturnal circling of that Irish purgatory, 'Station Island', its ghosts remind the speaker that the 'maternal Sublime' of the landscape in Ireland bespeaks a nationwide failure of nurture and emptying of place. To the speaker's nostalgic sensuality, his use of the jam jar once again to displace nurture – 'old jampots in a drain clogged up with mud' – Carleton wryly replies with an image of colonial settlement as purgation and interpenetrative incorporation as historical memory: 'another life that cleans our element. // We are earthworms of the earth, and all that / has gone through us is what will be our trace' (*SI* 66). Heaney's increasingly open discussion in *Field Work*, published in 1979, of cultural interpenetration in a colonial history of clearance and of hunger redefines the relationship that had fascinated him since 'Feeling into Words' and 'Viking Dublin: Trial Pieces'. Feeling and voice – and *words* and feeling – interpenetrate one another in ways close to the entry of another's words (or of words, generally) across the frontier of the body and into the imagination so that they feel as though they are possessed fully by the poet: 'Sensings, mountings from the hiding places, / Words entering almost the sense of touch / Ferreting themselves out of their dark hutch' (*FW* 34). Here and in such poems as 'Oysters' that quickening into word or verb feels more like violation (a 'split bulb') than inspiration, and the speaker is at once perpetrator and victim: 'Oysters' is deliberately set within the imperial power of consumer privilege in which, by the early 1980s, middle-class Irish Catholics were as likely to participate as their counterparts elsewhere across the globe. The bivalve, representative of a dispossessed diaspora, 'Millions of them ripped and shucked and scattered', forced from the mud of the North and hauled south on imperial conveyance, becomes uneasily contiguous to or even synonymous with the 'frond-lipped, brine-stung / Glut of privilege' that consumes it, the ambivalent, self-divided speaker who seeks to become, in near-rhyme to 'split bulb', quickened 'into verb, pure verb' (*FW* 11).

In *Station Island* vocalisation becomes, with such internment poems as 'The Loaning', associated with the forcible extraction of voice from the body, in a violent 'sounding'. Section III of this poem begins with the bodily, living tuning fork evoked by Heaney in 'The Makings of a Music' to emblematise the Wordsworthian poet (*P* 70): 'Stand still. You can hear / everything going on' (*SI* 52). But in 'The Loaning' what is heard through the heightened sense – and heard, recursively, as one's *own* voice – is the snapping of a twig from one of Dante's suicide trees:

> When you are tired or terrified
> your voice slips back into its old first place
> and makes the sound your shades make there ...
> When Dante snapped a twig in the bleeding wood
> a voice sighed out of blood that bubbled up
> like sap at the end of green sticks on a fire.
>
> At the click of a cell lock somewhere now
> the interrogator steels his *introibo*,

the light motes blaze, a blood-red cigarette
startles the shades, screeching and beseeching. (*SI* 52)

Thirty-two pages later, in Section IX of 'Station Island', Heaney connects the interned nationalist, the self that wilfully destroys its life (the self that *imitates*, one might say, the destructive feminine aspect of the land) with not the tree but the bog: 'My brain dried like spread turf, my stomach / shrank to a cinder and tightened and cracked' (*SI* 84).

These words, spoken by the hunger-striker Francis Hughes, introduce perhaps Heaney's most visceral, and visibly incorporative, self-inwoven simile: 'Often I was dogs on my own track / Of blood on wet grass that I could have licked' (*SI* 84). Yet when Heaney in his 1993 'Frontiers of Writing' (*RP* 186ff.) returns, in Wordsworthian fashion, to the moment in his own life that inspired this section (an essay in which, significantly, he also returns to 'Place and Displacement'), he brings to the fore his experience of being, as a poet who is also a cultural nationalist, uncomfortably in two places at once. Likewise in 'Station Island' Heaney returns, through the hunger-striker's powerful evocation of the place name 'Toome', to his own previous use of the Irish *dinnseanchas* in the sensuous lines (suggestive of incorporation) 'under the dislodged // slab of the tongue' in the poem 'Toome' (*WO* 26):

I saw country
I knew from Glenshane down to Toome
And heard a car I could make out years away
With me in the back of it like a white-faced groom,
A hit-man on the brink, emptied and deadly. (*SI* 84)

In being 'emptied', Hughes has not only literalised the purgation the speaker himself is failing to accomplish in this purgatory, but he also offers a model of that condition of meaningful absence that Heaney would displace into the interiority of memory (and into his daughter's) for future restoration of the self 'at the very centre of the empty city' in 'Changes' (*SI* 37).

In the stanza that follows, Heaney, imagining the martyr's inanition from the setting of festive satiation he describes in 'Frontiers of Writing', continues this act of, in effect, imaginative displacement. Detailing the ongoing life of his own body's senses, 'sensings' through which he, the poet, may displace himself into another's situation, Heaney subtly reminds the reader that these bodily senses ceased, one by one, for the hunger striker as death closed in:

This voice from blight
And hunger died through the black dorm:
There he was, laid out with a drift of mass cards
At his shrouded feet. Then the firing party's

Volley in the yard. I saw the woodworm
In gate posts and door jambs, smelt mildew
From the byre loft where he watched and hid
From fields his draped coffin would raft through. (*SI* 84)

In the final part of this stanza, Heaney not only returns once again to the bog; this poet who so often sounds such sites for an echo of his own voice now would silence – 'muffle' – Hughes, an 'unquiet soul', in 'the bog where you threw your first grenade'. But whereas in the previous section Heaney, in seeking repose for McCartney's muddied ghost, earned from that victim ridicule by 'dabbing' him with 'moss', he now gives over that funerary office to the bog, the 'moss' itself: 'and sphagnum moss / Could teach you its medicinal repose' (*SI* 84).

The lover of mud and dankness in the essay 'Mossbawn' must now confront his own 'mucky, glittering flood', as he drifts in the 'polyp' of 'self-disgust' that he calls, alluding again to a failed or perverse form of maternal nurture, 'surreal as a shed breast': 'I repent / My unweaned life that kept me competent / To sleepwalk with connivance and mistrust' (*P* 17ff.; *SI* 85). Although an instrument of sound – the trumpet he once found in an attic – is 'still there for the taking', such sounding, because it remains outside the body's own sounding devices, cannot yet redeem the speaker afflicted, notably, by 'place': 'I hate how quick I was to know my place. / I hate where I was born, hate everything / That made me biddable and unforthcoming' (*SI* 85). Significantly, at this moment Heaney's own device for mutually implicating poet and place – the self-inwoven simile – he now represents as futile, ending with an image from his own 'Belderg': 'As if the cairnstone could defy the cairn. / As if the eddy could reform the pool. / As if a stone whirled under a cascade, / Eroded and eroding in its bed, / Could grind itself down to a different core' (*SI* 86). Yet he concludes, nevertheless, with a linguistic device just as recursive, as implicative of the ends and their source (or of the object and subject) as the self-inwoven simile: the performative. 'Then I thought of the tribe whose dances never fail / For they keep dancing till they sight the deer' (*SI* 85).

NOTES

1. Patricia Coughlan, '"Bog Queens": The Representation of Women in the Poetry of John Montague and Seamus Heaney', in *Seamus Heaney*, ed. Michael Allen (New York: St Martin's Press, 1997), p. 187. Moynagh Sullivan has published a provocative, insightful essay that continues Coughlan's argument: see 'The Treachery of Wetness', *Irish Studies Review* 13:4 (November 2005), pp. 451–568.
2. Patrick Kavanagh, 'The Hospital', *Collected Poems* (London: Martin Brian & O'Keefe, 1972), p. 153.

3. Nicholas Roe in '"Wordsworth at the Flax-Dam": An Early Poem by Seamus Heaney' recapitulates the Romantic poet's relationship to Nature as one of transgression, guilt and personal redemption (*Critical Approaches to Anglo-Irish Literature*, ed. Michael Allen and Angela Wilcox [Gerrards Cross: Colin Smythe, 1989]).
4. Christopher Ricks, *The Force of Poetry* (Oxford and New York: Oxford University Press, 1984), p. 34.
5. Ibid., p. 51.
6. John Keats, 'Code to Psyche', *The Poems of John Keats*, ed. Miriam Allott (New York: Longman, 1970), p. 520.
7. Darcy O'Brien, 'Seamus Heaney and Wordsworth: A Correspondent Breeze', *Critical Essays on Seamus Heaney*, ed. Robert F. Garratt (New York and London: G.K. Hall, 1995), pp. 189, 187.
8. William Wordsworth, 1805 *Prelude*, Book XI, 342, in *The Prelude*, ed. J. Wordsworth, M.H. Abrams and S. Gill (New York: Norton 1979), p. 434.
9. Ibid., 1799 *Prelude*, Second Part, 7. Hereafter line numbers are in the text.
10. John Montague's *The Rough Field* was surely a model for Heaney's reading of this passage; see Heaney's 'The Sense of Place': 'It is just possible that John Montague, if he heard a fiddle played at one of those small-time dances, would be inclined to see in them the last twitch of his ideal culture' (*P* 144).
11. So important is this term 'soundings' to Heaney that he named a journal he founded in Belfast in the early 1970s by that title.
12. Nina Witoszek and Pat Sheeran, *Talking to the Dead: A Study of Irish Funerary Traditions* (Amsterdam and Atlanta: Rodopi, 1998).
13. Paul de Man, 'The Rhetoric of Temporality' in *Blindness and Insight: Essays in the Rhetoric of Contemporary Criticism* (1971), 2nd edn (Minneapolis: University of Minnesota Press, 1983), pp. 193, 197.
14. From M. H. Abrams, 'Structure and Style in the Greater Romantic Lyric', in *From Sensibility to Romanticism: Essays Presented to F. A. Pottle*, ed. F. W. Hills and Harold Bloom (New York: Oxford University Press, 1965), p. 551.
15. Mary Jacobus, 'Splitting the Race of Man in Twain', *Romanticism, Writing, and Sexual Difference: Essays on 'The Prelude'* (Oxford: Clarendon Press, 1989), p. 206.
16. Ibid., p. 272.

13

HEATHER O'DONOGHUE

Heaney, *Beowulf* and the Medieval Literature of the North

The publisher's blurb on the inside cover of *North* speaks of Seamus Heaney's 'idea of the north', a myth allowing him to 'contemplate the violence on his home ground in relation to memories of the Scandinavian and English invasions which have marked Irish history so indelibly'. In this essay, I want to show how Heaney has derived this 'idea of the north' – more properly, his idea of northern pasts – from Old Norse and Old English literary traditions, and how both the sameness and the alterity of these pasts are related to his own, and our, present. I will look first at *North*, and then take the poem 'Funeral Rites' as a detailed case in point. An important duality will emerge: the individual's engagement with an historical past, however it has been constructed, and the poet's engagement with, and reuse of, earlier literature. This double relation is of course central to the subject of the second part of this essay, Heaney's translation of *Beowulf*, an Old English poem on Scandinavian subject matter: the 'big thing', as Heaney himself has described it.

Not everyone has admired *North*.[1] And even its admirers have not warmed to all the poems in it. But one glorious exception is the first of the two opening poems 'in dedication for Mary Heaney'. 'Sunlight' is not only outside the body of poems in the volume, but also outside its central theme, the relation between past and present. Indeed, the picture of the poet's aunt baking on a sunlit afternoon is located outside time itself: she sits patiently waiting for 'the scone rising' in the space – temporal as well as spatial – between 'the tick of two clocks' (*N* 9). Mary Heaney, in the poet's memory, inhabits a no-man's-land between two time systems, aligned to neither of them. The rising she awaits has nothing to do with political history, that connotation (surely unavoidable in any Irish context) evoked only to draw playful attention to its significant absence.

In the second of the two dedicatory poems, 'The Seed Cutters', the passage of time – history – is denied in a different way. Two times are conflated. Contemporary farm-workers look as if they have stepped out of a picture by Breughel; our present and the past are visually indistinguishable. And the seed cutters are, like the scene in 'Sunlight', outside time (Heaney's apostrophe 'O calendar customs!' stresses that the agricultural year is cyclic, rather than linear). But the poem prefigures the violence which characterises, in *North*, both past and present. The silent farm-workers have 'time to kill', and their knives are sharp (*N* 10).

Heaney first alludes to the Vikings – the raiders from the north – in the poem 'Belderg'. Here, material objects from the past – prehistoric quernstones – 'just kept turning up / and were thought of as foreign', a suggestive echo of L. P. Hartley's description of the past as 'a foreign country'. But conversation with an unnamed archaeologist corrects this assumption: 'He talked about persistence, / A congruence of lives.' The great phases of Irish prehistory – 'iron, flint and bronze' – are not foreign places, but explained as 'growth rings', the organic metaphor powerfully stressing the contiguity of past and present. Place names too are evidence of this indivisible connection with the past, and Heaney is characteristically happy to recognise the 'forked root' of the second element of Mossbawn, the name of the townland where he grew up, which may be derived from either English or Irish. But the first element is troublesome: the word *mose* or *mos* means 'bog' in both Danish and Icelandic, and came into Ulster English via Scots.

The flow of dialogue in the poem suggests that Heaney as the poem's speaker is more reluctant to acknowledge this derivation; his interlocutor seems gently to prompt him: 'But the Norse ring on your tree?' The recognition that the Vikings are an organic part of Irish history causes a vertiginous, shocked, shift in perspective. For the Vikings mean violence, and the poem's speaker has a sudden epiphany, a vision of 'a world-tree of balanced stones' (*N* 13). In Old Norse mythology, the world tree – a great ash called Yggdrasill – is the central symbol of an imaginary cosmos, sustaining the world and its inhabitants, but creaking ominously as the violent apocalypse – Ragnarök – approaches.[2] In 'Belderg', Heaney re-imagines the tree as a tower of logs, chopped into cylinders and shaped like quernstones 'piled like vertebrae'. The domestic purpose of quernstones – to grind grain into flour – is hideously transformed into an image of destruction and violence: 'The marrow crushed to grounds.' Vikings used to be seen as a deplorable but mercifully transient plague on Irish society: pillage, plunder and departure. To allow a Scandinavian space in Irish history is to be forced to accommodate Viking violence too.

History has not been kind to the Vikings, especially in Ireland, where their reputation as savage heathen raiders, inimical to Celtic Christianity and civilisation, dominated until relatively recently. But archaeological work at such sites as Wood Quay in Dublin offered an alternative view: of Scandinavian settlers, craftsmen and homeowners who became part of medieval Irish society. 'Trial Pieces', in spite of its ominous title, seems at first to dwell on positive images of the Viking period: the delicately beautiful Viking artefacts excavated from the Norse settlement at Wood Quay. But murder and creativity are linked in the biblical echoes of the poem's opening lines – 'It could be a jaw-bone / or a rib' – and the poem's final, vile image is of the practice known as 'blood-eagling':

> With a butcher's aplomb
> they spread out your lungs
> and made you warm wings
> for your shoulders. *(N 24)*

Blood-eagling has been the occasion for a good deal of controversy amongst Old Norse scholars.[3] A highly cryptic stanza of early Old Norse verse seems to allude to an eagle being *skorit* – cut, or scored – on the back of an enemy's body, and this was understood (or elaborated) by later medieval writers as describing the action of excavating the lungs from a dead (or dying) body and spreading them out in a gruesome parody of wings, so that the victim apparently becomes a sacrifice to Óðinn, the Norse god of battle associated with birds of carrion such as eagles or ravens. It has been counter-argued that not even the Vikings could have been so sensationally barbaric, and that the stanza describes a body on the battlefield being ravaged *by* an eagle, a traditional image from Germanic battle poetry of birds of prey ripping carrion with their claws. Whatever the actuality of blood-eagling, in 'Trial Pieces' the allusion presents the Vikings as not merely mutilating the corpses of their victims, but transforming them into pagan sculptures, a gross extension of the aesthetic impulse.

This heady blend of violence and artistry can make the savagery seem almost exciting. But in the poem's penultimate section, Heaney shifts to a much grimmer picture of the Norsemen:

> Neighbourly, scoretaking
> Killers, haggers
> And hagglers, gombeen-men,
> Hoarders of grudges and gain. (*N* 23–4)

The Vikings are reduced from thrilling aliens to drearily familiar wrongdoers. The chilling paradox of a 'neighbourly killer' is powerfully suggestive of contemporary urban conflict, and is reused in precisely that context in 'Funeral Rites'.

In the title-poem, 'North', this crucial distinction between Viking raiders and settled Scandinavians is made even more forcibly. Following the evocative images from Norse mythology in its first stanza – the 'hammered' horseshoe-shaped bay and the 'thundering' Atlantic recalling the Norse myth of the god

Þórr – Heaney purposefully demystifies our idea of the north: the 'unmagical / invitations of Iceland' and the 'pathetic colonies / of Greenland'. The guiltily glamorised Vikings, whom the poet calls, with bitter irony, 'those fabulous raiders', warn him of what is to come. Their voices describe 'thick-witted couplings and revenges, / the hatreds and behindbacks / of the althing, lies and women' (*N* 19): a picture of settled Viking life derived not from popular histories, but from a literary source, the Old Icelandic sagas.

Old Icelandic family sagas are by and large thirteenth-century fictionalised accounts of life in Iceland from the settlement period – 870 AD – to the decades following the conversion of Iceland to Christianity in the year 1000 AD. They are naturalistic prose narratives, most akin to modern historical novels, in which the forces of order – the law, kinship, human virtue and fellow-feeling – are pitted, sometimes tragically, sometimes inspirationally, against their opposites: violence, betrayal, greed and the desire for vengeance.[4] Heaney's use of the Icelandic word 'althing' (literally, 'general assembly') conjures up the alterity of medieval Icelandic life, but in fact the Althing was nothing strange or exotic; it was a precociously and precariously democratic parliamentary and legal institution. As a reading of saga literature at once makes clear, saga society is unexpectedly familiar in its concerns and triumphs. It is a set-up we can compare with our own. And disturbing as it may be to include exotic raiders in one's national history, the similarities between saga society and the domestic violence of the Ulster troubles constitute an even more disquieting issue.

In his celebrated sequence of 'bog body' poems in *North*, Heaney considers a third image of the people of the North – the Danish bog bodies, which though paradoxically the furthest, geographically, from Northern Ireland, provide the most dramatic parallels with the political situation in the north. It was through P. V. Glob's celebrated book *The Bog People*, with its extraordinary photographs of the excavated bodies, that Heaney first encountered these bog bodies.[5] As the Yeatsian echo in 'Tollund Man', from the earlier collection *Wintering Out*, makes clear, the sight of the photographs affected Heaney long before he saw the bodies themselves: 'Some day I will go to Aarhus ... I will stand ...' (*WO* 47). 'Bog Queen' tells the story – through the speaking voice of the body itself – of a bog body exhumed from the Moira estate, just south of Belfast. But Heaney has clearly derived his knowledge of the Moira body from *The Bog People*, echoing many of Glob's phrasings in the poem.

The familiarity of the human bodies, relatively unchanged by cultural difference, reinforces the commonness of our, and Heaney's, humanity with them. From the stubble on his cheek to the half-smile on his face, Tollund Man – the body Heaney first described in *Wintering Out* – is vividly, shockingly, one of us, 'like an ancestor almost', as Heaney puts it. A visceral response to the photographs in *The Bog People* forces us and the poet to recognise our kinship with an otherwise strange and distant past, but the text of Glob's book introduces a much stranger idea; his thesis is that these bodies were sacrificial victims, ritually executed as an offering to an ancient *Terra Mater*: the goddess whom Tacitus, in his first-century AD *Germania*, an account of cultural practices of the Germanic tribes, names as Nerthus. In 'Kinship', which is spotted with allusions to the *Germania*, Heaney makes explicit the link between Ireland and the 'island of the ocean' which was how the classical historians figured Scandinavia. In this way, these bodies are paralleled with the victims of violence in Northern Ireland who are controversially presented as sacrifices to political ends – most notoriously, perhaps, in 'Punishment', in which the body known as Windeby Girl, with her shaved head, blindfold and noose, is regarded as a sister of the young women punished by the IRA for consorting with British soldiers.

To imply a 'sameness' with the past is to risk being accused of at the same time mystifying and naturalising political violence; as Ciaran Carson put it, 'it is as if [Heaney] is saying, suffering like this is natural; these things have always happened; they happened then, they happen now'.[6] But oddly enough, it may not be true to say that these things happened. Glob's interpretation of what happened to Tollund man, Windeby girl and the other famous bog bodies is not a matter of historical fact but a literary construct, based on literary sources, rather than on a strictly material, archaeological analysis (even if such a thing were feasible). The most recent scholarship on bog bodies offers a highly sceptical line on the whole idea of ritual killing – let alone sacrifice to an earth goddess. A good example is an aptly titled article in a collection about bog bodies, 'Did They Fall or Were They Pushed?', which thoughtfully worries at, amongst other things, the practical difficulties of combining ritual killing with deposition in a deep, wet bog; surely the executioners themselves would have been at some risk?[7]

Glob himself was well aware of the power of literary texts to influence interpretations: he is for instance sceptical of nineteenth-century Danish claims that a female body found at Haraldskjaer on Jylland could be identified as the Norse Queen Gunnhildr. She is represented in some Norse sources as a notorious and power-hungry nymphomaniac adulteress, and stories about her wrongdoings have no doubt been elaborated in the sagas. But Glob dismisses quite sober historical sources as 'fantasy', preferring to invoke Tacitus' account of the victims sacrificed to a Germanic fertility goddess. Our construction of the past is always directed by the politics of the present: the case against the Gunnhildr identification was challenged by a scholar whom Glob respectfully calls 'the founder of modern Danish archaeology as a science',[8] while the *Germania* has only recently been called into question as a calculated rebuke to Roman decadence rather than a disinterested account of Germanic practice. Heaney's idea of the Danish Iron Age is based on Glob's idea of it: 'what happened' is still a matter of debate.

I want now to explore more closely how Heaney's image of medieval Norse society, derived from his reading of family sagas, acts not only as a corrective to the popular image of transient Vikings, as we have seen, but also as a correlative to Northern Irish society during the Troubles.

In the poem 'Funeral Rites', Heaney follows a graphic account of memories of funerals in his childhood with an image of funerals on a national scale – the endless 'neighbourly murders' of the Troubles – and merges this with a vision of a prehistoric funeral rite snaking 'towards the mounds' in which

> the procession drags its tail
> out of the gap of the North
> as its head already enters
> the megalithic doorway. (*N* 17)

This shadowy image of a serpent or dragon leads us into the third part of 'Funeral Rites', in which the visionary scene shifts again in time and space, and the poet imagines the mourners imagining a scene from the Old Norse *Njáls saga*, in which the dead hero, Gunnarr Hámundarson, is seen chanting verses inside his burial mound: according to the translation Heaney read, Gunnarr 'was happy; his face was exultant'.[9] 'Funeral Rites' explores the relationship between feud and funeral: can the ceremony and custom of funeral rites 'placate' the urge to retributive violence? And the example of Gunnarr seems to suggest that it may: according to the poem, Gunnarr

> ... lay beautiful
> inside his burial mound,
> though dead by violence
> and unavenged. (*N* 17–18)

Heaney moves on to the verses Gunnarr was seen and heard speaking, and the four lights illuminating the inside of the burial chamber; even the saga's detail that Gunnarr had 'turned round to face the moon' is echoed in the poem's conclusion: '... he turned / with a joyful face / to look at the moon' (*N* 18).

This section of the poem has been read as refuting the inevitability of blood feud; for example, that 'the final section of this poem makes it the most positive and life-affirming work in *North*'.[10] The use to which the poet puts the past – negatively characterised by Ciaran Carson as a helpless condoning of the cycle of violence as irremediable – would here be completely different: a vision of what was and, therefore, what might be. But in the saga, Gunnarr is not left unavenged: vengeance follows hard upon the vision. Some critics have assumed that Heaney has 'changed the story' (though others have simply not known the saga). I will argue in what follows that Heaney leaves purposefully ambiguous his version of Gunnarr's story, neither misunderstanding nor deliberately distorting the saga's account.

Even without reference to *Njáls saga*, there are some slight hints in 'North' that may unsettle our reception of a purely positive image. That Gunnarr 'lay beautiful' in his mound recalls the sanctimony of what we might call 'professional mourners' – as in the comic Irish song 'Finnegan's Wake', in which the supposedly dead Tim Finnegan is 'such a lovely corpse [as] did you ever see'. And although because of the prehistoric funeral (also associated with resurrection, with the mound's 'stone / back in its mouth'), 'the cud of memory' is said in the poem to have been 'allayed', there is something odd about the parallel phrase, 'arbitration / of the feud placated': one might wish a feud, or the desire for vengeance, to be placated, not the arbitration of it.

Read in conjunction with the saga narrative, the full ambiguity of Heaney's text becomes apparent. The killing of Gunnarr is not the result of anything like a blood feud, and Gunnarr himself is neither martyr nor scapegoat. He is an old-style hero – brave, powerful and handsome – caught in the social transition between solving disputes in the time-honoured way, by violence, and relying on the law. He becomes involved, through family obligation and not through belligerence, with claiming back a dowry on behalf of a divorced female relative. Due legal process is stalemated, and Gunnarr, dismissing the advice of his wise friend Njáll, abandons the law, and challenges his opponent to a duel. The ex-husband concedes defeat and bows, somewhat resentfully, to the threat of superior force. But no blood feud follows: in fact, Gunnarr subsequently marries his opponent's niece, after perfectly proper and civilised negotiations with the family. Enmity towards Gunnarr comes from a quite different source: his female relative remarries shortly after regaining her dowry, and she and her new husband have a son who grows up to hate Gunnarr. The saga author, characteristically, gives no explicit reason, leaving us to imagine the boy's resentment about his family's indebtedness to a powerful, successful figure like Gunnarr. Violence is not promulgated through the mindless retribution of blood feud but through the psychological forces of family dynamics.

The next threat to Gunnarr comes in the shape of a darkly comic double act; two idly malevolent low-life characters called Otkell and Skamkell. A dispute arises when Gunnarr's wife Hallgerðr steals some cheese from Otkell: Otkell has refused to sell provisions to Gunnarr – for no good reason other than that for once, in this petty (though, in the harsh struggle for survival in medieval Iceland, far from trivial) domestic matter, he finds he is able to thwart the great Gunnarr – and Hallgerðr unwisely decides to get her own back. The almost inevitable eventual outcome is 'neighbourly murder'.

Skamkell, the more malicious of the two men, offers to consult their preferred arbitrator on his friend Otkell's behalf. This arbitrator predictably advises that Otkell should accept the generous compensation Gunnarr has offered. But Skamkell simply lies: he reports that the advice is to take Gunnarr to court, at the Althing, or general assembly, charging Gunnarr's wife with theft, and Gunnarr himself, preposterously, with receiving stolen goods. Otkell's brother sees at once what has happened: 'This is all an enormous lie,' he protests.[11] Such doings are what Heaney had in mind in 'North': 'the hatreds and behindbacks / of the althing, / lies and women' (*N* 20). In the sagas, lies and women are represented as powerfully disruptive forces in society.

Gunnarr, after a number of provocations, kills Otkell. Significantly, he does not triumph in this killing, reflecting instead on his own reaction to it: 'I wish I knew ... whether I am any less manly than other men, for being so much more reluctant to kill than other men are.'[12] But against the odds, and cynically set up by a coalition of petty enemies, Gunnarr does kill again. His friend Njáll manages to negotiate a settlement at the Althing, but Gunnarr violates its terms – three years' outlawry from Iceland. Again, Gunnarr acts not out of pride, or reckless heroism; he simply cannot bear to leave his home farm. He expresses this profound emotional attachment to what Heaney might call 'the home place' in words still celebrated in Iceland: 'How lovely the slopes are ... more lovely than they have ever seemed to me before; golden cornfields and new-mown hay. I am going back home, and I will not go away.'[13] His enemies kill him, in spite of an heroic defence.

The first response of his supporters is to turn to the law for reparation, but no legal proceedings can be taken against Gunnarr's killers, because he was legally an outlaw at the time of his death: technically, his killers acted within the law. In this curious vacuum, Njáll, the peaceable lawyer, is driven to contemplate unfocused retributive violence: he 'suggested it would be better to dishonour [Gunnarr's killers] by killing a few of them off'.[14] The law has failed society's need for justice, and Gunnarr's mother – in common with women elsewhere in the family sagas – falls back on the old ways, refusing to bury Gunnarr's weapon along with his body, so that a rightful avenger might take it up. Into this uncertain hiatus comes the vision of Gunnarr, sitting upright – not laid out – in his burial mound. Gunnarr is indeed 'unavenged', though neither deliberately left thus, as some critics who have read the poem but not the saga assume, nor destined to remain so. His verse, as quoted in the saga, is indeed about 'honour', as Heaney has it, but about the old kind of honour; Gunnarr describes himself in the verse – the traditional vehicle for gloating over violence – as 'distributing wounds gladly', as one who would 'rather die than yield'.[15] Gunnarr's joyful expression is not serenity, but exultancy that he died a hero, and in the confident expectation that he will be avenged. In life, Gunnarr is an unwilling killer, drawn into quarrels he has tried to avoid, and influenced by those who are trying to shape a new Iceland based on law and negotiation; and ultimately, Christian values. In death, he reverts to functioning as an old heroic type, transmitting a grim message to the next generation: his son, and the son of his best friend, Njáll, hear it, and plan their revenge.

Heaney's use of *Njáls saga* is intertextuality of a very high order. In 'Funeral Rites' he presents, with masterful ambiguity, an 'imagining' of what might have been, allowing the reader to suppose that the vision of Gunnarr offers hope and affirmation following violence, while *Njáls saga* demonstrates exactly the opposite. Indeed, the longer-term prospects in the saga are desperately bleak: though the violence set in train by the death of Gunnarr does finally wear itself out, this does not happen until the killings have engulfed the lawyers and the politicians, a shockingly pessimistic analogy to the Troubles in Northern Ireland.

Heaney's idea of the northern past scrupulously distinguishes between the Vikings – alien invaders renowned for savagery, and easy to imagine as 'other' – and a less familiar image of Scandinavians settled, whether in Iceland or Ireland, and living a closely-knit social life riven by the ever-present possibility of vengeance and violence in spite of an established legal framework. This image is derived from the Old Norse family sagas, and the analogy with contemporary Ulster is startling. Both images of the past are ultimately negative, but throughout *North*, Heaney figures these pasts as indivisibly, even organically, continuous with the present, a past which, as he puts it, we 'grew out of' ('Kinship', *N* 43).

In 'Bone Dreams' too, Heaney explores the way in which the past is indivisibly connected to the present, via language. Here, though, apart from Scandinavian connotation of the delicate image of a hollow made by a piece of bone in the ground as 'a small ship burial', the linguistic trail leads not to a Norse bloodbath, but more lyrically to an Anglo-Saxon philological past:

> to the scop's
> twang, the iron
> flash of consonants
> cleaving the line. (*N* 28)

The sound and form of Old English poetry, romantically imagined as recited, and perhaps composed, by the *scop*, the Anglo-Saxon word for an oral poet, is impressionistically evoked in material terms, a technique Heaney also uses in his prose, as in *Preoccupations*, for instance, in which he refers to the 'pointed masonry of Anglo-Saxon verse'. Heaney singles out for our attention the kenning *ban-hus*. A kenning is a characteristic feature of Old English poetic diction in which two nouns are linked together in a riddling way to denote a third, different referent. Thus *ban-hus* links 'bone' with 'house' to produce the idea of a house *for* bone: the kenning thus denotes 'body', the object which 'houses' and indeed shelters one's skeleton. Heaney's depiction of an Anglo-Saxon dwelling, 'its fire, benches, / wattle and rafters' as a sort of body, is then linked to the celebrated story told by Bede in his *Historia Ecclesiastica* (composed in Latin but translated into Old English). A counsellor of King Edwin of Northumbria is moved to convert to Christianity because of what he perceives as a failing in pagan doctrine:

> the fire is burning on the hearth in the middle of the hall, and all inside is warm, while outside the wintry storms of rain and snow are raging; and a sparrow flies swiftly through the hall. It enters in at one door and quickly flies out through the other ... So this life of man appears but for a moment; what follows or indeed what went before, we know not at all.[16]

This is the most sympathetic image of paganism in the whole of Old English literature. Heaney has poignantly and confidently developed the kenning *ban-hus* in conjunction with this story, figuring the sparrow as the human soul in the body which is the house: it 'fluttered a while / in the roofspace' ('Bone Dreams', *N* 28). Human life is fragile and transient, hardly more than a brief vision. I want now to turn to Heaney's translation of the Old English poem *Beowulf* in the context of this markedly positive idea of the Anglo-Saxon past.

Heaney's direct experience and knowledge of Old English literature derive primarily from his undergraduate studies at Queen's Belfast; he studied Old English poetry in the original language, and *Beowulf* was firmly situated at one end of a continuum of 'English Literature' (a canon to which Old Norse did not belong). *Beowulf* has been preserved in a poetic *koine* which has been described as the standard literary language amongst Anglo-Saxon poets, and in both tone and content it exudes centrality, authority, a profoundly wide-ranging and secure humanity. But *Beowulf* is not now regarded as the 'foundation stone' of the canon; its ever-increasing marginality is perhaps inevitable given that fluency in Standard English – or even facility with Shakespeare or Chaucer – is not enough to read the poem in the original. Ironically, although one of the arguments *against* the marginalisation of *Beowulf* in university syllabuses is the fact that modern poets such as Heaney once experienced it as part of the canon, Heaney himself has not shirked its curious status as a poem in a foreign language about sixth-century

Scandinavians: 'as an English poem it's a problematic poem, because it's actually European'.[17] *Beowulf*'s shift from centre to margin is a precise mirror image of Heaney's own position: though proudly conscious of writing and speaking from what is perceived by literary London as a linguistic and political margin, Heaney has himself centralised that margin, foregrounding the literature, languages and politics of Ulster. Heaney's translation of *Beowulf* is a dizzying amalgam of opposites: very distant meets very recent; centralised margin meets marginalised centre.

Old English poetry is written in alliterative long lines, each divided in two by a caesura, each half-line containing two stressed syllables. These half-lines are paratactically juxtaposed in an implicit grammatical relation to one another: the so-called 'appositive style'. Subtle metrical variations rescue the verse from formal monotony, what Heaney has called 'the thumping beat of Anglo-Saxon'. On the page of Heaney's translation, neither the caesura nor the alliteration are evident, though both are tactfully worked into the line (particularly attractive and effective is Heaney's tendency to alliterate on stressed second syllables, so that 'behind' alliterates with 'housed', and 'beyond' with 'yield'). But Heaney's great achievement is to translate the appositive half-lines, piled up and jumbled up in the Old English poetic technique called 'variation', into modern linear syntax. This is all easier to illustrate than to describe. Thus, the first three long lines in the poem –

Hwæt, we Gar-Dena	in geardagum
þeodcyninga	þrym gefrunon
hu đa æþelingas	ellen gefremedon

– may be glossed:

So, we Spear-Danes'	in days of yore
nation-kings'	glory have heard
how the princes	brave deeds performed.[18]

There are clearly a number of ways of linking these half-lines: have we heard about the glory of both the Spear-Danes and the nation-kings? Or are we celebrating the nation-kings *of* the Spear-Danes? Does the adverbial phrase 'in days of yore' qualify the glory or the brave deeds or both? Or even 'we ... have heard'? In fact, does the poet routinely exploit the absence of formal subordination in order to enable multiple senses?

Heaney produces two separate sentences instead of the ambiguous and heavy double genitive of the original:

So. The Spear-Danes in days gone by
And the kings who ruled them had courage and greatness.
We have heard of those princes' heroic campaigns. (*B* 3)

The solemn approbatory truth of the first sentence is underlined by its transformation into a simple statement of fact; the authority of the first-person speaker governs both. The long-term effect of this transformation is what Heaney describes in his introduction as 'a narrative line that sounded as if it meant business' (*B* xxix).

Translating the very first word in the poem – 'Hwæt' – has been the downfall of many earlier translations (the religious 'Lo'; the bathetic 'Well then'; the risible, if cognate, 'What Ho!'). Heaney has famously acknowledged the debt of his grave monosyllable to the colloquial Ulster language he grew up with. Irishisms abound in this translation, and sometimes, as here, they work unexpected miracles. Thus, the transformation of the warriors' experience in the great hall of Heorot from celebratory feasting to the terror of Grendel's attack is embedded in the way the hall timbers 'sing' as Beowulf and Grendel fight in an encounter Heaney calls a 'hall-session' (*B* xxv). The terminology of Irish music is also surprisingly appropriate for the many recitations in Heorot, as the otherwise barely imaginable Anglo-Saxon 'scop' is vividly realised as 'a traditional singer deeply schooled / in the lore of the past' (*B* 28). Sometimes, an Irishism is misleading; only those familiar with Hiberno-English will recognise Wealtheow's 'salute' to the warriors in the hall as a polite formal greeting, and some words – 'bawn', 'kesh', 'bolter', 'thole' – may be as unintelligible to some readers as the Old English. Heaney has himself discussed the special significance of 'thole', derived from the Old English verb *þolian*, to suffer or bear, describing it as 'the word that older and less educated people would have used in the country where I grew up ... And now suddenly here was "thole" in the official textual world' (*B* xxv). Such words are not anomalous; they are coded signals to remind the reader of the shared, but very different, marginality of two cultural and linguistic departures from Standard English: Ulster English and Anglo-Saxon.

Old English poetic diction is also marked by a plethora of compound words, and here Heaney's own poetic practice – probably itself influenced by his early reading of Old English verse – chimes with the Old English. Old English poetry is particularly rich in compound words because its poetic vocabulary is full of synonyms, and because of the freedom and inventiveness with which all these synonyms might be put together to form new words. In his great essay on poetics 'The Fire i' the Flint', Heaney celebrates the diction of Keats and Gerard Manley Hopkins, comparing the former – 'Close bosom-friend of the maturing sun' – with the latter – 'Warm-laid grave of a womb-life grey' – in terms of the quality of sound, but apparently taking for granted the remarkable compounding going on in both lines (*P* 84). Here we can see the complex pattern of poetic tradition and influence at work down through the canon of English Literature. This continuity mirrors and reinforces the often challenged linguistic continuity of English, Heaney's vision in 'Bone Dreams' of a journey 'back / through dictions' to Anglo-Saxon (*N* 28).

But in *North*, as we have seen, this idea of a past both contiguous with the present, and typologically symbolic of it, can be problematic – especially in the accusation that to claim that we have *not* grown out of the past is to condone – or at least resign oneself to – contemporary violence as somehow 'natural'. If, however, we bear in mind that the *Beowulf* poet himself was creating his particular 'idea of the past', for his own (and his society's) reasons, we can see an unexpected series of links between Heaney and him. For instance, the poet of *Beowulf* may well have used his Scandinavian subject matter to make a political point to his Anglo-Saxon audience that they might learn from his idea of the past. He too trod a narrow, acutely poised path between two cultures; in his case, he had to celebrate the achievements of his pagan ancestors while, as a Christian, deploring them as benighted. And though it's true that the poem is full of violence – violence long past, violence still to come, and the violence of the poem's present – the poet is far from condoning, still less celebrating it. To depict in less than intimate detail its far-reaching workings deep in the heart of society is to underestimate its power, and to fail to pay due respect to real heroism: the unremitting struggle by people of goodwill to slow its progress.

There are three kinds of violence in *Beowulf*: amongst family members, between warring tribes and between men and monsters. There are also three monsters: Grendel, his avenging mother and the dragon. These three monsters are surreal manifestations of the spirit of familiar, squalid human violence. Grendel is part of the legacy of Cain, who initiated the most intimate familial violence, fratricide – the mythic equivalent of neighbourly murder. His mother exemplifies the truism that violence begets violence, a fact disturbingly elevated to an ideal of vengeance in some societies. And the dragon represents a sort of solitary isolationism, nursing gold rather than sharing it; inward-looking rather than socially interactive; possessive, defensive and dug in, but given to sudden provocative and flamboyant displays of its power. By contrast, Beowulf and King Hrothgar are peacemaking statesmen, nurturing neighbourly affection and repaying debts of gratitude. But as Hrothgar will find, when he marries off his daughter to the leader of his old enemies, peacemaking is a thankless task.

It is clear that there are a number of resonant correspondences with the recent history of Northern Ireland here. The terminology of the Troubles – tit-for-tat killings, the peace process, mixed marriages, tribal warfare, the legacy of history – is what we reach for to recount the story of *Beowulf*. But Heaney never uses it in his translation. Although well aware of the danger of what he calls in his introduction to the translation 'the slightly cardboard effect that the word "monster" tends to introduce' (*B* xiii), Heaney refuses the chance to allegorise the poem into a costume drama version of the Ulster situation. Preserving the poem's cultural alterity, Heaney has not explicitly brought his 'idea of the [Anglo-Saxon] north' to bear on his and our present. His appropriation of *Beowulf* – establishing its indivisible continuity with the present – is an act of literary and linguistic politics.

NOTES

1. See, for instance, Edna Longley, '"Inner Emigré" or "Artful Voyeur"? Seamus Heaney's *North*', in *Poetry and the Wars* (Newcastle: Bloodaxe, 1986), pp. 140–65, or Blake Morrison, *Seamus Heaney* (London: Methuen, 1982).
2. E. O. G. Turville-Petre, *Myth and Religion of the North* (London: Weidenfeld & Nicolson, 1964).
3. See, for instance, Bjarni Einarsson, 'De Normannorum Atrocitate, or on the Execution of Royalty by the Aquiline Method', *Saga-Book of the Viking Society* XXII, Part 1 (1986), pp. 79–82, a reply to Roberta Frank's 'Viking Atrocity and Skaldic Verse: The Rite of the Blood-eagle', *English Historical Review* 99 (1984), pp. 332–43.
4. See Heather O'Donoghue, *Old Norse-Icelandic Literature: A Short Introduction* (Oxford: Blackwell, 2003).
5. P. V. Glob, *The Bog People: Iron-Age Man Preserved*, tr. R. L. S. Bruce-Mitford (London: Faber and Faber, 1969), from *Mosefolket: Jernalderens Mennesker bevaret i 2000 År* (1965).
6. Ciaran Carson, 'Escaped from the massacre?', *Honest Ulsterman* 50 (Winter 1975), pp. 183–6.
7. C. S. Briggs, 'Did They Fall or Were They Pushed? Some Unresolved Questions about Bog Bodies' in *Bog Bodies: New Discoveries and New Perspectives*, ed. R. S. Turner and R. G. Scaife (London: British Museum Press, 1995), pp. 168–82.
8. Glob, *Bog People*, pp. 70–1.
9. *Njal's Saga*, tr. Magnus Magnusson and Hermann Pálsson (Harmondsworth: Penguin Classics, 1960). The name of the eponymous hero, Njáll, is the Icelandic form of the Irish name Niall.
10. Nicholas McGuinn, *Seamus Heaney: A Student's Guide to 'Selected Poems 1965–1975'* (Leeds: Arnold-Wheaton, 1986), p. 100.
11. *Njal's Saga*, p. 128.
12. Ibid., p. 135.
13. Ibid., p. 166.
14. Ibid., p. 172.
15. Ibid., p. 173.
16. Bede, *The Ecclesiastical History of the English People*, ed. Judith McClure and Roger Collins (Oxford: Oxford University Press 1994), Book II, Chapter 13 (p. 95).
17. *Reading the Future: Irish Writers in Conversation with Mike Murphy* (Dublin: Lilliput Press, 2000), p. 95.
18. *Beowulf: A Student Edition*, ed. George Jack (Oxford: Clarendon Press, 1994).

14

JOHN WILSON FOSTER

Crediting Marvels: Heaney after 50

Accrediting Poetry

In his Nobel acceptance speech of 1995, Heaney recalled the burden for his art of recent violent events in Northern Ireland, then told his audience: 'I began a few years ago to try to make space in my reckoning and imagining for the marvellous as well as for the murderous' (*CP* 20). This is one of the several occasions on which the Nobel lecture and the recent poems expressly connect, for in 'Fosterling' from *Seeing Things* (1991), having characterised his earlier poetry as 'Sluggish in the doldrums of what happens' – a rewriting of a happier borrowed phrase of his, 'the music of what happens' – he suddenly refers to himself in apparent reproach: 'Me waiting until I was nearly fifty / To credit marvels' (*ST* 50). There is surprise expressed here, too, as when we ask of some event that stretches credulity, 'Would you credit it?' The surprise would seem to be the length of time it has taken for him to register the marvellous in his past (though the abbreviated syntax makes this ambiguous): 'So long for air to brighten, / Time to be dazzled and the heart to lighten'. So marvels happen too, but uncommonly enough to provoke wonder: *marvel*, via Middle English from Old French *merveille* from Latin *mirabilia*, 'wonderful things'. The miracle, from Latin *miraculum*, a thing wondered at, is not far away from the marvel though Heaney often avoids a specifically Christian (i.e. Roman Catholic) credence.

To 'credit' marvels is of course to *believe* in marvels, and belief is one of the impelling forces in Heaney's poetry. But it is also to *trust* in the marvellous (as the credit union trusts in our ability to pay back our loans), and in his recent poetry Heaney trusts so much in the marvellous that it can seem to the reader to have been almost commonplace in his boyhood and youth, capable of transforming – in memory if not at the time – even the apparently sluggish. He is (wittingly or no) following his fellow Ulster poet Patrick Kavanagh in this new heightened sensitivity to the marvellous and the ease of turning everyday brass into visionary gold, though it was as early as his first volume of poetry

(1936) that Kavanagh claimed to have found 'a star-lovely art / In a dark sod' ('Ploughman') and went on to report 'the thrill / Of common things raised up to angelhood' ('Pursuit of an Ideal').[1] Heaney's by contrast has been a delayed and, one feels, a more conscious receptivity to the wondrous inherent in the commonplace.

The incidence of marvels apart, a good deal of Heaney's recent poetry has been a revisitation of what he has already versified. But the revisitation is also a revision, made necessary, it would appear, through a recent accession of love or affection and what can even seem like late middle-aged nostalgia. ('I loved' is a common formulation in the emotional stocktaking of recent Heaney poetry.) It is also a translation into a vocabulary unfamiliar not in itself (the distinctive Heaney lexicon or 'word-hoard' is well known and is still being drawn on) but in the frequency of such words and inflections (and, therefore, ideas and images) as *air*, *light*, *water*, *space*, *sunlight*, *stream*, *waver*, *lift*, *soul*, *sky*, *spirit*, *river* – the language of the elemental, the transformative, the unconstrained. Such language was sometimes deployed in the past, and there was what amounts to a 'turn' towards it with *The Haw Lantern* (1987), but now it is commoner and more emphatic.

Heaney called his Nobel lecture 'Crediting Poetry' to imply his belief and trust in poetry, and for those who had read *Seeing Things* he was tacitly claiming to restore the marvellous to poetry. Explicitly, he was *acknowledging* and *thanking* poetry for making possible 'a fluid and restorative relationship between [his] mind's centre and its circumference', between his obscure Co. Derry childhood and his world recognition as a major poet (*CP* 11–12). By giving credit where credit is due, he was also *honouring* poetry that had in turn made possible the honour he was at that moment receiving from the Nobel committee and from the global community of readers for whom it undertook to speak.

He had of course been doing this for some time, seeking in his poems and criticism to *accredit* poetry; that is, to recognise the legitimate sovereignty of poetry as one government recognises the sovereignty of another country by accrediting its ambassador. He has been at pains for years to defend and advance poetry as an activity, accomplishment, language and experience apart, almost as an *estate*.[2] He was early roused to do so in part under the contrary pressure of those who during the Northern Ireland Troubles wished him to speak out in verse on behalf of those Ulster Catholics who considered themselves compelled to be British against their will and were seeking a newly constituted Ireland. In 'The Flight Path' from *The Spirit Level* (1996) he recalls a disaffected fellow Catholic asking him, 'When, for fuck's sake, are you going to write / Something for us?' and the poet replying, 'If I do write something, / Whatever it is, I'll be writing for myself' (*SL* 25, shades of

Stephen Dedalus resisting the artistic utilitarianisms of Davin and MacCann). Heaney has intended to write as a poet and for poetry and not as a citizen for a cause. The beckoning constitution which Heaney primarily ponders is poetic not political. What constitutes poetry? And what (to echo Shelley, as Heaney himself does) are its unacknowledged legislative powers? This consciousness of poetry, its definitions, capacities and obligations, is perhaps higher because Heaney came from an unliterary background (like Kavanagh) but became (unlike Kavanagh) a literary scholar. Less scholarly but no less widely read than Heaney, Yeats wrote the syllabus for high-minded poets that the later poet has attempted to follow with a dedication that distinguishes him among his contemporaries.

Heaney exploits the extended metaphors for poetry of sovereignty and constitution and therefore he can appear to be a political poet, in the way that the Keats of 'On First Looking into Chapman's Homer' can appear to the casual reader to be because of that sonnet's metaphors of realm, state, kingdom, fealty, rule and conquest. But if Heaney is a political poet, it is only in the way in which his larger poetic enterprise has assimilated politics. More overt political verse, such as the second part of *North* (1975) or the verse complaint *An Open Letter* (1983), has proven more difficult to absorb into the mainstream of his *oeuvre*. We could of course argue that Heaney's mission to constitute poetry is at bottom inseparable from his status as an Ulsterman of native and Catholic (and therefore minority) stock, who grew up on an island where questions of constitutional status have hung for centuries in the air and were particularly pressing just at the time when he came to maturity as a poet. I have myself made this argument, but even so, poetry receives Heaney's primary and virtually unswerving allegiance, and increasingly so.

To be sure, on several fronts, including the political, Heaney's work from the beginning was a kind of ongoing redress, and redress takes its place beside belief as a founding motive of his poetry. As an Irish poet published in volume form, he opened proceedings with 'Digging' (*Death of a Naturalist* (1966), 13), a 'big, coarse-grained navvy of a poem' (his words; *P* 43), as though like some Irish countryman he were tramping over the stately lawns of English verse in hobnailed boots, but thereafter had more subtle and intelligent designs on an English poetry that had seemed exotic and impossible, thereby adjusting or redressing a cultural imbalance.[3] And as an Ulsterman, and therefore with no apparent 'rights on / The English lyric' ('The Ministry of Fear', *N* 65) to be a player at all in the British literary scene was for him a remarkable cultural and implicitly political redress. (Kavanagh – like Heaney an actual man of the countryside – had tried and failed to insert himself in the metropolitan British scene.) But the most important form of redress for Heaney has come to be that which he spelled out in his Nobel lecture: asserting poetry's unique and too often unacknowledged 'truth to life' (*CP* 12).

Heaney's recent volumes have sought to entrench the sovereignty and self-determination of poetry he had already asserted. In *Preoccupations* (1980) Heaney was talking insightfully about Wordsworth, Hopkins, Yeats, Kavanagh and Larkin. By the time *The Government of the Tongue* appeared (1988) – the pun of the title allowing the notion of government *by* the tongue as well as regulation *of* the tongue – it had begun to seem as though Heaney might be talking *to* the dead poets: the practitioners listed above, plus Lowell, Mandelstam, Auden and Bishop (though he was still talking *about* Plath when he voiced some serious reservations about her poetry). As in Yeats's criticism, one can at times feel like an eavesdropper on an ongoing and high-minded conversation. In *Electric Light* (2001), the chosen exemplars have become a Yeatsian fellowship: Virgil, Dante, Hopkins, Hardy, Yeats, Auden among the long (or longish) dead, Hughes, Brodsky, Miłosz, Zbigniew Herbert among the living or recent dead. In *District and Circle* (2006), there are apostrophes to George Seferis, Pablo Neruda and Auden, conjurations or evocations of Wordsworth, Edward Thomas, Miłosz and Hughes, adaptations of Rilke and Cavafy. These are the citizens and ambassadors with whom Heaney is in primary colloquy, elite and fully accredited members of the most prestigious guild of human craft, that of Poetry.

But whereas the notion of a guild might imply a civic poetry, Heaney has recently (at least until *District and Circle*) become more consciously (perhaps *too* consciously and second-handedly) visionary in his utterances. Meanwhile, his sense of the civic now extends to a pronounced interest in the populated afterlife and even, in emulation and translation of the classical poets, the underworld. The sense of mission, of pilgrimage, has intensified, at least in expression. But now the journey has increasingly become the inward leg of the pilgrimage, the retracings of steps, as in 'The Golden Bough' and 'The Journey Back', the opening poems in *Seeing Things*. The first is a translation of those lines in the *Aeneid* (Book VI) in which Aeneas, despite his claim that he has 'foreseen and foresuffered all', seeks help from the Sibyl of Cumae to find his father and who forewarns him of the difficulty of return; the second is a fanciful encounter with Larkin's ghost who quotes Dante and whose underworld suitably resembles a workaday rush hour.

Heaney has Larkin describe his journey to the underworld as one 'like the forewarned journey back / Into the heartland of the ordinary' ('The Journey Back', *ST* 7). When in '"Poet's Chair"', Heaney remembers watching his father ploughing, he attributes to his young self 'all foreknowledge. / Of the poem as a ploughshare that turns in time / Up and over' (*SL* 47). It was in fact years later that Heaney discovered the etymological connection between *verse* and the movement of the ploughman as he finishes a furrow and turns on himself to begin another. Heaney can now revise previous versions of his earlier self in order to insert and inscribe awareness of the later self, such is his confidence in his persona, and it quietly implies a poetic destiny. Later still, in 'Desfina' from *Electric Light*, Greek roads are 'looped like boustrophedon' (*EL* 43): i.e. like that ancient reading or writing style that alternates direction on every line, the word itself meaning 'turning like an ox while ploughing'. This is an example of how each Heaney collection accrues value from previous volumes by a kind of compound interest. If Heaney praised Plath's 'interweaving of imaginative constants from different parts of the *oeuvre*' (*GT* 162), then his own weave has by now surpassed hers in intricacy – sometimes, one feels, at the risk of self-determination becoming undue self-allusion. Reading the recent poetry, I find myself remembering James Stephens's remark that Yeats sometimes clanked about too much in his own rhymes.

Foreknowledge is one of the woven attributes in Heaney but beyond that, what the poet wishes to say, and how he says it, is, when he begins to write, a kind of foreknowing, made explicit with the recurring theme of revisitation, the ghosts who populate his poems, the images and motifs that return. The first line in *Door into the Dark* (1969) asked the reader (or poet) rhetorically: 'Must you know it again?' Heaney's poems since then have been eloquent affirmations. Heaney's world is one that is distinctive and 'real' enough to tempt him to dwell *on* it, as well as *in* it. Inevitably, the threat of foreclosure hangs semantically over Heaney's verse. Action and even experience are, one senses, fated – 'Greek with consequence', to quote from 'Glanmore Revisited' (*ST* 35). And what must *be* is guaranteed by what *is*. What marvels there are irradiate less from events than from things.

The Real Things

It was with the captured weight of the rural world that Heaney made his reputation. This was the real world that challenged and provoked at a fundamental level poetry's 'truth to life'. He is still at home in the company of relishable objects – in *Seeing Things*, with a basket of chestnuts, a biretta, a settle bed, a cot, a schoolbag. In *Electric Light* we have a bookcase, a gate, a coffin, a bridge; in *District and Circle* a turnip-snedder, a sledgehammer, a railway sleeper, a fireman's helmet, a harrow-pin. The object may be symbolic, like the biretta that is tripartite like Gaul and the trinity, but it is chiefly the object in itself that Heaney wishes to celebrate, and he is particularly drawn to the palpable, the heavy and ungainsayable – for example, the 56-lb weight in 'Weighing In' from *The Spirit Level*. Such objects seem extraordinary at first only because they metaphorically occupy the deepest heartland of the ordinary and are the truest representatives of the quiddity of the world. But their weight is in challenging contrast to the lightness, otherworldliness and even wonder Heaney claims inheres in such things, or emanates from them, particularly when they are tools translated by skilful use, like the trowel in 'To Mick Joyce in Heaven' in *District and Circle*.

Heaney has never abandoned his early signature diction that tries to close the gap between word (and even syntax) and thing: 'Slack of gulped straw, the belly-taut of seedbags' (*EL* 16), we read in 'The Loose Box' from *Electric Light*, as though the poet had never read Wendy Cope's sport with his surplus reification in 'Usquebaugh'.[4] 'The Settle Bed' from *Seeing Things* verges on self-parody as the object in question demands that spondees collapse through their sheer weight the iambs of the blank verse, while the poet hammers his lines into three-line stanzas like planks:

> Willed down, waited for, in place at last and for good.
> Trunk-hasped, cart-heavy, painted an ignorant brown.
> And pew-strait, bin-deep, standing four-square as an ark. (*ST* 28)

('Ignorant' is an Ulster colloquialism and means crude or uncouth, and is pronounced with two crushed syllables – 'ig'nrnt'; it reappears in 'The Real Names' from *Electric Light*.) Objects have induced the curt serial phrases that press like Heaney's venerable hallmark in 'The Tollund Man in Springtime': 'My heavy head. Bronze-buffed. Ear to the ground. / My eye at turf level. Its snailskin lid' (*DC* 56).

This is reality at its least refutable: the kickable empirical world of Samuel Johnson that must be registered before the invisible idealist world of George Berkeley or Plato, or the Otherworld of Virgil, Dante or the medieval Irish saints, can be contemplated or experienced, and the kickable world is a precondition of such experience and contemplation. The rhythm of the phrasing in 'The Settle Bed' imitates the shortness of breath of anyone who would attempt to lift such a bed weighted down by legacy. Each of Heaney's chosen objects is 'the real thing', to borrow from both 'Hailstones' in *The Haw Lantern* and 'Whitby-sur-Moyola' in *The Spirit Level*.

To appreciate the real presence of the object is to have oneself 'ratified', as 'A Basket of Chestnuts' (*ST* 24–5) attests. To know the object, to *realise* it in an almost Hopkinsian way, to grasp its 'be-ing', is at the same time to be *self*-possessed. In 'Glanmore Revisited' from the same volume, the poet recalls his transition from tenancy to ownership of the cottage as one to 'full possession' (*ST* 32). Heaney in his preoccupation with objects, especially from his childhood, attempts to possess fully his world and is the precise opposite of Larkin's Mr Bleaney (in the poem of that name) who is the eternal lodger in the 'uncaring / Intricate rented world' ('Aubade') that Larkin humorously and chillingly depicts throughout his verse. But ownership in Heaney is typically inherited, gifted or bought: it is rarely, it seems, directly earned.

By extension, the work of art in Heaney's world also ratifies us, one example (in 'A Basket of Chestnuts') being the painting of Edward Maguire, whose portrait of Heaney composed the back cover of the paperback edition of *North*. Like Maguire, Heaney is an artist whose fidelity to the surface of the object is also a fidelity to the essence of the object, captured through an enhanced realism employed even in the service of the visionary: Heaney's visions, memories, afterlives and underworlds have the solidity of the here and now after the manner of classical mythology or medieval Christianity. But of course, Heaney's objective world moves through time (he is very conscious of family generations and inheritance) and space. If he is intrigued by the object handed down, he is also intrigued by the object that is a tool expertly used to engage the physics of the world: force, work, gravity, energy, equilibrium. That is why he cherishes the farming implement that feels like a javelin ('The Pitchfork' in *Seeing Things*): it does double duty in the world, a double shift, and this is perhaps why he cherished the pen that replaced his father's spade and was symbolically to perform spade-like work (in the service of which, through a kind of mimetic literalism, Heaney presumably cultivated his early tactile realism). But in 'Digging', the pen actually felt less like a spade than a gun and this got him into trouble with readers who saw gratuitous violence (as well as an inaccurate simile); it was perhaps the poet's love of basic physics that was at fault rather than an unnecessary sensationalism.

But when Heaney's similes and metaphors are right (and the poems are alive with them), things live in the reader's imagination even if they have never figured in his or her experience.[5] Indeed, from the start Heaney's figurative language was so self-confident it threatened to achieve an axiomatic quality that faintly suggested both passivity and preciousness.[6] This effect has re-inforced what we might call the conservative reverse thrust of his work and world; whatever *is* (and it indubitably *is* in his poetry) is, to adapt Pope, *right*. The first sonnet in 'Glanmore Revisited' begins: 'Bare flags. Pump water. Winter-evening cold ... It felt remembered even then, an old / Rightness half-imagined or foretold.' And a poem such as the twenty-fourth section of 'Squarings' (*ST* 31) shows that Heaney can like Pope switch between the cosmic and microcosmic in a trice.

In such a world view as this, politics are going to seem less like the art of the possible than the theology of the fated, foretold and foreclosed. Just as things cherished through time can become objects of worship, so actions repeated through time can become custom and ritual which are, as the idiom has it, *observed*, i.e. are passive forms of action. 'We pine for ceremony', Heaney claimed in 'Funeral Rites' (*N* 16) though surely he could only really speak for himself in the matter of Northern Ireland. Others pined for something a lot more proactive in response to murder and mayhem. It was the funeral and bog poems of *North* that prompted the accusation that by seeing the atrocities of rebellion and counter-rebellion in the 'Troubles' as prehistoric and ritualistic and thus virtually inevitable, perhaps even necessary (and the consolation – not remedy – for these as public ceremony and obsequies), Heaney was evading both the ethics and the politics of the situation. The 'beautiful prismatic counselling' to this effect ('Exposure', *N* 72), as Heaney had already sardonically called it in *North* itself, did not cause Heaney to pause and investigate the historical, reassess the ethical, ponder the political or re-insert the individual. Rather, he steadily became what appears to be at first glance a more religious, even vatic, less civic poet. Yet amidst the constant barrage of proffered solutions to the Ulster conflict, Heaney's 'long foray' back in search of archaic precedent, however inadequate as explanation, surely dignified us during the squalid internecine violence.[7]

Again, the recent poetry accentuates what was already attested. If poetry is a medium between the real world and ourselves (double-fastening the reality through right descriptions from memory or observation), it is also a medium between the real world and the other-world. Poetry's twin intermediary capacities are aspects of its sovereignty and power. The two lines of the epigraph poem of *The Haw Lantern* offered first the real then the unreal (yet, if anything, superior) version of the real:

> The riverbed, dried-up, half-full of leaves.
> Us, listening to a river in the trees.

Even more compactly, the pun in the title *Seeing Things* (also the title of a poem in the collection) combines objects and imaginings, seeing things that are very much there and seeing things that aren't. In 'The Real Names', the phrase is re-conscripted when he claims that there was 'airiness from the start' in his life, that as a child he stood on top of the family byre, 'seeing things / In a headier light from that much nearer heaven' (*EL* 46–7).

Heaney is now rebroadcasting, as it were, his earlier world and poetry in a broader-band frequency. 'Clearances' in *The Haw Lantern* celebrated the paradox of glowing absences, the most glowing absence being that of his dead mother. The 'bright nowhere' (*HL* 32) of sonnet 8 in the sequence is Larkinesque, if we have in mind the Larkin of 'High Windows' who sometimes crossed beyond the heartland of the ordinary and who entitled an early typescript collection 'In the Grip of Light', adapted by Heaney as 'The Main of Light' when he wrote about the English poet in *The Government of the Tongue*. The 'real thing' composed by both the ice pellets *and the poem itself* in the poem 'Hailstones' melts and smarts into its absence: the world and art authentically residing in their own kind of afterlife. One might think of Robert Frost (a Heaney exemplar) who thought a poem is like a piece of ice that rides on its own melting and who specialised not only in the imagery of rural life but also in what we might call the passive after-imagery of that life ('After Apple-Picking' would be the example readiest to hand). Frost, too, like Heaney gleaned 'the unsaid off the palpable' ('The Harvest Bow'; *FW* 58).

But the marvellous, even miraculous, has steadily asserted itself in Heaney and makes of him a more religious poet than Frost, even if, as in the case of James Joyce, the language of Catholicism is deployed by a residually Christian, even secular sensibility trying nonetheless to imagine through literature a world that somehow exists beyond this one: a vague, disestablished but intense religious feeling. Norse mythology, Greek mythology, Iron Age Scandinavian pagan ritual, Irish sagas, medieval Catholicism, in all of which Heaney at some serious level believes: these at another level have been in the hands of Heaney a kind of religious bricolage as the poet senses and seeks a faith that issues in poems but not in organised belief. It is in a peculiar way that we can speak of the theology of Heaney's poetry, though as in the case of Joyce, a lingering, indeed versatile Irish Catholicism has remained. When back in *North* he claimed to set as much store by the passive telling of rosary beads as by the more active commentary and pronouncements of journalism and politics in the matter of Ulster's troubles, he was clearly not being glib.

A Theme for Poetry

Heaney, then, is typically the rememberer and cherisher of objects, and only rarely the wielder of those that function as tools. Whether it be the Heaney process of reification, or of rarefication into which the objective world is increasingly remembered as passing, the poet receives more than he gives. But of course, the poet is paradoxically active in the rich expression of such passivity while the objects themselves can be paradoxically active as receivers or transmitters of miraculous force. As though that which is Aristotelian can be extended indefinitely until it becomes Platonic, everything in Heaney is going somewhere and eventually that somewhere is the world of light. (Henry Vaughan's famous first line about the dead opens poem xliv of 'Squarings'.) Along the way, everything lives an afterlife as memory, vision or ghost. The dead too are on their way, and having memorialised his dead mother in *The Haw Lantern*, it is the turn of his dead father in *Seeing Things*. The re-imagined father is associated with objects, most poignantly with his own ash plant in the poem of that title, and is poised to return from the world of the dead, the plant now a silver bough, lesser version of the golden bough that Aeneas needs to find and take with him in order to gain entrance to the otherworld. Objects, or some version of themselves, are in passage like the dead: a football and a fishing lure ('Three Drawings'); a hay fork ('The Pitchfork'); or a flat stone, earth's slipstream or figurative sailing boat (poem xlvi of 'Squarings') – all sailing 'into the longed-for' in *Seeing Things*.

Things, like people, are translated in Heaney's work into the elements of light and air. This lends a simultaneous weightlessness to the celebrated avoirdupois of his world. Heaney has of course been a translator in a literal sense, and has given us versions of some of his contemporary exemplars as well as of elder masterpieces, including Ovid's *Metamorphoses* (a book of bodily translations), Virgil's *Aeneid*, Dante's *Divine Comedy*, the medieval Irish tale, *Sweeney Astray* (*Buile Suibhne*, a translation of man into bird), *Beowulf*, Brian Merriman's eighteenth-century Irish poem, *The Midnight Court* (*Cúirt an Mhéan-Oíche*). The translator is an intermediary between the poet and the reader who cannot without intermediation understand the poet. He is also, in relation to the original impulse and imperative of the poem to be translated, passive. The poet might in 'Sonnets from Hellas' recall a Greek goatherd 'Subsisting beyond eclogue and translation' (*EL* 38); he might end 'Known World', a verse account recalling a 1978 visit to the Struga Poetry Festival, aboard a Boeing jet taking off ('All systems go'), but the enduring persona of his poetry is that of someone not directly involved or in full touch with action in its immediacy, nor yet a mere observer: but rather a later intercessor, the one who conducts, as it were, proxy talks among adversaries, who is the last to leave and who performs his office without being entirely neutral at any moment: in short, priest, bard or diplomat.

It is instructive, if bordering on the unfair, to contrast 'Lupins' (*Electric Light*) with 'Thistles' by Ted Hughes (*Wodwo* [1995]), each twelve lines long. The latter is a poem of fierce resistance whereas the former is a poem of mere persistence. Heaney's trademark resilient syntax of the first line ('They stood. And stood for something. Just by standing.') thaws into a Latinate and romance diction, while 'Thistles' flaunts its Anglo-Saxon inheritance until the defiant close. Of course, lupins are lupins, thistles thistles, but the respective choice of plant (wayside flower, unappeasable and unkillable weed) is itself telling. The urgency of Hughes's poem overtakes its figurations whereas in 'Lupins' one is aware of the embroidered dictions of Hopkins ('Rose-fingered dawn's and navy midnight's flower') and mock-Romanticism ('O pastel turrets') that succeed the distinctively Heaneyesque opening and reach a conclusion that acts, as so often in Heaney, like a blessing: 'And none of this surpassed our understanding' (*EL* 5).

Fittingly, the denial of understanding surpassed (perhaps a quiet rewriting of the last line of *The Waste Land*) occurs again in a poem in *Electric Light* written in memory of Ted Hughes, 'On His Work in the English Tongue'.[8] This oblique poem appears to be a justification of Hughes (perhaps in the wake of *Birthday Letters* [1998]) and, using the unlikely vehicle of Hughes, a restoration of passive suffering as a theme for poetry. (Is he siding with Hughes in the latter's lengthy and notorious apparent passivity in the face of hostile claims that he destroyed his wife Sylvia Plath?) Heaney asserts passive suffering as a theme for poetry, *pace* Yeats: 'Passive suffering: who said it was disallowed / As a theme for poetry?' (*EL* 62), a coy allusion to Yeats's banishment of Wilfred Owen and other Great War trench poets from his prospective *Oxford Book of Modern Verse* (1936) on that very ground. Yeats is immediately contradicted by allusions both to *Beowulf* (the tholings of Hrethel) and to Owen's 'Strange Meeting', elided in '*To sullen halls where encumbered sleepers groaned*'. The 'balked' love and life of the king seems to be a tale told by Hughes to Heaney on Dartmoor and echoes the lupins' refusal to 'balk', even when they whiten at summer's end, as though lupins were in their passive resistance one stage this side of mere passive suffering though far short of Hughes's thistle-feuds and 'revengeful' resurrections.

But although it is tempting to read 'Lupins' as an extended allusion to Irish passive suffering and resistance, since the thirty years 'war' in Northern Ireland had by 2001 (the date of *Electric Light*) ended, it makes more sense, if one must see human beings behind the flowers as we might see Vikings and other implacable feudists (including the blood feudists of Ulster) in 'Thistles', to see in 'Lupins' a half-conscious celebration of those who survive and bear witness, of those who 'Just by standing' are 'by-standers' in an admirable way. In 'Punishment' from *North*, Heaney notoriously pictured himself as standing by as Catholic girls in Northern Ireland were punished by their own side for fraternising with British soldiers (they were chained to church railings and had tar poured over their heads). Yet if he reproached himself, he did so with an eloquence that shrank the reproach: he was an '*artful* voyeur' (*N* 38; my italics: more poet than artful dodger) and in the sixth poem of 'Singing School' in the same volume he was an 'inner émigré, grown long-haired / And *thoughtful*; a wood-kerne // Escaped from the massacre' (*N* 73: my italics). These phrases and lines have since become famous among Heaney utterances. He was not, he implied, standing idly by even if physically passive. If he 'stood dumb' and connived 'in civilized outrage', he also understood 'the exact / and tribal, intimate revenge' (*N* 38). On balance, though, and worryingly for this reader, the understanding was of something real while the civilised reaction was contrived, worked up, though the silent inaction was the same in each case.

This final imbalance after the poet's seemingly painstaking weighing up of matters in which he has inherited a side, a bias, is itself a notable achievement in sustained equilibrium. In later poetry, Heaney has not upset the equilibrium at the level of statement, except at odd moments of bravado. In 'Weighing In' from *The Spirit Level* – and echoing the exasperation in 'Whatever You Say, Say Nothing' (*North*): 'Christ, it's near time that some small leak was sprung // In the great dykes the Dutchman made' (*N* 59) – there is a brief outburst. 'Weighing in' means getting one-sidedly stuck into an argument or fracas as opposed to the weighing in before sports contests, putting contenders on the scales.[9] This time the outburst is aimed it seems at poetry and himself rather than at others:

Still, for Jesus' sake,
Do me a favour, would you, just this once?
Prophesy, give scandal, cast the stone. (*SL* 18)

(In 'Punishment' he confessed he would have cast 'the stones of silence' [*N* 38] at the young Iron Age woman put to death for adultery. However, the cast stone is defensive in 'Weighing In' where it would have been offensive in the case of the Windeby girl or Catholic girls and a violation of Jesus' ironic commandment: 'He that is without sin among you, let him cast the first stone.') Before the outburst, Heaney equates 'passive suffering' (which 'makes the world go round'), 'bearing up' (like the lupins, one might say, and see also 'Keeping Going', also in *The Spirit Level*) and balance ('as long as the balance holds') with the angelic. But the equation is ironic in its neatness and is followed by the bitter memory of an occasion when he failed to avenge himself for some unidentified insult through 'A deep mistaken chivalry'. 'Red, White and Blue' from *Electric Light* is another poem about such a failed retaliation.

'Staggering for balance'

But it was equilibrium and balance that Heaney decided to explore, defend and even advocate in *The Spirit Level*, a title sharing the rhetorical figure of pun with *Seeing Things* and *Electric Light*. The poet's avowed desire is to be level-spirited even if, or especially when, he knows this condition, like peace, is as elusive or even fictional as the spirit-level's bubble which the poet's father once mischievously asked him to fetch. The morally dubious weighing of beauty and atrocity in 'The Grauballe Man' (in which the aesthetic allure of the bog victim's body – copy for the metaphor-hungry poet – like the statue of the Dying Gaul, makes art out of suffering) has not discouraged Heaney from repeatedly contemplating 'the scale of things' ('Squarings', xl; *ST* 100).

And unsurprisingly, this is an idea that he had already versified. In the third part of 'Terminus', a poem in *The Haw Lantern* named after the Roman god of boundaries, he recalls growing up figuratively between the two buckets he carried and had to balance, straddling as it were the border between warring physical forces. His ingenious but barely earned metaphor in this poem, and one evoking Elizabethan or Jacobean Ireland, is that of 'the last earl on horseback in midstream / Still parleying, in earshot of his peers' (*HL* 5: the previously mentioned diplomat or ambassador between opposing armies). Occupation of no-man's-land can cause, or be caused by, passivity and inaction, though on other metaphoric frequencies this can be a creative position as when he wishes to 'walk on air', conducting himself midway between the real world and art, between river gravel (mixed with cement, it is the ungainsayable) and a tune called 'The Gravel Walks' (in the poem of that name in *The Spirit Level*). On other frequencies it can be a movement from the middle to occupy two elements in quick succession or at once, a profitable amphibiousness. In 'Terminus', being in between is an opportunity for active mediation. But no mediation is possible between two lorries, one, a coal lorry, recalled from boyhood and associated with his mother and romance, the other a lorry with a deadly payload to cause havoc in Magherafelt ('Two Lorries', *SL* 13–14); nor ought there to be balance. Yet unfortunately Heaney, victim in this poem of his own intricate weave, is content with a hypothetical choice when surely the remembered terrorist lorry ought to provoke an imbalanced anger, not describe a metaphysical geometry.

Critics have commented on Heaney's slowness to anger. Helen Vendler thought it worth pointing out that the 'hitherto pent-up historical anger' in 'Mycenae Lookout', Heaney's centrepiece sequence in *The Spirit Level*, was unusual and a reaction to the poet's previous and responsible communication of hope.[10] Setting Heaney's anger aside for the moment, it is important to register the large achievement in dramatic poetry that this translation of Aeschylus' *Agamemnon* would be at any time, but specially on the heels of the IRA ceasefire of 1994, since the play and poem open with the ending of the Trojan War. One of its minor accomplishments is to extend the range of Heaney's subject positions from passivity towards activism. The idle bystander, the concerned bystander, the passive witness (and mere observer), the active witness (and recorder): these now extend to the wakeful lookout engaged in 'sentry work'. The lookout awaiting at Mycenae the return of Agamemon is 'Heaney' transposed: 'Still isolated in my old disdain', finding the war 'pre-articulate' (like the Ulster Troubles, as *North* implied), he himself 'balanced between destiny and dread' having seen the terrible events coming but reluctant to intervene:

The king should have been told,
but who was there to tell him
if not myself? (*SL* 34)

But with the ox on his tongue he did not. The sentry, describing Cassandra in language reminiscent of the murdered Windeby girl in 'Punishment' and in lines formally reminiscent of the thin bog poems of *North*, declares:

No such thing
as innocent
bystanding. (*SL* 30)

The tacit self-reproach seems as muted as the anger and indeed the poem ends with hope, with fresh water gushing bountifully from pumps that faintly echo the distant pump in 'Rite of Spring' from *Door into the Dark*.

If there is anger in Heaney it is largely submerged in expressions of the 'private self' where Adrian Frazier professes to find it. Frazier sees Yeats, the national question and the father as thematic and emotional cruxes in Heaney; they generate critical episodes in which two opposing attitudes are available, and during which anger is driven under and transformed. The first is provoked by what for Heaney, the Irish Catholic, is Yeats's alien race and religion crossed with the greatness of his art.[11] The third is, in Frazier's reading, provoked by the father's taciturnity and out-of-reachness. The second, which concerns me here, is provoked by sectarianism and frustration among Ulster Catholic nationalists (the 'slow, obstinate papish burn', as Heaney, quoted by Frazier, once described his feelings). Frazier makes a telling point about Heaney's famous balancing act and negotiations of the sectarian minefield (the poet is on record as admiring Yeats's own navigation through an earlier Irish minefield):

> it seems misleading to say, and it is often said, that when he speaks of dithering, equivocating, and Hamletizing about the Troubles, that he hesitates because he is unable to take a side. He is not unable to take a side between unionism and nationalism. What he stands between is two forms of intellectual nationalism ... between, if you like ... liberal nationalism and physical-force republicanism ... The riddle for Seamus Heaney is, 'What can a non-combatant do?' not 'On which side do you stand?'[12]

It is true that in Heaney's poetry (which is an uncommonly *populated* poetry), Ulster Protestants rarely figure and when they do are rarely sympathetic or if so, then marginal and merely glimpsed. In 'Weighing In', Heaney expresses the difficulty, even the tiresomeness, of 'having to // Balance the intolerable in others / Against our own' (*SL* 17), but even when his poems advocate doing this, and despite the fascination of what's difficult implied in it, one is not convinced that Protestant unionist behaviour is ever part of the equation or equilibrium. After all, Heaney's passport was always singular and green (even if his citizenship was and is unavoidably dual, British and Irish), and in his boyhood Protestants *were* marginal to him and his family: that was the way it was. But even if Frazier is correct, it is yet the case that the transformation and submergence of anger seem increasingly successful in the recent poetry. However, Frazier reminds us to great effect of the statement by Theodor Adorno that Heaney once accepted as applicable to his own poetry: 'the conciliatory nature of art is in direct relation to the rage which produced it'. Heaney has worked consciously, both formally and thematically, at conciliation, at balance.

Submergence of anger – if we accept Frazier's language – also means its sublimation (Latin *sublimare*, to raise). Heaney has continued to raise the balancing act higher off the ground and now broaches the sublime. Water is not turned into wine in Heaney; rather, the marvels occur when the world is turned into air, light or spirit. Achieving the air was defeat for Heaney's Antaeus back in *North* and a way by which the story of the giant could become 'pap for the dispossessed' ('Hercules and Antaeus', *N* 53), just as the story of Irish defeats paradoxically nourished the Irish. In the later poetry, achieving the air is success; it is as if the triumph now belongs to Antaeus, alive in both elements. That Heaney could not have planned the trajectory of his images and ideas as long ago as the early 1970s suggests his extraordinarily coherent development. If the political world is imbalanced for him (he seems unable sympathetically to embrace unionism or Ulster Protestants or the English),[13] he can nevertheless claim to achieve balance in a higher key. Up there, he no longer provides pap, even allegorically, for the dispossessed. But, then, he no longer needs to, the Troubles being over, Ireland now being an affluent country, as the poet's interlocutor acknowledges ruefully in 'Glanmore Eclogue' (*EL* 35). Once upon a time in Heaney, leaving or being caught out of your own element, engaging in what amounted to a mistranslation of yourself, creating a dangerous imbalance in tribal equilibrium, could be culpable folly, as 'Casualty' in *Field Work* testified. In *District and Circle*, Heaney remembers the dead Mick Joyce ('Out of your element'; 'To Mick Joyce in Heaven', *DC* 8) as he remembered the casualty of the Troubles who would not honour the tribal demarcations, but in this recent memory only a job is at stake – that, and the high, weightless flash of trowel when Joyce found his proper vocation.

It is always in Heaney a kind of translation of objects or actions between lower and higher elements: fishing and fishing rods are favourites in *Seeing Things*. It also frequently involves an exchange of voices that might be actual translation, adaptation or even the curious passivity of impersonation. In

Electric Light we hear Hopkins ('In the everything flows and steady go of the world' and 'the stunt and stress / Of hurt-in-hiding'; *EL* 4, 62); Eliot ('And then at midnight as we started to descend / into the burning valley of Gijon'; *EL* 24); Auden (in 'Audenesque', *EL* 64–6, echoing the third section of 'In Memory of W. B. Yeats'); Yeats himself ('All that was written / And to come I was a part of then', 'A woman changed my life. Call her Augusta' and 'Soul has its scruples'; *EL* 18, 35, 63): Lowell ('*Beria!Beria!Beria!* / Screeched Vladimir Chupeski, every time / He smashed a vodka glass and filled another / During those days and nights of '78', *EL* 19). The Heaney voice lately emerging is a chorus of other voices. But paradoxically this is creating a versatile and authoritative persona. At the same time, this persona seeks to achieve authority more directly through a growing stateliness, even old-fashionedness of diction by which the poet can 'aver' something or write these neo-Victorianisms: 'When I lift up my eyes at the start / Of Stanley Kubrick's film' – some bathos there in the second line; 'So I smiled straight back, as who should say, "Good God" …' (*EL* 17); 'I felt like one come out of an upper room / To fret no more and walk abroad confirmed.' There can also be an impression of faintly unearned addition. The title of his poem 'Conkers' ('Sonnets from Hellas', *EL* 39) puts me in mind of Wells's seasoned hacking chestnut ('conqueror of forty') in Joyce's *Portrait of the Artist as a Young Man*, and the way in which Heaney's poems can have value added by such borrowing of voices and lines, in the way a conker takes credit for all the victories of the enemy conker it has just defeated.[14] Could Heaney's line about Auden possibly be a disguised and hopeful self-reference: 'And the definite growth rings of genius rang in his voice' ('Ten Glosses', *EL* 55)?

But then, although Joyce's Stephen Dedalus might easily have anticipated Heaney's revelatory self-injunction in 'Pylos' (*EL* 40; the next sonnet from Hellas after 'Conkers') 'to be more myself', it is difficult if not impossible to show where in Joyce's prose he is not borrowing or imitating or at least adapting, or which of the innumerable styles in which he writes is the most authentically Joycean. The real Joyce does not stand up; this is a pure virtuoso with the spirit of a true original. His work is testament to the truth that everything has already been done but not in this particular permutation. But Joyce *demonstrates* this truth as well as having Bloom and Dedalus ponder multiple versions of it. One can have a sense in Heaney that there is not enough showing and too much telling, sometimes in slack lines and in poems, such as 'The Real Names', that seem to wish to flush themselves into vigorous prose but are constrained to be verse. But the borrowings and impersonations are at least attempts at showing. Heaney even communicates this indirectly. In 'Squarings' poem xxxvii, Heaney quotes from Han Shan and adds:

> Talking about it isn't good enough
> But quoting from it at least demonstrates
> The virtue of an art that knows its mind. (*ST* 97)

After all this time, it cannot be said that Heaney's art does not know its mind, especially when he is a poetry critic of the first rank; indeed, it knows it sufficiently to wish on more and more occasions to escape it by crediting the marvellous that might seem to reverse the foretold and foreknown. But Heaney's choice of the word 'crediting' may be telling. In terms of faith, crediting is a lesser act than believing: it is to believe through an act of will, to give the unbelievable the benefit of the doubt; crediting is to make the world tell its marvels – to believe is to let the world show its marvels. Crediting is weighing credence against incredulity or scepticism and tipping the balance towards the more venerable, traditional attitude of belief. Indeed, by wilfully *not* believing too readily in marvels, one can seem to induce them and thus undermine one's own disbelief. In 'The Bookcase', the poet braces himself to heft the case, to accept the earthboundedness of the thing, only to find, when 'staggering for balance, it has grown so light' (*EL* 57). *District and Circle* more than immediately preceding volumes accepts, anticipates and pays tribute to the heaviness of being.[15] Having done so, you can find yourself emancipated and airborne; even if you have tricked yourself in the beginning, you are primed for miracle.

NOTES

1. Patrick Kavanagh, *Collected Poems* (London: Martin Brian & O'Keeffe, 1972), pp. 3, 32.
2. I discuss this notion in *The Achievement of Seamus Heaney* (Dublin: Lilliput Press, 1995), pp. 25–7, 56–7.
3. In 'Feeling into Words', from which I've taken the navvy reference, Heaney quoted a review of *Death of a Naturalist* in which 'Digging' appeared: the reviewer saw the poem as representing 'mud-caked fingers in Russell Square' (*P* 43).
4. Wendy Cope, *Making Cocoa for Kingsley Amis* (London: Faber and Faber, 1986).
5. For example, 'The Grauballe Man' from *North* is a vertical procession of similes and metaphors, the rightness of which readers can check against the photographs in P. V. Glob's *The Bog People: Iron-Age Man Preserved* (see p. 205 n. 5).
6. I suggested this as long ago as 1974, in 'The Poetry of Seamus Heaney', *Critical Quarterly* 16 (1974), pp. 35–48, reprinted in *Critical Essays on Seamus Heaney*, ed. Robert F. Garratt (New York: G. K. Hall & Co., 1995), pp. 25–38.
7. I take the phrase 'long foray' from the title-poem in *North* (1975), the volume in which Heaney comprehensively staked out his mythic and ritual ground. 'Long foray' is a contradiction in terms, but Heaney no doubt meant to extend in time his early notion of poetry as a 'raid into dark corners'.
8. Heaney brings Eliot and Hughes together in 'Stern' (*DC*), a poem in memory of the latter.

9. The Dutchman is of course Prince William of Orange, later King William III, perceived champion of Protestantism and (by Ulster Protestants) of the Union of Great Britain and (Northern) Ireland.
10. Helen Vendler, 'Seamus Heaney and the *Oresteia*: "Mycenae Lookout" and the Usefulness of Tradition', in *Amid Our Trouble: Irish Versions of Greek Tragedy*, ed. Marianne McDonald and J. Michael Walton (London: Methuen, 2002), pp. 181–97.
11. I have attempted to analyse the difficulties Yeats represents for Ulster Catholic nationalists in '"Getting the North": Yeats and Northern Nationalism', *Yeats Annual* 12, ed. Edna Longley (London: Macmillan, 1996), pp. 180–212.
12. Adrian Frazier, 'Anger and Nostalgia: Seamus Heaney and the Ghost of his Father', *Eire-Ireland* 36 (2001), pp. 25, 29.
13. The 'English', of course, are not to be confused (oddly, we might think) with 'English literature' (greatly admired) or even with 'England', a relishable abstraction under certain circumstances. These ambiguities and ambivalences are part of the complicated freight carried by the Irish Catholic writer writing in English.
14. But in fact Heaney would have referred in his boyhood to 'cheesers', the Ulster word for the very English 'conkers'. (Indeed, I believe too he would have referred to his 'schoolbag' not to his 'satchel', as it occurs in 'Conkers'.) Heaney is developing in his poetry an increasingly public, de-regionalised poetic voice. The border between cultural development and cultural impersonation is not always clear.
15. In other ways, too, this volume is a return: there are further journeys in the underworld (including the title sequence), though here they seem more pretextual than substantive; Ann Saddlemyer is the dedicatee as she was in 'Glanmore Sonnets' in *Field Work*; 'Anahorish' from *Wintering Out* (1972) is revisited as 'Anahorish 1944'; 'The Tollund Man' from the same early volume is likewise revisited as 'The Tollund Man in Springtime'; even Miss Walls, who no doubt has featured in many a dissertation and article as a benign stooge in young Heaney's accession to the mud vision recorded in 'Death of a Naturalist' where it all began, returns as a less benign but somehow reduced figure in 'Senior Infants'.

GUIDE TO FURTHER READING

For an authoritative listing of works by Seamus Heaney, see Rand Brandes and Michael J. Durkan, *Seamus Heaney: A Bibliography 1959–2003* (London: Faber and Faber, 2008).

Primary Works

Volumes of Poetry

Death of a Naturalist (London: Faber and Faber; New York: Oxford University Press, 1966).

Door into the Dark (London: Faber and Faber; New York: Oxford University Press, 1969).

Wintering Out (London: Faber and Faber, 1972; New York: Oxford University Press, 1973).

Stations (prose poems) (Belfast: Ulsterman Publications, 1975).

North (London: Faber and Faber, 1975; New York: Oxford University Press, 1976).

Field Work (London: Faber and Faber; New York: Farrar, Straus and Giroux, 1979).

Selected Poems 1965–1975 (London: Faber and Faber, 1980); published as *Poems 1965–1975* (New York: Farrar, Straus and Giroux, 1980).

Sweeney Astray: A Version from the Irish (Derry: Field Day, 1983; London: Faber and Faber, 1984; New York: Farrar, Straus and Giroux, 1984).

Station Island (London: Faber and Faber, 1984; New York: Farrar, Straus and Giroux, 1985).

Hailstones (Dublin: Gallery Press, 1985).

The Haw Lantern (London: Faber and Faber; New York: Farrar, Straus and Giroux, 1987).

New Selected Poems 1966–1987 (London: Faber and Faber, 1990); published as *Selected Poems 1966–1987* (New York: Farrar, Straus and Giroux, 1990).

Seeing Things (London: Faber and Faber; New York: Farrar, Straus and Giroux, 1991).

The Spirit Level (London: Faber and Faber; New York: Farrar, Straus and Giroux, 1996).

Opened Ground: Poems 1966–1996 (London: Faber and Faber, 1998); published as *Opened Ground: Selected Poems 1966–1996* (New York: Farrar, Straus and Giroux, 1998).

Electric Light (London: Faber and Faber; New York: Farrar, Straus and Giroux, 2001).

District and Circle (London: Faber and Faber; New York: Farrar, Straus and Giroux, 2006).

Shorter Poetic Publications

Eleven Poems (Belfast: Queen's University of Belfast, 1965).

A Lough Neagh Sequence (Didsbury: Phoenix Pamphlet Poets Press, 1969).

Soundings '72: An Annual Anthology of New Irish Poetry (Belfast: Blackstaff Press, 1972).

Bog Poems, with illustrations by Barrie Cooke (London: Rainbow Press, 1975).

An Open Letter (Derry: Field Day Theatre Pamphlets, 1983).

The Tree Clock (Belfast: Linen Hall Library, 1990).

A Shiver (poetry pamphlet) (Thame: Clutag Press, 2005).

Translations and Adaptations

The Midnight Verdict, translations from *Cúirt an Mheán Oíche* by Brian Merriman (*c.* 1780), and Ovid's *Metamorphoses* (Oldcastle: Gallery Press, 1993).

Laments, by Jan Kochanowski, tr. Seamus Heaney and Stanisław Barańczak (London: Faber and Faber; New York: Farrar, Straus and Giroux, 1995).

Beowulf (London: Faber and Faber, 1999; London and New York: W. W. Norton, 2000); published as *Beowulf: A New Verse Translation* (New York: Farrar, Straus and Giroux, 2000).

The Diary of One Who Vanished: A Song Cycle by Leoš Janáček (London: Faber and Faber, 1999; New York: Farrar, Straus and Giroux, 2000).

Drama

The Cure at Troy: A Version of Sophocles' 'Philoctetes' (Derry: Field Day Theatre Company; London: Faber and Faber, 1990; New York: Farrar, Straus and Giroux, 1991).

The Burial at Thebes: Sophocles' 'Antigone' (London: Faber and Faber; New York: Farrar, Straus and Giroux, 2004).

Prose

(This very brief list is an attempt to include, as well as the four major collections of prose writings, some of the most important separately published items.)

Preoccupations: Selected Prose 1968–1978 (London: Faber and Faber; New York: Farrar, Straus and Giroux, 1980).

'A Tale of Two Islands: Reflections on the Irish Literary Revival', in *Irish Studies*, 1, ed. P. J. Drudy (Cambridge: Cambridge University Press, 1980), pp. 1–20.

'Among Schoolchildren', John Malone Memorial Lecture (Belfast: Belfast University Press, 1983).

'Envies and Identifications: Dante and the Modern Poet', *Irish University Review*, 15:1 (Spring 1985), pp. 5–19.

The Government of the Tongue: The 1986 T. S. Eliot Memorial Lectures and Other Critical Writings (London: Faber and Faber; New York: Farrar, Straus and Giroux, 1988).

The Place of Writing (Atlanta, GA: Scholars Press, 1989).

'William Butler Yeats (1865–1939)', in *The Field Day Anthology of Irish Writing*, ed. Seamus Deane (Derry: Field Day Publications, 1991), vol. II, pp. 783–90.

The Redress of Poetry: Oxford Lectures (London: Faber and Faber, 1995); published as *The Redress of Poetry* (New York: Farrar, Straus and Giroux, 1995).

Crediting Poetry, The Nobel Lecture 1995 (Oldcastle: Gallery Press, 1995; New York: Farrar, Straus and Giroux, 1996).

'Time and Again: Poetry and the Millennium', *European English Messenger*, 10:2 (2001), pp. 19–23.

Finders Keepers: Selected Prose 1971–2001 (London: Faber and Faber; New York: Farrar, Straus and Giroux, 2002).

Collaborations

Homage to Robert Frost, by Seamus Heaney, Joseph Brodsky and Derek Walcott (London: Faber and Faber, 1997).

The Rattle Bag, ed. Seamus Heaney and Ted Hughes (London: Faber and Faber, 1994).

The School Bag, ed. Seamus Heaney and Ted Hughes (London: Faber and Faber, 1997).

Interviews with Seamus Heaney

'Interview' (Harriet Cooke), *Irish Times* (28 December 1973), p. 8.

'Poets on Poetry' (Patrick Garland), *Listener* (8 November 1973), p. 629.

'The Sunday Interview' (Caroline Walsh), *Irish Times* (6 December 1975), p. 5.

'Unhappy and at Home' (Seamus Deane), *New York Times Book Review* 84:48 (1979), pp. 79–101; reprinted in *The Crane Bag Book of Irish Studies 1977–1981*, ed. Mark Patrick Hederman and Richard Kearney (Dublin: Blackwater Press, 1982), pp. 66–72.

'An Interview with Seamus Heaney' (James Randall), *Ploughshares* 5:3 (1979), pp. 7–22.

'Raindrop on a Thorn: Interview with Seamus Heaney' (R. Druce), *Dutch Quarterly Review* 9:1 (1979), pp. 45–6.

'Meeting Seamus Heaney: An Interview' (John Haffenden), *London Magazine*, (19 June 1979), pp. 5–28; reprinted in *Viewpoints: Points in Conversation with John Haffenden* (London: Faber and Faber, 1981), pp. 57–75.

'An Interview with Seamus Heaney' (Frank Kinahan), *Critical Enquiry* (Spring 1982) pp. 405–14.

The South Bank Show (Melvyn Bragg), London Weekend Television (27 October 1991).

Seamus Heaney in Conversation with Karl Miller (London: Between the Lines, 2000).

Reading the Future: Irish Writers in Conversation with Mike Murphy (Dublin: Lilliput Press, 2000), pp. 81–97.

'On Elegies, Eclogues, Translations, Transfusions: An Interview with Seamus Heaney' (Rui Carvalho Homem), *European English Messenger* 10:2 (Autumn 2001), pp. 24–30.

John Brown, *In the Chair: Interviews with Poets from the North of Ireland* (Co. Clare: Salmon, 2002).

Secondary Works

Collections of Essays

Allen, Michael (ed.), *Seamus Heaney*, Macmillan Casebook Series (London: Macmillan, 1997).

Andrews, Elmer (ed.), *Seamus Heaney: A Collection of Critical Essays* (London: Macmillan, 1992).

Bloom, Harold (ed.), *Seamus Heaney: Modern Critical Views* (New Haven, New York and Philadelphia: Chelsea House Publishers, 1986).

Broadbridge, Edward (ed.), *Seamus Heaney* (Copenhagen: Danmarks Radio, 1977).

Curtis, Tony (ed.), *The Art of Seamus Heaney* (Bridgend: Poetry Wales Press, 1982; Dublin: Wolfhound Press, 1994; 4th edn, Bridgend: Poetry Wales Press, 2001).

Garratt, Robert F. (ed.), *Critical Essays on Seamus Heaney* (New York and London: G. K. Hall & Co., 1995).

Malloy, Catherine and Phyllis Carey (eds.), *Seamus Heaney: The Shaping Spirit* (Newark: University of Delaware Press; London: Associated University Presses, 1996).

Critical Books

Andrews, Elmer, *The Poetry of Seamus Heaney: All the Realms of Whisper* (London: Macmillan; New York: St Martin's Press, 1988).

(ed.), *The Poetry of Seamus Heaney*, Icon Critical Guides (Cambridge: Icon Books, 1998).

Burris, Sidney, *The Poetry of Resistance: Seamus Heaney and the Pastoral Tradition* (Athens: Ohio University Press, 1991).

Buttel, Robert, *Seamus Heaney* (Lewisburg, PA: Bucknell University Press, 1975; reprinted 1988).

Clark, Heather, *The Ulster Renaissance: Poetry in Belfast 1962–1972* (Oxford and New York: Oxford University Press, 2006).

Corcoran, Neil, *The Poetry of Seamus Heaney: A Critical Study* (London: Faber and Faber, 1998).

Durkan, Michael J., and Rand Brandes, *Seamus Heaney: A Reference Guide* (New York: G. K. Hall, 1996).

Foster, John Wilson, *The Achievement of Seamus Heaney* (Dublin: Lilliput Press, 1995).

Foster, Thomas C., *Seamus Heaney* (Dublin: O'Brien Press; Boston: Twayne Publishers, 1989).

Hart, Henry, *Seamus Heaney: Poet of Contrary Progressions* (Syracuse, NY: Syracuse University Press, 1992).

McGuinn, Nicholas, *Seamus Heaney: A Student's Guide to 'Selected Poems 1965–1975'* (Leeds: Arnold-Wheaton, 1986).

Morrison, Blake, *Seamus Heaney* (London and New York: Methuen, 1982).

Murphy, Andrew, *Seamus Heaney*, Writers and Their Work (Plymouth: Northcote House, 1996).

O'Donoghue, Bernard, *Seamus Heaney and the Language of Poetry* (Hemel Hempstead: Harvester Wheatsheaf, 1994).

Parker, Michael, *Seamus Heaney: The Making of the Poet* (Iowa City: University of Iowa Press, 1993).

Tamplin, Roland, *Seamus Heaney: Open Guides to Literary Studies* (Milton Keynes: Open University Press, 1989).

Vendler, Helen, *Seamus Heaney* (Harvard: Harvard University Press; London: HarperCollins, 1998).

Articles, Essays and Chapters in Books

Brown, Terence, *Northern Voices: Poets from Ulster* (Dublin: Gill and Macmillan, 1975).

Coughlan, Patricia, '"Bog Queens": The Representation of Women in the Poetry of John Montague and Seamus Heaney', in *Gender in Irish Writing*, ed. Toni O'Brien Johnson and David Cairns (Milton Keynes: Open University Press, 1991), pp. 88–111.

Deane, Seamus, 'Seamus Heaney: The Timorous and the Bold', in *Celtic Revivals* (London: Faber and Faber, 1985), pp. 174–86.

Fennell, Desmond, 'Whatever You Say, Say Nothing: Why Seamus Heaney is No. 1', *Stand* 32:4 (Autumn 1991), pp. 38–65.

Lloyd, David, '"Pap for the Dispossessed": Seamus Heaney and the Poetics of Identity', in *Anomalous States: Irish Writing and the Post-Colonial Moment* (Dublin: Lilliput Press, 1993), pp. 13–40.

Longley, Edna, '*North*: "Inner Emigré" or "Artful Voyeur"?', in *Poetry in the Wars* (Newcastle: Bloodaxe, 1986), pp. 140–69.

Paulin, Tom, 'Political Anxiety and Allusion: Seamus Heaney', in *Crusoe's Secret: The Aesthetics of Dissent* (London and New York: Faber and Faber, 2007), pp. 349–73.

Ramazani, Jahan, 'Seamus Heaney', in *Poetry of Mourning: The Modern Elegy from Hardy to Heaney* (Chicago: University of Chicago Press, 1994), pp. 334–60.

INDEX

Cambridge Companions to ...

AUTHORS

Edward Albee edited by Stephen J. Bottoms
Margaret Atwood edited by Coral Ann Howells
W. H. Auden edited by Stan Smith
Jane Austen edited by Edward Copeland *and* Juliet McMaster
Beckett edited by John Pilling
Aphra Behn edited by Derek Hughes *and* Janet Todd
Walter Benjamin edited by David S. Ferris
William Blake edited by Morris Eaves
Brecht edited by Peter Thomson *and* Glendyr Sacks (second edition)
The Brontës edited by Heather Glen
Frances Burney edited by Peter Sabor
Byron edited by Drummond Bone
Albert Camus edited by Edward J. Hughes
Willa Cather edited by Marilee Lindemann
Cervantes edited by Anthony J. Cascardi
Chaucer, second edition edited by Piero Boitani *and* Jill Mann
Chekhov edited by Vera Gottlieb *and* Paul Allain
Kate Chopin edited by Janet Beer
Coleridge edited by Lucy Newlyn
Wilkie Collins edited by Jenny Bourne Taylor
Joseph Conrad edited by J. H. Stape
Dante edited by Rachel Jacoff (second edition)
Daniel Defoe edited by John Richetti
Don DeLillo edited by John N. Duvall
Charles Dickens edited by John O. Jordan
Emily Dickinson edited by Wendy Martin
John Donne edited by Achsah Guibbory
Dostoevskii edited by W. J. Leatherbarrow
Theodore Dreiser edited by Leonard Cassuto *and* Claire Virginia Eby
John Dryden edited by Steven N. Zwicker
W. E. B. Du Bois edited by Shamoon Zamir
George Eliot edited by George Levine
T. S. Eliot edited by A. David Moody
Ralph Ellison edited by Ross Posnock
Ralph Waldo Emerson edited by Joel Porte *and* Saundra Morris
William Faulkner edited by Philip M. Weinstein
Henry Fielding edited by Claude Rawson
F. Scott Fitzgerald edited by Ruth Prigozy
Flaubert edited by Timothy Unwin
E. M. Forster edited by David Bradshaw
Benjamin Franklin edited by Carla Mulford
Brian Friel edited by Anthony Roche
Robert Frost edited by Robert Faggen
Elizabeth Gaskell edited by Jill L. Matus
Goethe edited by Lesley Sharpe
Thomas Hardy edited by Dale Kramer
David Hare edited by Richard Boon
Nathaniel Hawthorne edited by Richard Millington
Seamus Heaney edited by Bernard O'Donoghue
Ernest Hemingway edited by Scott Donaldson
Homer edited by Robert Fowler
Ibsen edited by James McFarlane
Henry James edited by Jonathan Freedman
Samuel Johnson edited by Greg Clingham
Ben Jonson edited by Richard Harp *and* Stanley Stewart
James Joyce edited by Derek Attridge (second edition)
Kafka edited by Julian Preece
Keats edited by Susan J. Wolfson
Lacan edited by Jean-Michel Rabaté
D. H. Lawrence edited by Anne Fernihough
Primo Levi edited by Robert Gordon
Lucretius edited by Stuart Gillespie *and* Philip Hardie
David Mamet edited by Christopher Bigsby
Thomas Mann edited by Ritchie Robertson
Christopher Marlowe edited by Patrick Cheney
Herman Melville edited by Robert S. Levine
Arthur Miller edited by Christopher Bigsby
Milton edited by Dennis Danielson (second edition)
Molière edited by David Bradby *and* Andrew Calder
Toni Morrison edited by Justine Tally
Nabokov edited by Julian W. Connolly
Eugene O'Neill edited by Michael Manheim
George Orwell edited by John Rodden
Ovid edited by Philip Hardie
Harold Pinter edited by Peter Raby
Sylvia Plath edited by Jo Gill

Edgar Allan Poe edited by Kevin J. Hayes
Alexander Pope edited by Pat Rogers
Ezra Pound edited by Ira B. Nadel
Proust edited by Richard Bales
Pushkin edited by Andrew Kahn
Philip Roth edited by Timothy Parrish
Salman Rushdie edited by Abdulrazak Gurnah
Shakespeare edited by Margareta de Grazia *and* Stanley Wells
Shakespeare on Film edited by Russell Jackson (second edition)
Shakespearean Comedy edited by Alexander Leggatt
Shakespeare on Stage edited by Stanley Wells *and* Sarah Stanton
Shakespeare's History Plays edited by Michael Hattaway
Shakespearean Tragedy edited by Claire McEachern
Shakespeare's Poetry edited by Patrick Cheney
Shakespeare and Popular Culture edited by Robert Shaughnessy
George Bernard Shaw edited by Christopher Innes
Shelley edited by Timothy Morton
Mary Shelley edited by Esther Schor
Sam Shepard edited by Matthew C. Roudané
Spenser edited by Andrew Hadfield
Wallace Stevens edited by John N. Serio
Tom Stoppard edited by Katherine E. Kelly
Harriet Beecher Stowe edited by Cindy Weinstein
Jonathan Swift edited by Christopher Fox
Henry David Thoreau edited by Joel Myerson
Tolstoy edited by Donna Tussing Orwin
Mark Twain edited by Forrest G. Robinson
Virgil edited by Charles Martindale
Voltaire edited by Nicholas Cronk
Edith Wharton edited by Millicent Bell
Walt Whitman edited by Ezra Greenspan
Oscar Wilde edited by Peter Raby
Tennessee Williams edited by Matthew C. Roudané
August Wilson edited by Christopher Bigsby
Mary Wollstonecraft edited by Claudia L. Johnson
Virginia Woolf edited by Sue Roe *and* Susan Sellers
Wordsworth edited by Stephen Gill
W. B. Yeats edited by Marjorie Howes *and* John Kelly
Zola edited by Brian Nelson

TOPICS

The Actress edited by Maggie B. Gale *and* John Stokes
The African American Novel edited by Maryemma Graham
The African American Slave Narrative edited by Audrey A. Fisch
American Modernism edited by Walter Kalaidjian
American Realism and Naturalism edited by Donald Pizer
American Travel Writing edited by Alfred Bendixen *and* Judith Hamera
American Women Playwrights edited by Brenda Murphy
Australian Literature edited by Elizabeth Webby
British Romanticism edited by Stuart Curran
British Romantic Poetry edited by James Chandler *and* Maureen N. McLane
British Theatre, 1730–1830, edited by Jane Moody *and* Daniel O'Quinn
Canadian Literature edited by Eva-Marie Kröller
The Classic Russian Novel edited by Malcolm V. Jones *and* Robin Feuer Miller
Contemporary Irish Poetry edited by Matthew Campbell
Crime Fiction edited by Martin Priestman
The Eighteenth-Century Novel edited by John Richetti
Eighteenth-Century Poetry edited by John Sitter
English Literature, 1500–1600 edited by Arthur F. Kinney
English Literature, 1650–1740 edited by Steven N. Zwicker
English Literature, 1740–1830 edited by Thomas Keymer *and* Jon Mee
English Poetry, Donne to Marvell edited by Thomas N. Corns
English Renaissance Drama, second edition edited by A. R. Braunmuller *and* Michael Hattaway
English Restoration Theatre edited by Deborah C. Payne Fisk

Feminist Literary Theory edited by Ellen Rooney
Fiction in the Romantic Period edited by Richard Maxwell *and* Katie Trumpener
The Fin de Siècle edited by Gail Marshall
The French Novel: from 1800 to the Present edited by Timothy Unwin
Gothic Fiction edited by Jerrold E. Hogle
The Greek and Roman Novel edited by Tim Whitmarsh
Greek and Roman Theatre edited by Marianne McDonald *and* J. Michael Walton
Greek Tragedy edited by P. E. Easterling
The Harlem Renaissance edited by George Hutchinson
The Irish Novel edited by John Wilson Foster
The Italian Novel edited by Peter Bondanella *and* Andrea Ciccarelli
Jewish American Literature edited by Hana Wirth-Nesher *and* Michael P. Kramer
The Latin American Novel edited by Efraín Kristal
Literature of the First World War edited by Vincent Sherry
Literature on Screen edited by Deborah Cartmell *and* Imelda Whelehan
Medieval English Theatre edited by Richard Beadle *and* Alan J. Fletcher (second edition)
Medieval French Literature edited by Simon Gaunt *and* Sarah Kay
Medieval Romance edited by Roberta L. Krueger
Medieval Women's Writing edited by Carolyn Dinshaw *and* David Wallace
Modern American Culture edited by Christopher Bigsby
Modern British Women Playwrights edited by Elaine Aston *and* Janelle Reinelt
Modern French Culture edited by Nicholas Hewitt
Modern German Culture edited by Eva Kolinsky *and* Wilfried van der Will
The Modern German Novel edited by Graham Bartram
Modern Irish Culture edited by Joe Cleary *and* Claire Connolly
Modernism edited by Michael Levenson
The Modernist Novel edited by Morag Shiach
Modernist Poetry edited by Alex Davis *and* Lee M. Jenkins
Modern Italian Culture edited by Zygmunt G. Baranski *and* Rebecca J. West
Modern Latin American Culture edited by John King
Modern Russian Culture edited by Nicholas Rzhevsky
Modern Spanish Culture edited by David T. Gies
Narrative edited by David Herman
Native American Literature edited by Joy Porter *and* Kenneth M. Roemer
Nineteenth-Century American Women's Writing edited by Dale M. Bauer *and* Philip Gould
Old English Literature edited by Malcolm Godden *and* Michael Lapidge
Performance Studies edited by Tracy C. Davis
Postcolonial Literary Studies edited by Neil Lazarus
Postmodernism edited by Steven Connor
Renaissance Humanism edited by Jill Kraye
Roman Satire edited by Kirk Freudenburg
The Spanish Novel: from 1600 to the Present edited by Harriet Turner *and* Adelaida López de Martínez
Travel Writing edited by Peter Hulme *and* Tim Youngs
Twentieth-Century Irish Drama edited by Shaun Richards
Twentieth-Century English Poetry edited by Neil Corcoran
Victorian and Edwardian Theatre edited by Kerry Powell
The Victorian Novel edited by Deirdre David
Victorian Poetry edited by Joseph Bristow
Writing of the English Revolution edited by N. H. Keeble